HOLLYWOOD
THE DREAM FACTORY

An Anthropologist Looks at the Movie-Makers

Published by

Little, Brown and Company · Boston

by

Hortense Powdermaker

Published by
Little, Brown and Company · Boston

HOLLYWOOD

the Dream Factory

AN ANTHROPOLOGIST LOOKS
AT THE MOVIE-MAKERS

A

TO
DR. PAUL FEJOS

Acknowledgments

AN ANTHROPOLOGIST incurs so many obligations in the field, and in the course of writing, that it is impossible to list all those to whom he is indebted. However, I do want to express my deep gratitude to the literally hundreds of people in Hollywood who so generously gave me of their time and interest, and without whose co-operation the field study could not have been made.

Many scholars have contributed to my intellectual orientation, through personal contact or writings, or both. Among these, I should like to particularly mention the late Bronislaw Malinowski and Edward Sapir; Ralph Linton, Alfred Kroeber, Theodor Reik, Erich Fromm, and the late Harry Stack Sullivan. I am much indebted, likewise, to friends and colleagues in Los Angeles and New York for stimulating and helpful discussions and special thanks are due to Carl Withers, Geraldine Emily Smith, Paolo Milano and Ian Watt.

The project was sponsored by the Viking Fund. I am exceedingly grateful to the Board of Directors for making it possible and for their generous support. The dedication to Dr. Paul Fejos does not adequately express my appreciation for his contributions of time and critical interest and for his unique qualities of insight.

HORTENSE POWDERMAKER

New York, *1950*

Contents

Contents

HOLLYWOOD
THE DREAM FACTORY

An Anthropologist Looks at the Movie-Makers

INTRODUCTION
Why an Anthropologist Studied Hollywood

I SPENT A YEAR in Hollywood, from July 1946 to August 1947, a more normal year than those which followed. I went there to understand better the nature of our movies. My hypothesis was that the social system in which they are made significantly influences their content and meaning. A social system is a complex co-ordinated network of mutually adapted patterns and ideas which control or influence the activities of its members. My hypothesis is hardly original, although it has not been applied before to movies. All art, whether popular, folk or fine, is conditioned by its particular history and system of production. This is true for Pueblo Indian pottery, Renaissance painting, modern literature and jazz as well as for movies. These are a popular art concerned with telling a story. They differ from folk art in that while consumed by the folk, they are not made by them; and they are unlike the fine arts, since they are never the creation of one person. But although movies are made by many people in the setting of a big industry, certain individuals have power to strongly influence them, while others are relatively powerless.

My field techniques had some similarities to and some differences from those I had used on an island in the Southwest Pacific and elsewhere. As in other communities, I had to establish and maintain the same role: that of a detached scientist. While in Hollywood I was a part-time visiting professor of anthropology at the University of California in Los Angeles, a useful local sanction for this role. More important, however, was the absence of any desire on my part to find a job in the movie industry or to become a part of it. This was unique for anyone living in Hollywood for a year. Then, too, I had no ax to grind in a situation where everyone was very busy grinding his own; instead, I was trying to understand the complicated system in which they worked and lived. I saw people neither as villains nor heroes, but as playing certain roles in this system.

I took the inhabitants in Hollywood and in the South Seas seriously, and this was pleasing to both. To me the handsome stars with their swimming-pool homes were no more glamorous than were the South Sea aborigines exotic. All, whether ex-cannibal chiefs, magicians, front-office executives, or directors, were human beings working and living in a certain way, which I was interested in analyzing.

In Hollywood there were the great advantages of a well-documented history and of not having to learn a new language or work through an interpreter. The matter of a "sample" — selection of people to study — was more difficult. That problem had hardly existed in the South Seas, since there I lived in a village of about two hundred and fifty people and knew them all well. In Hollywood this was obviously impossible.

I arrived there with a few letters of introduction, and during the first month I met everyone I could. Gradually I became better acquainted with key people who were helpful in making necessary contacts as well as giving me data. My sample was approximately three hundred people, and was representative of the various functional groups such as producers, writers, directors, actors and so on, and included the very successful, the medium successful and the unsuccessful. Since political opinions may influence attitudes, the sample also cut across left, right and center groups. It was not the ideal random sample of the statistician, which while theoretically perfect would have been impossible to use in this type of field work. Taking every nth name in a directory would simply not have worked. But I endeavored to make the sample as representative and as complete a picture of working relationships as possible. A producer would tell me how he worked with his writers, and this would be supplemented by interviews with five or six writers who had worked with him. A director would talk about his relationships with actors; later I would interview a number of actors with whom he had worked.

Some people I saw once, many others two, three, or a half-dozen times. There were some sufficiently interested in the study whom I could see almost any time I wished. The number of interviews were approximately nine hundred.

The first interview with anyone was "set up" — that is, I came by appointment after an introduction which both explained what I was doing and more or less vouched for me. The place for the interview varied and studios, restaurants, and homes were all used. Leisurely luncheons and evening or week-end visits in homes were the best and most frequent settings and were always used for interviewing actors. It was the custom for successful actors to be interviewed on the set by representatives of magazines and newspapers, with a publicity man present, but this would have been an impossible interviewing situation for me. Executives, producers and directors could be interviewed in their offices without anyone else present. Some of these I saw also outside the studio. Writers were interviewed in their homes or at lunch.

Everyone knew the purpose of my study, and that the names of those called on would be held in confidence. I usually began by getting the interviewee to talk about whatever picture he was working on, or the last one he had finished. This enabled me to get specific data on one situation. From there we could go on to his experiences since coming to Hollywood, to his background before that, and to a discussion of other problems. Sometimes the interview would go off on tangents, depending on the particular interests of the respondent. I had a detailed outline of problems, but it was left at home; the conversation was directed in a seemingly casual manner. However, it was never completely *directed*, because it was important to encourage spontaneity. Many times I was given data on problems which I would not have known existed if I had hewed too closely to a certain line of interviewing.

I took no notes during the interview except when I was given statistical data which I asked permission to write down. Among a primitive people who had no writing, I could write continuously in front of them. I have experimented on this point in contemporary field studies in other places as well as in Hollywood, and have found that when I want fairly intimate data, I get more by not writing during the interview, even at the risk of forgetting some details. In Hollywood, as soon as the interview was over I drove around the corner and, sitting in my car, wrote it up roughly. Then, as soon as possible, usually within twenty-four hours, each interview became part of a dictaphone record, which was later transcribed by a secretary.

Hollywood people made excellent interviewees for a number of reasons. The level of frustration was high, and frustrated people love to talk. There were also a small but appreciable number who were helpful because they saw Hollywood in comparison with other societies. A few were Europeans; others had come recently from Broadway. Some people were good for exactly the opposite reason. They knew only Hollywood and, unaware of other standards, made excellent respondents because of their naïveté. There were also the reflective people, who had long been disturbed by the chaotic complexity of Hollywood and who enjoyed serious discussions about it. But the most important reason for being able to get data is one that underlies success in any field work, whether in primitive or modern societies: all human beings love to talk about themselves and are flattered at having their opinions taken seriously.

One afternoon I had a particularly fruitful interview with a producer, who had given me very generously of his time. The interview lasted about two hours, and he had told his secretary that he was in conference and not to be interrupted by phone calls. He did practically all the talking with only an occasional question from me. When I finally got up to go he said, "You know, this has been simply fascinating. You must come again."

While much of the data came from interviews, there were other important sources. Motion Picture Association of America made available to me its complete files on the implementation of its Production Code, which I have called "Taboos." The Screen Writers' Guild permitted me to read its files on the arbitration of screen credits. Both sources were invaluable for factual data. Executive secretaries of the Writers' Guild, Actors' Guild and various other guilds were all most helpful in giving statistical and other data.

During the year in Hollywood, I read most all of the trade papers. But long before that, I had become acquainted with the weekly *Variety*, which was the most important single source of printed information. Its frank, detailed news was and continues to be an invaluable source of data; and its colorful language of "pix's" and "nix's" is a pleasure.

As in any field trip, my role was that of participant-observer. In the beginning, I went on the sets a number of times and watched the directors, actors and others while a picture was being shot, primarily to familiarize myself with this process. I went to a number of guild meetings and listened to the members discuss their problems.

Just as I sat around campfires in the evening with my native friends in the South Seas and participated in their feasts, so in Hollywood I had leisurely evenings with friends, and went to some of their parties. As in other field trips, this was my life for the time being and I was completely immersed in it. I was always taking notes, mentally or otherwise. I continuously thought about and lived with the problems of the study, and I was constantly getting new ideas, reformulating hypotheses on the basis of new data, and clarifying ideas through discussion. This is the background of any intensive research.

The data are not all of the same order. A large part of the material is a factual account of the mores and the way they work. An equally important part is concerned with attitudes to the mores. While I tried to get the norm for each of the major patterns, whether of behavior or attitude, I was equally interested in the exceptions which often clarify the norm. In a changing situation, the exceptions may also represent new trends. For most of the material there is strong documentation, while — as in all field studies — there is some based on impressions only, which I have so labeled. The emphasis was always on the relationships between the data, rather than just collecting it. The study as a whole may be regarded as an example of applied anthropology, that is, using an anthropological point of view to observe and understand a contemporary institution.

The anthropologist has a measure of objectivity from having lived in and studied cultures other than his own. But he cannot escape completely from his own society and its values. As Gunnar Myrdal writes:

> Full objectivity, however, is an ideal toward which we are constantly striving, but which we can never reach. The social scientist, too, is part of the culture in which he lives, and he never succeeds in freeing himself entirely from dependence on the dominant preconceptions and biases of his environment.[1]

The value premises are themselves subject to study, and, again as Myrdal writes, they "should be selected by the criterion of relevance and significance to the culture under study."[2] The choice of the social scientist is between being aware of his values and making them explicit, or being unaware and letting the reader get them by inference. It seems more scientific openly to present the values, which can then be rejected by a reader if he chooses, than to have them hidden and implicit.

The very selection of a problem indicates a value. Underlying much of the scientific work of biology is the concept that health is better than sickness. The fact that among one primitive tribe epilepsy is a necessary condition for the prestige position of *shaman* does not negate the validity of our goal of health. Just as most of us think that health is better than sickness, so we consider maturity better than immaturity. It is good to grow up psychologically as well as physiologically. Maturity is, of course, a very large concept with many characteristics. Among them is the ability of the individual to face life, to make decisions, to be flexible and able to adapt to changing situations, and to utilize a considerable number of his potentialities. The human species is relatively very young, a million years or so in more than a billion years of life on earth. Indi-

[1] Gunnar Myrdal, *An American Dilemma*, Vol. II, App. 2, p. 1035. New York: Harper and Brothers.
[2] *Ibid.*, p. 1045.

viduals and groups are in different stages of growing up, and I know of none who could be considered really mature. To me a democratic society represents a more grown-up way of living and one more likely to encourage maturity in its members than does a totalitarian society.

My interest in American society is both as an anthropologist and as a citizen. The interpretation in this book is based on a way of thinking conditioned by twenty years of anthropological training and experience and the particular orientation of my personality. Other interpretations are possible. It is, however, the anthropologist's job not only to describe but to say also what he thinks his data mean.

But while values influence, as they always do, the choice of problem and interpretation of data, they do not affect its collection or choice. This, whether from interviews, written, or printed sources, is recorded as objectively and accurately as possible.

The book tries to explain in nontechnical language how the social system underlying the production of movies influences them. This, of course, does not preclude the existence of other conditioning factors, such as financing, exhibition and distribution, and still others. It is, however, part of the nature of all scientific work to limit a problem and to work intensively on certain aspects selected for study. Much was learned in the writing of the book, which was combined with college teaching, mostly part-time.

In my thinking and in the book I have asked more questions than I could answer. There are some fairly definite answers, and others which are hypotheses. The emphasis has been on trying to understand the complexities of the Hollywood social system rather than on reducing it to an oversimplified formula and, likewise, to see the relationship between Hollywood and the society in which we live.

I did not try to do a complete study of Hollywood as a community or to analyze all aspects of movie production. Neither would have been possible in the time at my disposal or necessary in terms of my problem. My questions were concerned with what aspects of the system of production and which individuals most influenced movies. The answers were found in a study of the locus of power and its exercise, in the taboos which circumscribe all production, in the values as represented in goals, in historical and economic factors, and in the introduction of new technology and new ideas with resulting conflicts between old and new.

As in any society, the myths, folk tales and gossip were all relevant to understanding it. Since no social system can be understood without a knowledge of the people through whom it functions, the personalities of those who sit in the front office, of producers, directors, actors, writers, and others, were observed. Their backgrounds, goals, ways of thinking, frustrations and compensations were all significant. Equally important were their relationships with each other, and among the key ones were those of producer-writer, director-actor, and of all with the front office. All influence the creative aspects of movie production and leave their imprint on the movies. Although no movie could be made without cameramen, set designers, musicians, costume and make-up departments, carpenters, electricians and many others, these have relatively little influence on the content and meaning, and so were not studied in any detail. Related problems of distribution and exhibition are discussed only incidentally, since the study was focused on *production in Hollywood*.

In analyzing the data, the most important criteria were, first, the degree to which the Hollywood system of production was oriented to maintain and strengthen the qualities essential to its product, which is storytelling, and, secondly, how well the system utilized its resources. This kind of analysis is necessary from the point of view of movies both as a big industry, and as a popular art form.

Obviously, no anthropologist could study Hollywood as an isolated phenomenon. It is part of the United States. But Hollywood is no mirrorlike reflection of our society, which is characterized by a large number of conflicting patterns of behavior and values. Hollywood has emphasized some, to the exclusion of others. It is the particular elaboration and underplay which is important for this study.

Although an expedition to Hollywood has some resemblance to other field trips, it is not quite the same as studying a tribe of headhunters in New Guinea, who have never before been observed. Much is known about Hollywood and much has been written about it. But no anthropological lens had been focused on it. This brings a certain frame of reference — namely, the social system — as well as the knowledge, techniques and insights gained from comparative studies of the human species from the Stone Age until to-day. The purpose of the study is to understand and interpret Hollywood, its relationship to the dreams it manufactures, and to our society.

I am concerned with opening up the general problem of movies as an important institution in our society. A unique trait of modern life is the manipulation of people through mass communications. People can be impelled to buy certain articles and brands of merchandise through advertising. Columnists and radio commentators influence political opinions. Movies manipulate emotions and values. Just as advertising can and does promote anxieties to increase consumption, movies may increase certain emotional needs which can then only be satisfied by more movies. In a time of change and conflict such as we experience today, movies and other mass communications emphasize and reinforce one set of values rather than another, present models for human relations through their portrayal by glamorous stars, and show life, truly or falsely, beyond the average individual's everyday experiences. The influence of the movies touches the lives of 85,000,000 American men, women and children who sit in the audience and likewise extends into remote corners of the earth. The inventions of printing press, radio, and movies have probably been as revolutionary in their effect upon human behavior as were those of the wheel and the coming of steam.

Opinions on the influence of movies range from viewing them as the hope for a better world to the fear of their degrading mankind. Some critics hold them responsible for practically everything they disapprove of, from juvenile delinquency to drunkenness and divorce. These problems, however, have a long and involved history in the life of individuals and society, and the causal factors are complex and not completely known. More important are the millions of people who weekly and monthly go to movies and who do not become delinquents, criminals, or drunkards. These more or less normal everyday people may over a period of time be influenced subtly, but deeply, in their ideas of human relations, and in their values.

Movies are successful largely because they meet some of modern man's deepest needs. He has long known increasing insecurity. He is filled with apprehension about the present and the future. The atomic bomb brings fear of destruction, and the struggle between democracy and totalitarianism throughout the world is truly frightening. Even before these two epochal happenings, the anxieties of modern man had increased because of his growing feeling of isolation and consequent loneliness. This feeling occurs not only in big cities with their intensive concentration of people and industry; it has spread even to agricultural areas, where the traditional rural attitudes have been replaced by those usually associated with the city.[3] Anxieties are further deepened by difficulties in understanding national rivalries, the conflicts in ideology, the complex theories of psychoanalysis and of relativity and so on, which whirl about the average man's head. The popularity of any book which attempts to relieve this situation gives further evidence. Joshua Liebman's book, *Peace of Mind*, was on the best-selling list of non-fiction books continuously for several years after its publication, and so also was the latest Dale Carnegie volume, *How to Stop Worrying and Start Living*. But the book-buying public represents only a small fraction of the population; for the masses of people, the reading of books is not the way out of their confusion and apprehension.

In this age of technology and the assembly line, many people wish to escape from their anxieties into movies, collective daydreams themselves manufactured on the assembly line. To some people, the word "escape" connotes a virtue; for others it is derogatory. But escape, *per se*, is neither good nor bad. All forms of art offer some kind of escape, and it may well be that escape is a necessary part of living. The real question is the quality of what one escapes into. One can escape into a world of imagination and come from it refreshed and with new understanding. One can expand limited experiences into broad ones. One can escape into saccharine

[3] Cf. Carey McWilliams, *Factories in the Field*. Boston: Little, Brown. Also Walter Goldschmidt, *As You Sow*. New York: Harcourt, Brace.

sentimentality or into fantasies which exaggerate existing fears. Hollywood provides ready-made fantasies or daydreams; the problem is whether these are productive or nonproductive, whether the audience is psychologically enriched or impoverished.

Like all drama and literature, movies extend the experiences of the audience vicariously, and translate problems which are common to mankind into specific and personal situations, with which identification is easy. Results from some preliminary research with audience reactions provide the hypothesis that audiences tend to accept as true that part of a movie story which is beyond their experience. A low-income group of workers, for instance, were very critical of part of one movie which touched their own experiences, saying, "That's just Hollywood!" — but in the same movie they accepted as completely true the portrayals of a successful girl artist and her two wealthy boy friends, the counterparts of whom they had never met. Those whose associations are restricted to law-abiding respectable members of a community will get their picture of gangsters, thieves, and "bad" women from their movies. This happens even to quite sophisticated people. In a graduate school seminar on case work, a social worker reporting on the case of an unmarried mother said that the mother spoke very casually of being pregnant again. The instructor asked what she had expected, and the student replied: "W—ell, I thought she'd act more like the way they do in the movies!" For people who have never traveled, the movies give them their ideas of what foreigners are like; and the latter may get their pictures of Americans in the same way. The ideas of young people with relatively limited experience about love and marriage may be influenced by what they see in the movies: a young girl in a small Mississippi town complained about the local beaus as compared to the movie heroes.

Almost every movie, even a farce, deals with some problem of human relations, and the manner in which glamorous movie stars solve these problems may affect the thinking of people about their own problems. A middle-aged woman whose husband had recently left her changed her mind three times about how to handle the situation, after seeing three movies in which she could identify her own problem.

Movies have a surface realism which tends to disguise fantasy and makes it seem true. This surface realism has steadily grown from the old days of the silent flickers to the modern technicolor talkies, with their increasing use of the documentary approach. If the setting is a New York street, the tendency today is to film an actual New York street. There is, of course, no necessary correlation between surface reality and inner truth of meaning. But if one is true, the other is more likely to be accepted. On the stage, often the inner meaning is accepted and the obviously false settings lose some of their pseudo quality. In the movies, it is frequently the reverse: since the people on the screen seem real and "natural" and the backgrounds and settings honest, the human relationships portrayed must, the spectator feels, be likewise true. It is this quality of realness which makes the escape into the world of movies so powerful, bringing with it conscious and unconscious absorption of the screen play's values and ideas.

The statement that the primary function of movies is entertainment is clearly not the end of the question. All entertainment is education in some way, many times more effective than schools because of the appeal to the emotions rather than to the intellect. "Precisely because they wear the warmth and color of the senses, the arts are probably the strongest and deepest of all educative forces." [4] Any consistent patterning in the mass communications of human relations, of attitudes, of values and goals, is education in the broader sense of the term.

South Sea natives who have been exposed to American movies classify them into two types, "kiss-kiss" and "bang-bang." Love and violence are two major themes not only in the motion picture but in all drama and literature. The significant question is: How are love and violence portrayed? According to the movies, love is the be-all and end-all of existence. The triumph of love against all obstacles and contrary to normal expectations is an ancient fantasy (but unknown to primitive man), and its use as an anodyne against unsatisfying reality — which was a prevailing theme in the medieval

[4] *General Education in a Free Society*, Report of the Harvard Committee, with an Introduction by James Bryant Conant, p. 30. Cambridge, Mass.: the Harvard Univ. Press.

tales of chivalry — is a motif in many movies. Murder and suspense have long been an essential part of tragedy; but they are present in movies which are devoid of tragedy. In both the kiss-kiss and bang-bang movies, the roles are played with little emotional impact. Only the exceptional movie conveys any deep emotion underlying either a love relationship or a murder. Love is usually limited to an immediate infatuation, and murder is committed by automaton-like actors.

The importance of the motion picture in our society is not confined to the darkened cathedral-like theaters: movies have given us new heroes who are tending to replace those of the quite recent past. The folk tradition that any American boy could be president of the country or become a Henry Ford was once often projected in the ambitions of parents for their sons. Today these ambitions tend to take a different form: "I'm going to bring up my boy to be a Bing Crosby. . . . All he'll have to do is open his mouth and sing, and he'll become a millionaire and support me in my old age!" represents a contemporary trend. Who would want to be president of a country in these troubled times, or to become a great industrialist or a successful inventor — which usually means a lifetime of hard work — if, instead, he could have a glamorous life of wealth and ease in Hollywood, merely by opening his mouth and singing or passing before a camera and acting?

These are some of the many ramifications of the motion picture in our society. Movies meet, wisely or unwisely, man's need for escape from his anxieties; they help assuage his loneliness, they give him vicarious experiences beyond his own activities; they portray solutions to problems; they provide models for human relationships, a set of values and new folk heroes.

It would be difficult to underestimate the social and psychological significance of movies. Like all institutions, they both reflect and influence society. It is hoped that a future project will be concerned with learning about this two-way process, including both an analysis of culture patterns in movies and detailed field studies of audience reactions. The present study of Hollywood and the system in which movies are made is the first step in the larger project.

CHAPTER I
Habitat and People, Mythical and Real

THERE IS ONLY ONE HOLLYWOOD in the world. Movies are made in London, Paris, Milan and Moscow, but the life of these cities is relatively uninfluenced by their production. Hollywood is a unique American phenomenon with a symbolism not limited to this country. It means many things to many people. For the majority it is the home of favored, godlike creatures. For others, it is a "den of iniquity" — or it may be considered a hotbed of Communism or the seat of conservative reaction; a center for creative genius, or a place where mediocrity flourishes and able men sell their creative souls for gold; an important industry with worldwide significance, or an environment of trivialities characterized by aimlessness; a mecca where everyone is happy, or a place where cynical disillusionment prevails. Rarely is it just a community where movies are made. For most movie-goers, particularly in this country, the symbolism seems to be that of a never-never world inhabited by glamorous creatures, living hedonistically and enjoying their private swimming pools and big estates, attending magnificent parties, or being entertained in famous night clubs. The other symbols belong to relatively small groups of people.[1]

Of all the symbols, sex and wealth are the most important. Every Hollywood male is supposed to be a "wolf" and every Hollywood female a tempting object easily seduced. The movie fans, worshiping their heroes, believe this. The members of a church

[1] The majority of novels dealing directly with Hollywood (Bud Schulberg, *What Makes Sammy Run.* New York: Random House. Carl Van Vechten, *Spider Boy:* A scenario for a moving picture. New York: Knopf. Francis Scott K. Fitzgerald, *The Last Tycoon:* An unfinished novel. New York: Scribners. Caroll and Garrett Graham, *Queer People.* New York: Grosset and Dunlap. Ludwig Bemelmans, *Dirty Eddie.* New York: Viking — and others) are cynical or depressing in tone and characterized by disillusionment. Some of these novels have been popular, but not on the top of best-seller lists. The group they reach is comparatively very small, a section of the intelligentsia.

missionary society in Iowa who write indignant letters to the Producers' Association also believe it. For the conservative or radical, sex over and beyond the traditional mores and codes is part of their idea of Hollywood. The other characteristic — easy Hollywood money, an enormous fortune quickly made — is the contemporary Cinderella theme for the naïve youngster in Alabama who has just won a beauty contest, as well as for the sophisticated New York writer who has been asked to come for six months to a Hollywood studio. No matter what the other symbols, or for whom they have meaning, the accent is on sex and money, for the Hollywood inhabitants as well as for the world outside.

Many other communities have a symbolic character. Paris, New York, a farming community in the Midwest, a town in the Deep South, an island in the South Seas, all mean many things to many people. For some, a South Seas island is thought of as an escape from a troubled world, for others as a place where money can be made by exploiting natural resources; for some it is a place where natives live a peaceful life, for others one where savages roam about in head-hunting expeditions. The anthropologist tries to find out what the place and people are really like. In studying Hollywood, he asks: Which of the myths and symbols have a basis in reality, which are fantasy, and which are a combination? What is their effect on the people who work and live there? What are significant elements about which the world outside does not even know enough to develop a folklore or mythology?

The geographical location of any community always has important social implications, and Hollywood is no exception. The semitropical climate gives a certain soft ease to living. Beaches, desert and mountains are all within easy reach, and the almost continuous sunshine is an ever-present invitation to the outdoors. Although Los Angeles stretches in distance for eighty-five miles and has a population of approximately four million, the whole of it is dominated by Hollywood. If the center of movie production had been in New York, the metropolis would probably have influenced the making of movies, rather than being dominated by it. Its location on the West Coast successfully isolated the movie colony in the past. Today, however, this insularity no longer exists, since many movies are being made on location in different parts of the country and abroad. There is also among the upper-bracket people considerable trekking — more literally, flying — back and forth between Los Angeles and New York. But these actors as well as the many others who do not travel have their roots in Hollywood, and the new trend has not materially changed the colony's essential character.

Hollywood's domination of Los Angeles comes out in many ways. The most trivial news about personalities in the movie world are front-page headlines in the city newspapers. Many of the local mores have been strongly influenced by the movie industry. The standard technique for a "pick-up" in Los Angeles is for the man to suggest to the desired female that he knows someone who will give her a screen test. Pretty girls, working in the popular drive-ins, live in hopes that a producer or director will notice them. School-teachers, doctors, white-collar workers and many others who have never shown any talent for writing, and who in another com-munity would have quite different goals, spend their spare time writing movie scripts. Earnest little groups meet an evening a week to criticize each other's work, expecting soon to reach the pot of gold at the end of the Hollywood rainbow. The people who work at the making of movies refer to those unconnected with the industry as "private people," the implication being that such individuals are unimportant.

Hollywood itself is not an exact geographical area, although there is such a postal district. It has commonly been described as a state of mind, and it exists wherever people connected with the movies live and work. The studios are scattered over wide dis-tances in Los Angeles, and are not particularly impressive-looking. They combine a bungalow and factory in their appearance, and many give the feeling of being temporary. The homes of movie people are found in Beverly Hills, Bel-Air, Westwood Village, the San Fernando Valley, the original Hollywood district, and other areas. I use the term "Hollywood" in this larger sense.

The myth of enormous and elaborate homes set in the midst of big estates turns out to be generally untrue. Beverly Hills, Bel-

Air and the others are quite charming, conventional, well-kept, upper-class suburbs, not too different from the Roland Park of Baltimore, the Shaker Heights of Cleveland, Westchester, Connecticut, or any attractive upper-class residential district near a large city. The actual Hollywood-situated homes seem less ostentatious, since many of them are in an informal, modern style. A home surrounded by an acre or less may be dignified as an "estate," while "ranch" is frequently used to describe any informal house with only an acre or less of land. The swimming-pool part of the popular myth has more basis for reality, and swimming pools are more common here than in the East. But they are not a Hollywood invention; their utility in the all-year-round semitropical climate of southern California is obvious.

The atmosphere of Hollywood both resembles that of a village and differs from it. There is the same extroverted cordiality, but more stress on status as determined by income and power. This is reflected in the use of first names. Those in the upper brackets call everyone beneath them by their first name, but this is not always reciprocal. Mr. Very Important will be addressed by some as "Mr. Important, sir," by others as "Mr. Important," as "V.I." by those earning over $1200 a week, and as "Very" by only a few close associates. But Mr. Very Important calls everyone by his or her first name. As in villages, the same people are at the same parties, the same restaurants, the same clubs and the same week-end resorts. But again there is more emphasis on financial status. With rare exceptions, the people at a party are all in the same income bracket, and there is very little association with private people. The stimulus of contact with those from other fields of endeavor, which is so accessible in most big cities, is lacking in Hollywood. For the most part, people work, eat, talk and play only with others who are likewise engaged in making movies. Even physical contact with the private people is exceptional, for the residential suburbs such as Beverly Hills and Bel-Air are far removed from the working-class and industrial districts. Each suburb has its own select shopping district, and it is relatively easy to live within its boundaries, driving outside only to the studio, to the home of friends in other secluded suburbs, or to Sunset Strip for the night clubs. An occasional brief excursion beyond these is made in one's own automobile, never in a public conveyance. A woman who painted as a hobby, the wife of a successful writer living in Beverly Hills, complained that she never saw any faces there to paint, and made a comparison with New York where there is an unescapable contact with faces interesting to a painter.

This quality of isolation is regarded as a disadvantage by a few of the more thoughtful people who live and work in Hollywood. Frank Capra, in a newspaper interview on the advantage of production on location, said:

> Shooting away from Hollywood also gives a producer or director a chance to get acquainted with the lives of other people. In Hollywood we learn about life only from each other's pictures. [2]

But this point of view is not typical. Most of the inhabitants seem to enjoy and receive a certain security from being only with people like themselves. Members of a Melanesian tribe in the Southwest Pacific likewise cannot imagine living anywhere else and are fearful of going beyond their own small community.

Although the proportion of gifted people in Hollywood is probably as great as, if not greater than, it is anywhere else in the world, Hollywood's cultural and social life does not reflect this group as does that of New York, London or Paris, where there is also an aggregation of talent. World-famous composers and performers reside in Hollywood, yet they almost never perform in public.

Los Angeles, a city of four million, which includes the largest concentration of actors, has been described as having a

> . . . near-absence of legitimate theater. The city's lone theater, the Biltmore, is largely a plaything of the United Booking Office, drawing today the tag end of a Broadway hit, tomorrow Blackstone, the Magician, replete with gazeeka box. Various small groups of actors, directors and others try to irrigate this "theatrical aridity" through productions such as those of the Actor's Laboratory and the Coronet Theater. [3]

[2] Interview in *Variety*, April 14, 1948.
[3] *New York Times*, June 1, 1947; article by Gladwin Hill with a Los Angeles byline.

To date, however, they remain "little theaters."

Nor does social life have the brilliance and sparkle that is found among talented people in other cities. A number of such people coming to Hollywood for the first time from Europe, or New York, have commented on the dullness of Hollywood parties. There are, of course, the usual exceptions; a few homes where intelligent and gifted people, regardless of their financial status, gather for good conversation and fun, not dependent on elaborate food, heavy drinking or ostentatious entertainment. But Hollywood is not dominated by the artists, or even influenced by them, any more than is the larger community of Los Angeles. Social influence seems to lie with many of the big executives and producers, and some but not all of the stars, whose social life away from the studio consists mostly of horse racing, gambling, yachting and big parties, which are reported the next day in the gossip columns. A "sunny Siberia" is the phrase used to describe it by some of the more critical inhabitants. The weekly show-business trade paper, *Variety* (May 21, 1947), has a headline **Hollywood May Be Heaven to Yokels but Thesps Want to Live Elsewhere,** followed by a story of actors who prefer to make their homes in the East and "commute" to Hollywood when they are doing a picture.

There are, of course, the exceptions — small groups of people who live much the same kind of life as they would in New York or Philadelphia: a few musicians meet weekly in each other's homes for chamber music; a group of actors, most of whom knew each other in New York, play charades until two A.M.; three or four writers, whose friendships date back to New York, and their wives, have an evening together in the rather simple style they enjoyed in the East. There is also a lively political activity, with lines drawn between left, right and center. For a few there is guild activity. Prominent actors give their time to try to settle a jurisdictional strike between two sets of rival carpenters, and are busy on negotiating committees for their own guild. The writers have preliminary caucusing, and a big turnout for the annual election of their guild officers. But these are not the dominating themes of Hollywood social life.

The majority revel in the sunshine and lush climate, enjoy a middle-class comfort or an upper-class luxury they never knew before; live in the intense hope that success is around the corner, if they have not already achieved it; bask in the excitement of the current studio crises; and think and talk only about movies with other movie people. The world outside is considered by them mainly in terms of box office, domestic and foreign. One successful man, who still retained a remembrance of another existence, said that Hollywood was like a "sealed chamber," and that one gradually accepted its standards and values, forgetting about others. There are many there who seem never to have had any other standards, and for whom Hollywood was and is the ultimate, for whom the glamour is real. Rupert Hughes in an article in the annual New Year edition of *Variety* (January 7, 1948), describes his picture of the attitude towards Hollywood three hundred years from now. He writes:

> What if, three hundred years from now, the people of Los Angeles should make shrines of the graves and birthplaces of moving picture writers, actors and directors? Pay tens of thousands for their scenarios?
>
> What will people three hundred years from now say of us who lived next door to the great geniuses who have created and perfected the world-shaking art of the cinema? . . .

For most people, successful and unsuccessful and regardless of their background, the tendency is to get caught in the Hollywood maze.

The emphasis upon sex in the popular mythology about Hollywood has perhaps more influence on the attitudes and conversation of the inhabitants than on their behavior. They have a standard to live up to. There is much talk about sex, and direct or indirect allusions to it are frequent in the gossip columns. Around the studios are more beautiful young women and handsome young men than can be found probably in any other place in the world. Nor are they just beautiful or handsome. Having a screen personality usually means that the actor or actress has a sex appeal obvious enough to come through on the screen. Sex and sexiness are in the air. Pretty young girls who come to Hollywood hoping for careers as actresses are prepared and ready to use sex as a means of getting ahead. It is part of the prevailing attitude of manipulation of people for career purposes, and sex is just one of several techniques. This attitude seems more common than the Bohemian one of sex for fun or pleasure. Among some of the group who have already achieved success, there does exist the attitude of bored rich people who hunt for new sensations and variations in sex patterns. But those same unconventionalities are found in New York and in Paris.

In studying peoples of different cultures, the social anthropologist is usually more concerned with attitudes towards sex than with a statistical enumeration of the frequency of the biological act. To those who know life in Mississippi or Vermont villages, in New York, or in any European capital, there seems, without statistical data, to be no more or less sexual activity in Hollywood than anywhere else. Those who talk most about the greater amount of sexual "goings-on" in Hollywood are either puritanical or ignorant of sex life in other places. Actually, a large number of Hollywood people live more or less "normal" family lives, and it is the current studio policy to do everything possible to publicize this. Publicity and fan magazines have been concentrating on pictures of "normal" family life. The April 1950 number of *Modern Screen* showed the following: Shirley Temple bringing up her young daughter, Susan, with five pictures of mother and daughter playing together; Olivia de Havilland in "She Knew What She Wanted," with pictures of her in an affectionate pose with husband, and other poses with her baby, serving lunch to her husband, playing croquet with him, and reading a script on her patio; John Derek and his wife in "Bluebird on the Window Sill," with seven pictures showing their domesticity. June Haver was featured in another story, "Winning a New Peace in Her Unselfish Devotion to Others." Gail Russell and Guy Madison were in a story called "They Don't Belong" (because they are just small-town folks wanting the simple things of life). Another tale was about Gene Kelly and his wife Betsy Blair; this was called "It Must Be Love," and described them as "the plainest, simplest, most unaffected couple in Hollywood. They don't even own a swimming pool." Still another was about the "exceptionally happy marriage" of Jeanne Crain and Paul Brinkman. Some of the Holly-wood stars have themselves been infected, and among these there is a cult for the "normality" of upper-class suburbia — which, of course, need not preclude extramarital relations. The myth of Holly-wood's greater sexuality, however, still prevails; its symbolism runs strong and deep both inside and outside of Hollywood. Attitudes there are primarily those of an adolescent type of boasting about sexual power and the use of sex to further careers, which of course is not confined to Hollywood, but is merely more open and frequent there.

The myth of easy and big Hollywood money also has consider-able basis in fact, but there is much that is not correct about it. Statistics may be published about the number of unemployed; the public remembers only the headlines about the enormous annual earning of stars and executives. In Hollywood itself the myth is completely believed. A man may be unemployed for years, or em-ployed in very minor jobs, but his strong belief that a fortune is just around the corner does not weaken. Since many of the fortunes are made by men with little training or special ability, the idea that they can be made by anyone persists.

Actually, the truth underlying the myth of easy money is that everyone in Hollywood is paid more than his counterpart outside, whether he be actor, writer, producer, publicity man, cameraman, carpenter, or electrician. Salaries are very high. This makes the fact that there is only one Hollywood in the United States and in the world particularly significant to anyone who loses his job. There is then almost no place for him to go to find the equivalent of Holly-wood money.[4] This strengthens the existing structure in Hollywood.

While Hollywood represents a monopoly there is, unlike other monopolies, competition among its members — the "big five" studios — for stories, stars, directors, producers and others. This competi-tion makes for some flexibility in the structure and occasionally

[4] A businessman, a teacher, a scientist, an artist, a journalist can usually work under much the same conditions and earn about the same amount of money in Chicago, San Francisco, Denver or New York.

permits an outstanding individual to influence it. The independent producer is another anomaly in this monopolistic structure, although his independence is by no means complete.

Perhaps the most fundamental and striking characteristic of the motion picture as an institution is that the making of movies is both a big business and a popular art. Certainly its financing, its relationships with banks, boards of directors and stockholders, its distribution and advertising, its problems of markets, domestic and foreign, and its labor relations are all the well-recognized parts of any big business. But its product is not like those of other businesses. The product of the movie industry is a story, told primarily in visual imagery and movement, and, since the introduction of the sound track, with dialogue. The movie shares the function of all storytelling, of all literature, of all theater: that of a comment on some phase of existence. Artists — including directors, writers, actors, photographers, musicians, cutters — are necessary to fulfill this function.

The general attitude in Hollywood, and out of it too, is to try to escape this essential dualism: Making movies must be either business *or* art, rather than both. For most people in executive positions it is a business, where, according to the folklore, "for a nickel you get a dollar." The goal is profits, large and quick ones. They call themselves "showmen," and any talk about the movies as art is for them the height of absurdity and unreality. Their problem is to find the least common denominator that will please the most people, and therefore bring in the most profits. For them there is a search for a "sure-fire" formula which will always work, in the same way that a certain formula for steel can be counted on to produce the best steel.

This point of view is well expressed in the following editorial by W. R. Wilkerson in the *Hollywood Reporter* (September 29, 1947):

> The drawing-room set is yelling: "Stop making pictures for Glendale. Stop catering to the morons and bring pictures up to an intelligent level." . . .
> We believe the majority of men at the head of this business

— showmen that they be — are possessed of as much intelligence as the drawing-room set. We feel that they too would like to lift our pictures up to a higher plane but every time they have shouldered that load they have found it too much to carry. As a consequence, they move down into the bracket that most of our theater customers patronize — shooting stories without too much of a problem, yarns that are easy to understand, making pictures that WILL entertain instead of making their audiences unhappy.

Pictures are essentially for entertainment. That's what has built this great industry — ENTERTAINMENT. Pictures are made for Glendale, for Kansas City and New York. Our pictures are made for the whole world, and that whole world has been buying them, which affords the tremendous pay checks handed out here every week and makes it possible for tremendous story costs. . . .

Glendale has been good enough for us for thirty years. It should be good for another hundred.

For the artist there is another traditional goal. He tries to give his interpretation of a segment of experience he has either known or observed, which he wants to communicate to others. This need for the individual artist to communicate his ideas to an audience seems far removed from the need to accumulate large profits. But the contradiction is not a true one. If the audience is large and the artist succeeds in communicating with it, profits follow naturally. Much money has been made by successful artists fulfilling their functions in the theater, and in literature, music and painting. The artists and the executives in the studios are both unrealistic in insisting on an "either . . . or" point of view. Movies are a mass medium and to remain as such in our society they must make a profit. In the end this may be desirable, since otherwise they might become esoteric. There can, however, be a considerable difference of opinion on what constitutes a fair or good profit and on the amount of experimentation desirable within a profitable business.

The producers and executives seem somewhat unbusinesslike in not recognizing the true nature of their medium and exploiting it to the utmost. To be sure, they employ artists and pay them high salaries, but instead of permitting them to function as such, they insist that the work be done according to the businessman's formula. For this reason the studio frequently does not get its money's worth from the artist. The chemist working in industry is allowed to function more within the framework of his training and background than is the artist in the movies. The most independent people in the latter industry are the cameramen, sound engineers and technicians, who can experiment and follow through their own ideas.

The position of the "expert" who is called in for temporary consultation on a picture is frequently like that of the artist. He is usually paid a high fee, and then very little or no attention is paid to his opinion. A psychoanalyst used as a consultant on a picture with a psychiatric theme is disturbed because his name appears in the list of "credits" for the picture, and contrary to his previous understanding with the studio. After seeing the picture, it is easy to understand this psychoanalyst's anxiety about his professional reputation. On the other hand, the movie *Snake Pit* clearly showed that there the expert's advice had been followed. As a result, the picture rang true and, it might be noted, was a far bigger box-office attraction than the phony one.

The conflict between business and art is not confined to different groups of men, but may be found within the same individual. The most businesslike executive is pleased when a reviewer praises his picture in terms other than box-office, and as drama. But in almost the same breath an important producer likens the product of the industry to cans of beans, pointing to some rolls of film lying in his office to make his allusion more striking, and a minute later says that he feels "like a god" with the capacity to make men laugh or cry. He then extols the movies as a combination of all the art forms, and talks of their world-wide significance.

For some men there seems to be continuous conflict, repeated for each picture, between making a movie which they can respect and the "business" demands of the front office. It is assumed, although there are many examples to the contrary, that a movie which has the respect of the artist cannot make money. The fact that a number of pictures — such as *Snake Pit* and *Best Years of Our Lives* — regarded by most critics as good from a dramatic point of view have also been big box office has not yet ousted front-office beliefs and traditions. Thus in a primitive society many natives may still cling to their magical cures after modern medical practices have been introduced. Their conservatism may be due to lack of understanding of the new medicine, and to resistance to change, and to fear, on the part of medicine men and elders, of losing prestige and power. Technically, this is called "cultural lag," more colloquially known as "not keeping up with the times."

The domination of the business executive over the artist in Hollywood is not surprising either in view of the history of the movies or in terms of American culture. Movies began as small business, an extension of the Coney Island type of entertainment. The men who started them — some still in control — were usually small entrepreneurs, some from the field of cheap entertainment, some from other small businesses. The artist was not even present. Later, when he arrived on the scene, he came as the employee of those men, who by this time were big business and who still remain firmly in control.

In the values of our culture as a whole, business has always been regarded as more important than art. To say someone is "arty" is a term of opprobrium, while to say he is businesslike is a compliment. Art and artists belong to the extravagances and to the periphery of society. Business and businessmen are the essentials which make the wheels go round. Intellectuals in general occupy much the same role as the artist, unless they can contribute directly to technological improvements or to the business of making money.

From an anthropological point of view, this order of importance has no God-given sanctity; nor is it necessarily valid to make such a clear-cut separation between the two. It is possible at least to conceive that the artist, who enriches our imagination, deepens our understanding of our fellow men, broadens our experiences and sharpens our sense of moral values, is as important as the businessman. Actually the whole problem — which is the more important — is a false one. Man is a complex creature and differs from other animals in that he cannot live by bread alone. For him the spirit, whether it is called imagination, ideas, morals, or goals, is necessary for survival. While there is some general awareness of this point of view, it is usually relegated to small esoteric groups.

The conflict between business and art in Hollywood is a reflection of the conflict within our culture, but it is more sharply focused there than elsewhere. It is not inherent or necessary in the production of movies, but rather a point of view culturally determined and exaggerated there.

Since the making of movies is a highly collaborative enterprise, in which no one works alone, a study of the relations between the people who share the undertaking is essential. The writer's situation cannot be understood unless his relationship with the producer is known; and the actor's problems are unintelligible without a knowledge of his relationship with directors; all these are interrelated with front-office executives, agents, publicity writers, and many others. While each group recognizes the collaborative nature of the medium, and gives it frequent verbal obeisance, each thinks its own function the most important. There is an obvious dependency of each group on the other, and at the same time a constant struggle for control and domination.

The overt verbal behavior in all these relationships is that of love and friendship. Warm words of endearment and great cordiality set the tone. But underneath is hostility amounting frequently to hatred, and, even more important, a lack of respect for each other's work. To the casual observer all relations seem to be on a remarkably personal level. But this is merely a sugar-coating for a deep impersonality. This impersonality comes out in two important ways. People are property in no uncertain terms, usually valuable property, and everyone has his price. Underlying the endearing terms of every conversation are the questions: "What can I get from him?" . . . "What does he want from me?" . . . "Will I need him in the future, if not now?" Human relationships are regarded as basically manipulative and are lacking in all dignity.

There is a constant "jockeying" for a superior position and power. But while the competition is hard and severe, there is among the competitors a great need for each other. In the struggle and competition for power within the industry, no one can knock his opponent completely out, because in the end all of them are needed to produce a movie. Another reason for not permitting hostilities to go too far is that status positions are transitory. One never can be sure how long any individual will remain at the top, middle, or bottom of the ladder. There is always the fear of antagonizing someone who may be important tomorrow. This could characterize only a relatively new industry. In an older one, power and status are more firmly entrenched and there is less questioning of it. The movies represent a last frontier in industry, with quick and sudden shifts. This intensifies competition, but at the same time makes it necessary to keep the adversary in a position of dependency, rather than to oust him.

The shifting nature of relationships in Hollywood is also seen in the relatively few stable partnerships. The relationships between writer and producer, director and actor and producer, usually last only for the duration of one picture. It is this situation which makes the gossip column in the daily trade paper, the *Hollywood Reporter*, and other similar columns, important and widely read; for it is in the gossip column that the news and intimations of new alignments may be first given. If two people are reported as dining together, that may mean they are making a deal of some kind. It was reported in one of these columns that the three-year-old girl of a producer was playing with the four-year-old child of a star who lived across the street. On the day this item appeared, the producer had some twenty-odd calls, including one from his lawyer, asking whether he was making some kind of deal with the actor.

Accompanying the transitoriness of personal relationships is the impermanence of friendships. Associates for evenings and week ends are drawn from the working companions of the day at the studio. Three months later there is a new set of associates. A man out of a job is usually a man out of friends. There seems to be a belief that success or failure is contagious through contact, a sort of sympathetic magic.

Although the production of movies, with its reliance on gossip columns and its lack of stability, is unbusinesslike in many ways, at the same time it has some of the characteristics of the assembly line. Producer, writer, director, actor, cameraman, cutter, musician, make-up man, set designer, and many others all have a set place and timing in the production. A unit manager endeavors to keep all efficiently geared to a schedule and a budget. The filming of sequences in a different order from that in which they finally appear contributes to the assembly-line analogy. So also does the breaking up of the writing of the script into many separate and seemingly disconnected elements. One man adapts from the novel or play, another rewrites this adaptation in the form of a script, another supplies gags or comedy touches, still another adds some characterizations, and finally the dialogue is polished by several more. All these work "under the thumb" of the producer. The emphasis given to technical details such as lighting and the great concern with appearances — costuming, sets and make-up — as compared to the meaning of the picture as a whole or its emotional validity are other characteristics similar to those of the assembly-line factory.

But closer examination reveals many other elements of movie making that are foreign to the assembly line. The raw material is not a piece of steel but a product of imagination, and there is an excitement in translating it into celluloid film to be seen by millions of people. Nor does this assembly line run with the smooth precision of careful planning. Rather it operates in an atmosphere of constant crisis, towards which there are differences of attitude. Some glory in it. This feeling is well expressed in an article by Maurice Bergman, whose theme is **Crisis Is the Backbone of Our Industry.** To prove his point the author makes a number of interesting statements, such as:

> Our adrenalin glands are more stimulated because we never know how good we are until the picture opens. . . . We are better conditioned to hysteria. We worry a lot, but our systems are attuned to worry. It's like other people being susceptible to the common cold. Our occupational disease is the stomach ulcer. If we escape the actuality of the ulcer, we always are reconciled to its imminence.
>
> That's why so many of us are hypochondriacs. Living in a two-dimensional world of profitable shadows that talk and make noise, we suddenly go into shock when we get exposed to the third-dimensional world.
>
> If a world economic crisis lurks around the corner, we con-

tinue our abstract but imaginative skirting around it, finding solace in the dream world we build to harmoniously fit in with the dreams of our customers (God bless them). It isn't that we like such crises. Existing as we do on the people's hopes and making films evocative of these hopes, we just can't let a crisis affect our creative efforts. We have to function in our own atmosphere of crisis. Betting $400,000,000 or so a year that the pictures will please is what we term a crisis *ab initio*.

When someone says, "Bergman, you look worried," I always answer by saying, "No wonder; I worry all the time."

But my worries are well channeled and logical and never get out of hand. Lacking blueprints, our minds (who's that heckler?) are flexible to the degree that we necessarily have a new intellectual wardrobe every week. . . . Let's remember that crisis is the backbone of our business.[5]

Mr. Bergman represents a point of view held by many.

There are others, a smaller number, who see that many of the crises are unnecessary and artificially stimulated, and who do *not* enjoy them. These people resent the almost complete lack of planning and the day-by-day opportunistic attitude. They would prefer business executives who did not pride themselves on being showmen running their business by "instinct," and whose behavior did not frequently resemble that of a prima donna following erratic whims. However, the atmosphere of continuous crisis helps create the illusion of everyone's and everything's being of the greatest importance. The star refuses to play the part as it was written — and there is a crisis on hand. The Motion Picture Association office has insisted on the deletion of something which the director thinks is necessary — and this is a crisis. The producer is tearing his hair because his $3000-a-week writer is not turning out the kind of script he wants. There is a big blow-up between two important people that leaves repercussions all around. A crisis next occurs in the publicity department, because it is discovered that a secretary has sent the wrong negative for a magazine cover to meet a New York date line; she is afraid that she will be fired, and the head of the department fears that this will be a black mark against him. There

[5] *Variety*, January 17, 1948.

are difficulties in shooting on location, and the unit manager is swearing over the phone to the director about the delay. . . . All are crises, part of the daily atmosphere. They are resolved; but everyone goes home at the end of the day exhausted. A few know, deep down, that the crisis is not really important and that the film will go on.

Sometimes, of course, the crisis *is* important, but often a trifling incident is blown up so as to appear a crisis. A studio limousine with two men in it drives twenty miles to an actor's home at midnight on Saturday to deliver one page of minor changes in the script of a film in which he will play a secondary role. He is not due to report to the studio for another two weeks. But — "Crisis is the backbone of our business."

Closely related to this crisis atmosphere is the lack of planning for training directors and actors and writers for their jobs. Instead, there is a parasitic reliance on stage, radio and literature, and on accidental "finds." As one might expect in such an atmosphere, there is also an anti-intellectual point of view, and the research done by the industry as a whole is negligible. Mr. Eric A. Johnston, the president of the Motion Picture Association of America, stated that the "film industry knows less about itself than any other major industry in the United States." [6] In the same interview he points up a number of questions to which the industry has no answer. Among them are: "What is the relationship between the cost of films and their drawing power?" . . . "Why do some people go to movies, and why do others stay away?" . . . "What sort of people are in each group?" The answers would be of inestimable value to the industry. But the research department, situated in New York, is small, operates on a meager budget and is not equipped to undertake extensive work.

The lack of both planning and useful research may be due, in part, to the phenomenal success of the movies and their big profits, which come so easily and in spite of the methods of production, rather than because of them. Moviegoing happens to be a popular habit that fills a real need, and it takes a lot to stop it.

[6] *Variety*, March 27, 1946.

Another part of the anti-intellectual attitude is revealed in the superstitions which abound. These are not just the traditional ones of actors, but the untraditional ones of executives. For instance, one producer had an enormous box-office success from a script which numbered two hundred and three pages. After that, all the scripts of his movies had to have two hundred and three pages, even if this result could be obtained only by the stenographic department through such devices as spacing and margins.

Every social system operates under a number of institutionalized controls, economic, religious, family, political, legal and others. In a Stone Age Melanesian society, one of the most important of these is the kinship system, which regulates all economic and social life. The power of the elders is another control; still another lies in the taboos handed down by tradition.

Hollywood has its controls, too, which influence the method of production, the relationships between people, and leave their stamp on the movies.

One of the Hollywood controls is that of the contract between any of the various talent guilds and the studio — which, while legalistic and economic in nature, contributes much to the psychological atmosphere. Everyone, except the front-office executive and producer, is in a guild or union.

The contracts which guilds have with the studios vary in details — such as in the range of salaries — but all have one very essential feature in common: the option clause. The option contract is usually made for a period of seven years, and the studio has the privilege of renewing or dropping the option — that is, firing the employee — at the end of each six months. (In some cases it is a year instead of six months, with sometimes an increase in salary if the option is taken up.) The employee cannot, however, leave the studio of his own volition until the seven years have expired. As a union contract which gives the employer the right to fire a worker every six months, but binds the latter for seven years' service, it is unique in trade union history. Hollywood presents the picture of a 100 per cent union community, paying the highest salaries in the country (not to mention the world), but with the atmosphere of a company town. It can also be viewed as a modern big industry, utilizing the very latest technological developments, with the air of a medieval manor and its relationships between master and serf.

In this case the master is the front-office executive; and behind him are the banks and financial interests with their goal of quick, sure and large profits. When the question is asked, "Does a picture make money?" it usually means, "Does the picture make money in the first six months?" — not over the two or three years it may be playing throughout the country.

"What are the net profits on any picture?" is the sixty-four-dollar question in Hollywood, and one of the most difficult on which to get exact data. Ideas on what is a good net profit range from 25 to 300 per cent, and 100 per cent is regarded as only average. The *Variety* headline of April 9, 1947 — **Film Biz Dips to Only "Terrific" from Used-to-Be "Sensational"** — is, according to the same paper, an "industry cliché."

The unusually high salaries are as important a control as the big profits. It is extremely difficult for the writer, the actor, the director, to do other than the bidding of the studio heads. He is paid highly for his docility, and it is an unusual man who will take a chance on losing a salary of two thousand dollars a week in order to keep his personal and creative integrity. Beverly Hills houses have been described as the "most beautiful slave quarters in the world." . . . With the best-paid slaves, it might be added.

A very important control is the star system, a keystone on which the social structure rests. The star is not only an actor, but one of the gods or folk heroes in our society. It is on his looks and personality that the picture is primarily sold, and he often takes precedence over every other element in the making of the movie. Scripts are frequently written with a particular star in mind; on the set it is his will, whether logically or temperamentally exercised, which is supreme. The ramifications of the star system permeate the entire structure and leave their indelible mark on the final product, the movie.

Censorship, both direct and indirect, is another active control.

There is the well-known Code in regard to subject matter and details of treatment — with its list of taboos that the producers impose upon themselves, a code carried out through the Production Code Administration of the Motion Picture Association of America — formerly known as the "Hays Office" — now headed by Eric Johnston and administered by Joseph Breen. More indirect is the control exercised by heterogeneous organized groups such as churches, temperance leagues, parent-teachers' associations, professional and occupational groups, national and racial groups and political parties. No one can say that the American public does not take its movies seriously, and no one could be more convinced of the profound influence of the movies than members of these organized groups. Their propaganda has two themes, both negative: (1) No member of their group must be portrayed in an unflattering manner, or as the "heavy." (2) No movie should emphasize drinking, delinquency, divorce, or immorality (on the premise that movies are the cause of these social ills, or at least of their frequency). The State Department has added its critical notes: (1) No picture should show in an unflattering light the members or institutions of a foreign country with which we have cordial relations. (2) Pictures designed for export abroad should "sell" the American way of life.

All these forms of direct and indirect censorship influence the script before a word is set on paper.

The producers' rule "Give the audience what it wants" is still another control. Many producers tend to see the audience in their own image. This does not, however, prevent some of them from also employing polling organizations to tell them what the audience wants in terms of plots, titles and stars.

The fears and anxieties which pervade all of Hollywood likewise function as controls. From top to bottom, no one is sure that his job or reputation will continue. "A man is only as good as his latest picture" is another saying of the industry. Even when his latest picture is successful, it does not insure the continuation of a job. Studio heads mysteriously "blow hot and cold" about their creative personnel. A man is in great favor one day, but not the next; reasons can only be speculated upon. Or, there may be a reorganization at the top of the studio or in a department; the folk proverb "A new broom sweeps clean" is frequently carried through in personnel policy. Even important executives may be "dropped" with very little notice. There is no security in employment for anyone.

Most people feel that they owe their positions and big salaries to "getting the breaks" rather than to their own ability and hard work. Anxiety is a natural accompaniment of such a situation. Luck and the breaks are by their nature transitory, and what comes in this way can go just as easily. Only a sense of one's own real ability can give a feeling of true security. Many people give the impression of Cinderella at the ball, just before the clock strikes midnight. They are scared that their chariots will be turned back to pumpkins and that the fairy godmother will disappear.

Every picture is regarded as an enormous gamble, surrounded by the greatest uncertainties of success at the box office. Whether or not this attitude of the gamble is justified by reality is, at least, open to question. Producers who talk most about the gambling aspects rarely experiment with a new kind of film or do anything not based on either a Broadway hit or a best-selling novel, or not insured by the presence of popular stars and a big exploitation campaign. But the attitude of uncertainty pervades the whole studio, and everyone — from the front-office executive, producer, director, actor, writer, to script girl and secretary — works under conditions of anxiety and tension.

To live in this situation individuals must, of necessity, develop ways of relieving the tensions, and some of the methods become institutionalized. The manner in which both the anxieties and the ways of meeting them leave their marks on the movies is seen in the more detailed discussions of writing, acting and directing in later chapters.

Frustrations and anxieties are not unique to Hollywood. They occur in every industry and society, and each society provides its compensations, too. Among the latter, in Hollywood, are the satisfactions which accompany any creation, although in the making of movies this satisfaction is frequently in inverse proportion to the creativeness of the individual. There is the camaraderie, the "kibitzing," the "smell" of the set. There is the excitement — particularly for little people — of being associated with something big, different and glamorous, something "new every day." There is the constant titillating experience of being with beautiful women and handsome men and in the general atmosphere of sexiness. But most important are the big salaries and enormous profits.

Some of the over-all important characteristics of the social structure of Hollywood have been briefly indicated. My hypothesis is that they determine, to a considerable degree, the kind of movies we see. I have mentioned the deep symbolism of Hollywood for the world, the importance of its situation in Los Angeles; I have pointed out that the movies are both big business and a popular art with widely differing goals and values, that the locus of power is in the front-office executives who control the artists, that the relationships are highly personalized on the verbal plane but impersonal on the deeper exploitive and manipulative level, that production resembles in some ways a modern factory assembly line and is at the same time characterized by constant crises, and that there are many controls — among which are big business, big profits, big salaries, censorship, the star system, "what the audience wants," and the ever-present fear and anxiety. All these leave their marks on the movies.

There is nothing in Hollywood which cannot be found elsewhere in the United States, or the rest of the world. Contradictory and conflicting patterns are part of our society. What is significant in Hollywood is the particular type of thinking and behavior which it elaborates at the cost of the kind it underplays.

Like all modern societies, Hollywood is in flux, and represents a changing situation. It has deep roots in the past, which dominate the present; but there are also new tendencies, not yet very strong, some of which may be merely aberrations — and others, signposts to the future.

CHAPTER II

Mass Production of Dreams

Hollywood is engaged in the mass production of prefabricated daydreams. It tries to adapt the American dream, that all men are created equal, to the view that all men's dreams should be made equal. Movies are the first popular art to become a big business with mass production and mass distribution. It is quite obvious that movies cannot be individually produced, and that some form of mass production is inevitable. But the assumption is that for any sort of mass production more than one kind of social system is possible. The question is therefore asked, Is the Hollywood system the most appropriate one for the making of movies — one form of an ancient and popular art, storytelling, in which the storyteller's imagination and understanding of his fellow men have always been a necessary ingredient?

The invention of the movie camera and the use of celluloid film brings the art into direct contact with a modern technology and makes it dependent on mass rather than individual production. New technology always precipitates changes in the method and system of production, whether it is of storytelling or agriculture. But the essential old elements do not completely disappear. In a primitive society, when new agricultural techniques are introduced, the nature of the soil and climate and the customs of the people cannot be negated, if the new techniques are to be successfully used. New technology in any society must be adapted and integrated with former patterns and adapted to the basic nature of the product to be produced. But instead of integrating, the old and new are sometimes in conflict; or they may run in parallel lines without much effect on each other. Of the three possibilities, Hollywood production of movies represents conflict.

A feature of all mass production is the uniformity of the manu-factured product. Hollywood has tried to achieve this by seeking formulas that it hopes will work for all movies and insure their success. It is ironical that this was more possible in the early days, when movies were small business, for then just the novelty of movement on the screen fascinated an audience. The common de-nominators of pantomime, slapstick and romance could be under-stood and enjoyed by uncritical audiences almost anywhere in the world. Since all members of the human species have the same basic needs and have some characteristics in common, there are certain simple forms of entertainment to which they can all respond. But now, when movies are big business, and the mass production and uniformity in the prefabricated daydreams more desirable to the manufacturer, such uniform products have become less salable. The only motion picture with a stereotyped plot which has met with a fairly consistent success over a long period of time is the Western. The formulas for other pictures have been a series of constantly changing *do's* and *don'ts*, such as, "You cannot make an A picture about a prize fight," "No picture with any kind of message can make money," "The love story must be the most important part of an A picture." Each one of these formulas has been successfully broken and shown to be false at one time or another through a box-office success. This was accomplished by someone with imagina-tion, courage and faith in his own judgment, usually a director or producer with sufficient prestige to get his own way. But each time anyone departs from the formula and meets with success, the de-parture then becomes another formula.

When *Lost Weekend*, made despite the misgivings of studio ex-ecutives by an imaginative team of director and writer, was very successful, the formula changed. It had been, "The leading character in a serious picture cannot be a drunkard. Drunkards are for comedies." After the success of *Lost Weekend*, there were attempts to repeat the new formula. *Smash-Up* with a woman alcoholic as its main character, was one of the repetitions, but had neither the power of *Lost Weekend* nor its profit at the box office.

The movie *Body and Soul* broke the formula that "You cannot make a successful A picture about a prize fight." *Snake Pit*, a serious film about insanity — which most executives would have regarded as an unprofitable theme — was one of the top-grossing pictures in 1949, and, according to *Variety* of January 12, 1949, was almost as "strong" in smaller towns as in big cities such as Chicago and New York.

Crossfire, one of the first pictures with a definite message about anti-Semitism, made money. Since then there have been a whole cycle of pictures like *Home of the Brave*, *Lost Boundaries* and *Pinky*, with messages about the Negro problem, and these have all been profitable. Contrary to expectations they have been O.K.'d for distribution and were successful in the South, in spite of its well-known resistance to pro-Negro themes. *Variety* (October 5, 1949) says: "The career of *Home of the Brave* in the South was a virtual walkover."

Pinky was the second-largest top-grossing picture of 1949.[1] The industry then changed its formula to "Any message picture will make money" and produced a cycle of anti-Communist pictures. Certainly the anti-Red pictures were congenial to the prevailing political atmosphere, and their box office should have been helped by their timeliness with the headline news plus the strong exploitation campaigns. Yet *I Married a Communist*, *The Iron Curtain*, *The Red Menace* and *Red Danube*, the major anti-Communist movies, have not been successful either at the box office or with the critics. Their lack of success, which was contrary to all expectations, had nothing to do with their message but much to do with their poor quality: "The public will buy 'message' pix, but they gotta be good."[2]

The criteria of good entertainment might be applied to any picture, with or without a message. But good entertainment is not harmonious with the following of formulas and the use of stereotypes. Year after year, the list of top box-office hits indicates great diversity in audience tastes, and includes musicals, serious dramas, adventure and suspense stories, comedies, farces, war and historical themes. The four top-grossers of 1947 were such different pictures as: *Best Years of Our Lives*, *Duel in the Sun*, *The Jolson Story*, and

[1] *Variety*, Jan. 4, 1950.
[2] *Ibid.*, Oct. 5, 1949.

Forever Amber. The top-grossers of 1948 also showed diversity. According to *Variety* of January 5, 1949, they were: *Road to Rio, Easter Parade, Red River, Three Musketeers, Johnny Belinda, Cass Timberlane, Emperor Waltz* and *Gentleman's Agreement*. In 1949 the five largest box-office hits, all grossing over $4,000,000, were widely different: *Jolson Sings Again, Pinky, Male War Bride, Snake Pit,* and *Joan of Arc.* Those movies which have been acclaimed by the more serious critics also show diversity. But in spite of this demonstrated many-sided character of the taste of movie audiences, the industry continues to look for formulas, and to produce cycles of pictures dealing with the same theme. This continues even though the exhibitors, the businessmen who operate the theaters, protest. "One of the biggest squawks now being voiced by circuit ops [operators] is that their theaters are being deluged by an unbroken string of cycle pix." [3] The particular complaint voiced in this article is against the six musicals released and made available by majors within four or five weeks.[4] This followed a prior cycle of ten A pictures which were Westerns.[5]

Theater operators say that cycles are bad business and that the law of diminishing returns starts working long before the end of one is reached. The audience gets tired of the same theme over and over again.

The industry attempts not only to use formulas for movie plots, but to use star actors as another formula for success, and to stereotype actors, those who play secondary roles as well as stars. Both these practices are considered in the discussion of actors and acting.[6] The points are only briefly mentioned here as examples of the industry's attempt to substitute formulas for the storyteller's imagination and skill.

A well-known maxim in the industry is, "We give the public what it wants." The technique of the polling organizations used to

[3] *Ibid.,* Aug. 3, 1949.

[4] *Look for the Silver Lining, It's a Great Feeling, You're My Everything, Yes Sir, That's My Baby, In the Good Old Summertime* and *Top o' the Morning.*

[5] *Whispering Smith, Yellow Sky, Streets of Laredo, Canadian Pacific, El Paso, Colorado Territory, The Younger Brothers, Red Canyon, Tulsa* and *South of St. Louis.*

[6] See Chapters XI, XII, XIII.

find out what the public wants is to ask members of a "sample" a question, such as, "Would you like to see a movie based on a story about —— ?" following with a condensation of the proposed plot in a few sentences. In some polls the names of stars who will play in the films are used. Other polls are taken for preferences in titles and for the depth of audience penetration reached by the publicity and advertising campaigns. I am particularly concerned with the first type of polling, designed to find out what kind of story the public likes, because it is this which affects the content of movies.

From the point of view of good business and as a way of producing movies, this type of research appears both unsuitable and wasteful financially. Consumers' research on such problems as whether people prefer this or that type of automobile has been useful. But the underlying principles are quite different from those involved in audience research. The average person does not know what movie he likes to see until he has seen it. If asked by the polling expert, his answer may depend on what he has last seen. If he liked the last psychological murder thriller, he is apt to say that he will like another one. But the movie on which he is being polled will not be finished and ready for distribution for a year or a year and a half later. By that time he may be bored by a long succession of similar plots, or his taste may have changed. It is also very doubtful if the plot is the primary reason for an audience liking or not liking a picture. A very good plot may be ruined by a poor script and bad direction and acting, while a slim, inconsequential one may be delightful because it is well written and acted.

The movie industry has taken over the polling devices of other big businesses without even realizing that they may even be detrimental to making movies. Mr. Sidney Buchman, the producer of *A Song to Remember*, a picture based on the life of Chopin, said that he wondered what would have happened if the surveyors on story content had asked, "Would you go to see a picture full of classical music?" or "Would you go to see a picture about an eighteenth-century composer?" "Answers, he felt, would be largely in the negative, yet the film proved a b. o. [box-office] success." [7] The film caused an enormous increase in the sale of Chopin records, and

[7] In an interview quoted in *Variety*, May 6, 1946.

my question is, "How could people know if they wanted to see a film with a lot of Chopin music in it, if they had never heard any?" Good ideas for films, which might have been successful if well done, may be shelved because the polling organization advises that they are "poison." How many successful novels would never have been written, if they had been subjected to the same pre-testing?

Underlying this whole process of polls is a lack of understanding of the creative process underlying storytelling and an attempt to imitate practices of other big businesses. If a poll of prospective customers for a new automobile indicates that they prefer one with four doors rather than two, this would in no way interfere with the functioning and efficiency of the workers in an automobile factory. But a gifted writer or director loses much of his efficiency and creative skill if he works not out of his own knowledge of what is true, but according to what a polling organization tells him the public wants. The production of movies is a creative process, and this characteristic does not disappear even when it is denied. It is illogical to carry the premises underlying the manufacture and merchandising of automobiles to the making and selling of movies, because the problems involved are essentially different.

The polling experts conduct their surveys not only on the content of films, but also on how they should be edited or cut. A preview is held before a sample of about eighty people who hold a little gadget in their hands which they press at times of greatest interest, and this is electrically transferred to a graph, which will determine whether scenes stay in or come out. The gadget takes over part of the cutter's job, one of the most skilled operations in production of movies. A story circulated around Hollywood about a pre-testing graph which gave no indication of any audience reaction to intensely exciting scenes. It was later found out that the audience had been so excited that they forgot to press the gadget. Again it seems to be a mistake in business judgment to think that there can be any substitute for knowledge and judgment. Only the lazy or ignorant man wants a substitute. For others there is a pleasure in the exercise of judgment. Machines may and do reduce man's labor and even take its place, but they are not substitutes for thinking and knowledge.

Instead of adapting the use of polls and gadgets in an undiscriminating fashion from other big businesses, the industry might find it more profitable in terms of dollars and cents if it attempted to learn about relevant changes in behavior and attitudes among the American people. A knowledge of its market, present and potential, is needed by any big industry, but this kind of study is not within the province of polling organizations. The world in which audiences lived during the first quarter of the century is obviously very different from the one of today. Therefore, they need and enjoy different kinds of daydreams, fantasies and stories. The movie audience has not only increased numerically but has become increasingly more diversified from the early days of working-class audiences who went to the first silent movies. Today, the audience differs widely in age, experience and background and all these condition the kind and quality of movies it wants to see. Nor is any individual so restricted that he can enjoy only one type of movie.

The increasing spread of college education, which received such an impetus after World War II from the financial aid extended by the government to former G.I.s, cannot help but further modify standards and tastes in all the popular arts. Likewise, one can predict changes in the future when the present generation of children becomes adults. Movies for them are not confined to "entertainment" in the neighborhood theater. They are continuously being exposed to 16 mm. educational and documentary films, in schools, clubs and even churches. Courses in film making and lectures on film appreciation are being given in many schools. Making movies is a pastime in some homes and a Handbook of *Basic Motion-Picture Techniques* [8] has been published for amateur movie makers. "Cinema 16" and other noncommercial movie societies continue to increase. This kind of familiarity is bound to produce innovations in both standards and attitudes concerning movies. But a knowledge of such changes cannot be gained through the use of mechanical polls and gadgets.

One man, Mr. Maxwell Shane, a writer-producer-director, decided to do some personal research on what kind of movies the

[8] New York, Whittlesey House.

public wants. He took a two months' eight-thousand-mile automobile tour through twenty-four states, talking to several thousand people about the kind of movies they wanted to see. Mr. Shane came back with several important conclusions which he reported in an article. Conclusion Number One was:

> The Hollywood belief that there is a difference between the big-town and the small-town market is an absolute myth. A gas station attendant in Sidney, Nebraska, had the same approach to the same badly made melodrama as a haberdasher in the Chicago Loop. Lumberjacks in Fort Bragg, Calif., had the same admiration for *Champion* as the formally attired hotel manager whom I queried in Seattle. A general store clerk in Cook, Minn., surprised me with the same Bob Hope wisecrack I'd heard from a taxicab driver in Los Angeles. . . . Don't decline to make an adult picture solely on the absurd theory that the folks out around Bumpkin Corners won't go for it.

His second conclusion was:

> Above all else, American audiences want motion pictures to be honest. Again and again I heard the complaint that, in effect, too many pictures are based on patently false premises or that they fall apart through shabby contrivance and completely unrealistic character motivations. . . . It pretty much comes down to the fact that audiences simply do not want to be told at the outset of a film that what they are about to see is a mirror of life, only to be shown characters who act like idiots and are inspired by emotional drives incomprehensible to all but advanced psycho-pathologists. I concluded that the public at this time will "buy" two kinds of pictures: those which state at the outset that they concern real human beings reacting to recognizable situations and which follow through to recognizably valid conclusions, and those which state in one way or another at the outset that they are really kidding and intend to entertain without reflecting life. These are the fantasies, the farces, the fairy tales. They must be labeled as such. In other words, the ticket-buying public will no longer accept those Hollywood concoctions which pretend to be reflections of real life but which spectators recognize as be-

ing real only to certain writers and directors and producers, who get all their ideas of real life from each other and from other movies.[9]

When Mr. Shane returned to Hollywood, he attended a convention of the Theater Owners of America and told them about his findings and conclusions. Mr. Shane said, however, *that no one would believe him.*[10] The theater owners are an important part of the industry; but on this occasion, at least, they appeared to have a closed mind even to learning about their customers.

The anthropologist wonders if the general attitude of the industry towards its audience represents a survival from the past, to which it stubbornly and unrealistically clings. A newspaper columnist put it another way when he said:

> No longer should films be conceived as an exchange of baby talk between far-flung masses. Important people listen in to the conversation now and switch off, if it is not to their liking. . . . Movies, let the moguls recognize, have become the conversation of nations. By the quality of its conversation a nation is judged.[11]

However, when movies became big business, the heads of the industry did quickly adopt some of the monopolistic characteristics of large-scale mass production. The desire for uniformity in its product and the use of formulas and of polling devices are all part of the same trend. The business functions of movie production reach far beyond Hollywood, extending not only to New York and Chicago and every town in the United States where there is a motion picture theater, but also to every part of the world where American films are shown.

The five major companies, Metro-Goldwyn-Mayer, RKO Radio Pictures, Inc., Twentieth Century-Fox Film Corp., Inc., Warner Brothers Pictures, Inc., and Paramount Pictures, Inc., control a large number of subsidiaries such as film laboratories, lithographing con-

[9] *New York Times*, Oct. 16, 1949.
[10] *New York Times*, Oct. 16, 1949. Italics ours.
[11] James Mason, guest columnist in Leonard Lyons's column, *N. Y. Post*, Feb. 13, 1948.

cerns, radio manufacturing subsidiaries, music publishing houses, real estate companies, booking agencies, broadcasting corporations, recording studios and television companies.

This diversity of interest is represented on the board of directors of each large motion picture company by bankers, real estate men, theater owners and heads of production. Executive personnel are men of high finance and real estate interests, as well as those in charge of production.

However, the real backbone of the monopoly has been in the control by one company of production, distribution and exhibition. The top executives of the three departments relating to theater, sales and production have decided on "the number of pictures to be made, the total amount of money to be spent, the distribution of funds between the various classes of pictures, the budgets of the individual pictures, and the dates when they are to be finished." [12] The distributor has been the middleman who rents the film to the exhibitor or theater owner. Since the majors have owned the first-run theaters which provide a large part of the film rentals, they have been their own best customers.

This three-way control has been investigated by the Federal Trade Commission and the Anti-Trust Division of the Department of Justice for more than twenty years.[13] An antitrust suit was brought against the majors with the aim of divorcing exhibition from production and distribution. A consent decree in 1940 provided for modifications, by restricting rentals in the block-booking [14] to five films at a time, the elimination of blind selling by having trade showings of all films before their release, and an agreement by the five majors not to expand their theater holdings.[15]

A new federal decree regulating the film industry was issued in 1946. It further banned block-booking and was designed to

[12] Mae D. Huettig, *Economic Control of the Motion Picture Industry*, pp. 59–60. Phila.: Univ. of Penn. Press.

[13] The first antitrust suit against legitimate theater interests was filed February 21, 1950. This charged the Shubert Brothers with controlling thirty-seven theaters in the United States and also controlling a large part of all bookings.

[14] Block-booking is "the simultaneous leasing of groups of films at an aggregate price fixed upon the condition that all the films in the given block be taken." (Huettig, *op. cit.*, p. 116.)

[15] Huettig, *op. cit.*, p. 140.

break monopolistic practices and encourage competitive ones. It also aimed at the partial divorcement of studios from theater ownership.

Since then the Department of Justice has been trying to compel the major motion picture companies to split into separately owned theater companies and producing-distributing ones, thereby weakening monopolistic practices. All the major companies have fought the trend to divorcement and there have been endless negotiations, litigations, compromises and revisions of the original decree. Some of the ties between production and ownership of theaters have been broken, but others remain. Independent theater companies have been established by some movie companies, while others are still in the midst of negotiations and court cases.

Monopolies seem to continue in our country in spite of all the antitrust legislation. Sometimes the laws are not fully enforced. At other times, while the forbidden practices are stopped, different devices with the same goals take their place. How far legislation can keep strongly entrenched customs, particularly profitable ones, from functioning is an interesting but difficult question to answer for any society.

While the relationship between the production and distribution phases of the industry has been close, it has not been harmonious. Instead, there has been complete distrust. The trade papers have carried many stories about how distributors, exhibitors and producers have all been victims of each other. Theater exhibitors complain about the poor quality of the films, how bored their audiences are, and how poor business is. This seems to be an almost chronic state of mind among exhibitors, particularly small-town ones. A Hollywood definition of an exhibitor is "a man who goes to Florida for the winter on his losses." The editor of the *Hollywood Reporter*, a spokesman for the producers, had the following to say about the exhibitors on August 20, 1947:

> In the present over-all effort to save picture money to plug any gaps that might be created by losses in foreign markets, it might be well for our company heads and their distributors to go on an all-out drive to stop the thieving of

their monies by crooked exhibitors, who, we are told, have been taking an estimated $10,000,000 to $15,000,000 a year from box-office receipts, on percentage pictures, that should justly be resting in the bank accounts of the distributors. It has become quite evident that this business of giving our majors wrong reports on the ticket sales of their pictures has jumped to enormous proportions, with the checking systems employed by the distributors lacking in efficiency. Too, once an exhibitor is caught, our distribution heads have let him off too easily, accepting some small settlement. Then the distributor goes right back, sells him more pictures and will probably get the same treatment.

Two years later, however, Mr. Eric Johnston, president of the MPAA, made a plea at an all-industry public-relations conference, held in Chicago at the end of August 1949, for the end of intra-mural feuds. He said: "We are often our own worst enemies . . . This industry is as riddled with inter-industry strife as any I have ever seen." [16] It was pointed out that this "internecine sniping" contributed to bad public relations, the subject of the Chicago conference. The intra-industry squabbles, also, according to Mr. Johnston, make the industry the "most lawsuit-ridden" one in the country, and the "lack of unity weakens the industry's position in Washington." [17] A Conference Committee consisting of representatives of the participating groups of the Chicago conference was formed "to spread the gospel of intra-industry unity." [18] No one can tell how successful their efforts will be.

But whether exhibitors or producers quarrel or make up, they are dependent on each other. The producers must have theaters as an outlet, and the exhibitors are dependent on films. The exhibitors' influence tends to be on the conservative side; they are reluctant to experiment with anything different from the sure and tried box-office hits.

The monopolistic character of the industry has been challenged not only by federal antitrust decrees, but also by the growing

[16] *Variety*, Aug. 31, 1949.
[17] *Ibid*.
[18] *Ibid*., Sept. 7, 1949.

development of independent producers. In 1946 more than a third of all films in production were being shot by independent units,[19] and according to *Variety* (January 7, 1948) in 1947 more than one hundred independent companies were formed carrying budgets of over four million.

This development continues from two quite different causes. One comes from the Treasury Department. "The artists, dismayed by wartime income-tax rates, went into business for themselves as independent producers in order to pay a capital gains tax rather than income tax." [20] The other, according to the same writer, is the itch of the director, writer, actor, and producer to gain more control over the medium, to be in the driver's seat. However, their independence is circumscribed, since the outlets for distribution are limited to the major companies. The latter therefore exercise a considerable control, in that they still put their O.K. on the kind of pictures they wish to distribute and refuse their O.K. for others. Many of the independents use the production facilities of a big studio, and expenses and profits are shared. The independents, who have their own organization, have been active in fighting co-operative buying-booking combines, and have welcomed the decisions of the Department of Justice that favor separating the exhibition and the production activities of the major companies.

Like any other big business, the motion picture industry is dependent on capital, which can be defined as a potential for production.[21] More than most, Hollywood operates on borrowed funds.[22] The Bank of America, which handles an estimated 70 per cent of the film-making loans in this country, makes some credit advances . . .

as high as eighty and even ninety per cent in the cases of producers having strong stories and casts, and backed by records of previous successes and the number of their features still

[19] Borneman, Ernest, "Rebellion in Hollywood. A Study in Motion Picture Finance," *Harper's*, October 1946.
[20] Borneman, *op. cit.*, p. 337.
[21] Roger Burlingame, *Backgrounds of Power*, p. 192. New York: Scribners.
[22] Mae D. Huettig, *op. cit.*, p. 98.

bringing in income. . . . A few of the banks which formerly went up to sixty-five per cent of a picture's total cost, cut the amount to fifty per cent. . . .[23]

Since the banks and motion picture finance corporations which supply these funds require regular fixed charges, the tendency to experiment is restricted. The banks lend money only for those films which they consider good risks.

A vice president in charge of film loans for a large New York bank is quoted as saying: "Whenever we lend a producer money, we insist on seeing the shooting script. We make sure it fits our idea of what will make a good picture. That is only common business prudence." [24] By a "good picture," the vice president indicated later in the interview that he meant a film entertaining enough to pay its way. Bank executives therefore have an important voice in the decision on what kind of entertainment will be popular. However, it is the men in charge of the Hollywood studios who implement the decision and who control the actual spending of the money. The lavish and often unnecessary extravagance which, until the present economy wave, characterized the entire industry is not exactly a secret.

Money is, of course, not the only form of capital. Most businessmen know that special skills, knowledge, intelligence and a strong drive are also potentials for production. In the motion picture industry, in addition to the capital supplied by banks or other sources, there are the intangibles, such as the highly specialized crafts and arts involved in telling a story in film.

The skills of the writers, directors, actors, and other artists are as necessary to the production of movies as are the funds borrowed from the banks. The question of whether Hollywood gets its money's worth from these employees, and whether it utilizes their special gifts as well as do the big businesses which employ chemists, physicists or other scientists, interests the anthropologist but is rarely heard in Hollywood.

All these are the problems of any large industry. Yet of prime

[23] *Hollywood Reporter*, April 21, 1947.
[24] *Variety*, Aug. 4, 1948.

importance remains one fact: The product of the dream factory is not of the same nature as are the material objects turned out on most assembly lines. For them, uniformity is essential; for the motion picture, originality is important. The conflict between the two qualities is a major problem in Hollywood.

CHAPTER III

Taboos

Every part of movie production is circumscribed by a very specific Code of taboos. We know all societies, from primitive ones to modern Hollywood, have their "thou-shalt-nots." In the South Seas they are a way of dealing with the supernatural to avoid certain dangers and to insure success, particularly in those situations in which luck or chance play a part. In Hollywood they are also a technique to escape dangers which, although of this world, are so fearful as to appear almost supernatural; and here too they are part of a formula for trying to make success more certain.

Among Stone Age Melanesians in the Southwest Pacific there is a taboo on sex relations before a fishing expedition, to insure a good catch. In Hollywood there is a taboo on portraying in a movie any indication that a marriage has been consummated, and for the same reason: to prevent hostile forces from interfering with the catch — at the box office. The most important and universal taboo in all primitive culture is the prohibition of incest far beyond the limits of the immediate family; in some places half the females are forbidden to the males, and vice versa. If individuals are caught in an incestuous act, they either commit suicide or are killed by their relatives. The breaking of this taboo is thought to endanger the very life of the society in some terrible but indefinable way, and the death of the violators serves as a kind of appeasement. In the Hollywood production of movies, there is an equally important taboo prohibiting any reference to the biological nature of man or other animals. There can be no dialogue, serious or farcical, about the mating of men, elephants, horses, moths, or butterflies; even a wet baby in need of being diapered is absolutely forbidden. Violators of these taboos do not commit suicide nor are they killed by members of their clan. But they are refused its seal of approval, which is considered a form of business suicide.

Among primitive peoples there is an implicit and absolute belief not only in their taboos, but also in the way of thinking and living which they represent. No one takes them lightly or facetiously and there are rarely any heretics. A few taboos in our own society, such as incest in the immediate family, or any threat to private ownership of property, are likewise maintained with a high degree of conviction and belief in the seriousness of their violation. In the Deep South, the taboos on social relations of equality between white and colored people are also earnestly observed. Most of our taboos spring out of a desire to maintain the *status quo* and from some deep fear, similar to that of primitive men, that something terrible will happen if the prohibitions are broken. Values underlying these taboos are a strongly intrenched part of our customary thinking and behavior and men believe that life as they know it, whether in the South Pacific or in Mississippi, depends on obeying. So naturally all feel safer when the taboos are maintained.

The Hollywood taboos embodied in the self-imposed Production Code have the same psychological origin as do those of primitive man, fear. But they differ in that they do not represent the actual beliefs, values, or behavior of the people practicing them. Taboos in Hollywood apply not to the personal lives of the makers of movies, but to the content of the movies, and the fears are not of the supernatural, but of a quite specific threat in this world, censorship. This threat existed earlier, but became more serious after the First World War, in the early twenties, when opposing social trends were in conflict. On the one hand, there was then a general loosening of sex standards in behavior, conversation, books and plays, and some producers eagerly exploited the risqué and daring; on the other hand, there were strong reformist groups who believed they could cure social ills through legislation such as the prohibition amendment. Spurring on those groups who were already critical of movies and fearful of their influence was the well-publicized notorious conduct of certain movie stars who flaunted traditional sex mores. The court case of "Fatty" Arbuckle, in which he was charged with manslaughter occurring at a riotous party, increased the vigor of the reformers. Although Arbuckle was acquitted after several trials, public indignation was so intense that his film career was ended.

At this time there was considerable debate on the extension of censorship on state and community level. Various groups wished legislation to prevent whatever they considered immoral and unsuitable in films. The definition of immorality and unsuitability varied from one community to another, and if this kind of censorship were extended, the number of cuts and rejections would be so increased as to seriously threaten mass production. It would even be difficult for the industry to survive, if each one of the forty-eight states and a number of municipalities had their own separate censorship laws. The answer to the industry was a new trade association, headed by Mr. Will Hays and later, by Mr. Eric Johnston.[1] It was natural for an industry which had developed from an early period of rivalry and competition between studios, and had then expanded and consolidated to the point of becoming a trust, to act as a unit when it was threatened by an extension of censorship. But its united action was not to fight this ominous danger, utilizing the strong American traditions of freedom from censorship which have always applied to newspapers, books and other forms of mass communication. Instead, the fear of the studio executives was so great that they seemed to endow their adversaries with a supernatural power, and the industry's answer was appeasement through a self-imposed set of taboos.

Like primitive man, Hollywood prefers magic to either fighting or reasoning with menacing forces. The forces of censorship seem to most Hollywood people so powerful and so unreasoning as to take on the quality of a black magician aiming malevolent spells. A set of taboos, while it does not destroy this threatening power, seems to the industry to ward it off, just as primitive man thinks magic and taboos lessen the dangers of the supernatural and the evil intentions of other beings.

[1] For a detailed history of the "Hays" office, see R. A. Inglis, *Freedom of the Movies, A Report on Self-regulation from the Commission on Freedom of the Press.* Chicago: Univ. of Chicago Press.

The trust now took on a moral face, and Mr. Will Hays was in charge of the face-lifting. The beginning of this process was called a "formula," which consisted of a rather loose arrangement to prevent certain types of books and plays from being filmed. The next was a list of "Don'ts and Be Carefuls," which were superseded in 1930 by the Motion Picture Production Code; this with certain additions is in operation today. It is concerned with morality and taste. Among its specific taboos are those related to sex, crime, vulgarity, religion and the feelings of racial, national and religious groups.

The office of the Production Code Administration of the Motion Picture Association of America is empowered to give a certificate of approval when the prohibitions are obeyed. Formerly, there was a fine for any exhibition of pictures without such a certificate; but since 1942, the fine has applied only to production and distribution. This office regards itself as a service organization to studios and works with a producer from the time he considers buying a novel, play or story, or suggestion for a story, until the completion of a film. Staff members of the MPAA read each script presented and analyze it for two main points: the theme and the details. The solution of the problem in a story will frequently determine its acceptability or unacceptability. If sin or crime go unpunished, the theme is not acceptable. Once the theme is accepted, there is detailed criticism of dialogue and scenes in terms of the various taboos of the Code. The MPAA staff members confer with the studios, giving them a list of unacceptable points and often suggest changes which would make the film acceptable. The seal of approval is not given, however, until the finished film is seen.

But after all the changes have been made and the seal of approval granted, it is decidedly questionable whether the large majority of pictures are the "correct" entertainment defined in the preamble of the Code — one which "raises the standards of the whole nation" — or whether they meet the aim of the Code, "to recreate and rebuild human beings exhausted with the realities of living." Discounting the window-dressing of the noble-sounding preamble, it can be further questioned whether the Code succeeds in its specific restraints on sex, crime and violence. In primitive societies

the taboo on incest is actually a restraining force, decidedly limiting
incestuous relations. But although the MPAA Code of taboos is more
or less obeyed, everyone inside and outside of Hollywood knows
that sexiness is a prime requisite for all actors and for most movies,
and that crime and violence dominate a very large number of
them. The anthropologist is skeptical as to whether the Code is
really concerned with morality. Biological facts of life are not
necessarily synonymous with morality, and are certainly not the
whole of it. Truthfulness is usually considered an essential part
of morality, but honesty is completely missing from most movies.
Neither the office of the Production Code Administration nor most
of the movie makers are concerned whether characters are presented as passive robots moved about by the exigencies of a plot, or
as human beings of dignity, whether solutions to problems are
phony or honest. It is further questionable whether either morality
or taste can be achieved through following a set of taboos imposed
out of fear. Both have a way of seeping through rules and taboos.

The manner in which the Code is implemented helps explain
why it is so unsuccessful. It is particularly concerned that no one
be incited by movies to either sexual or criminal behavior and that
the feelings of no group of people be hurt through their characterization in a film. The MPAA tries to achieve these ends by minute attention to details which insure the technical appearance of
virtue, the negation of all biological aspects of the human species
as well as other animals, the punishment of all crime and sin, and
the omission of its details. It also tries to keep to a minimum unfavorable characterizations of members of any racial, religious, national or occupational group, and to offset them by favorable portrayals.

The nominal appearance of virtue is maintained in a number of
ways. No prostitute can be shown in a movie. If a script calls for
prostitutes they are changed to dancing girls, barmaids, or hostesses.
In a movie set of the early days of a Western frontier town, filled
with gun toters and whiskey drinkers, the town's rough spot, a
combined saloon and house of prostitution, was changed to a
boardinghouse and the prostitutes to dancing girls. In a similar

movie the prostitutes, in a saloon, were called hostesses — a peculiar use of the word in that time and setting. It is probably now taken for granted by most movie-goers over the age of twelve that dancing girls and hostesses in saloons and cafés are prostitutes. (Those under twelve would probably not know what a prostitute was, even if she were plainly labeled.) But the MPAA has been successful in maintaining the appearance of virtue.

All suggestions of sexual intimacy in and out of marriage are taboo. Producers are regularly cautioned that a married man and woman should not be "overly eager to exercise their marital privileges." In one film, the MPAA asked for the deletion of dialogue which indicated that a husband wanted to sleep with his wife. In another, it recommended that the studio omit the "dissolve" which might imply that a man and his wife would consummate their marital relationship, and it was further recommended that the breakfast scene the next morning not play up the fact that they had enjoyed themselves. In one movie, there was disapproval of a sign DO NOT DISTURB being placed on the stateroom door of a young married couple and also of a reference to the "first night." In another picture a scene showing a soldier who has been away for several years as glad to see his wife and wanting to sleep with her is regarded as too "intimate." Even gestures of affection between a man and wife are taboo. The MPAA asked for omission of a scene in which a man was buttoning his wife's dress and kissed the back of her neck, and of another showing a husband giving an affectionate pinch to his wife's posterior.

The suggestion of frustration in marriage is just as taboo as that of the enjoyment of marital privileges. In one picture the MPAA disapproved of dialogue which suggested that a husband and wife could not satisfy their sexual desires because he worked at night; and in another, of a scene which indicated that the heroine was frustrated because her husband was excessively preoccupied with his business affairs.

Any suggestion of sexual intimacy or physical contact outside of marriage is completely taboo. The code insists that when the hero and heroine are not married, it must be clearly shown that the male does not stay overnight. In one romantic comedy, the hero

was shown leaving the girl's apartment at night and sleeping some-
where else. When he returned in the morning, he had to be plainly
seen coming from his hotel. Equally great care was taken in a
murder mystery without romance and in which the two leads had
not as much as held hands. The hero was a private detective trying to find a murderer and doing his best to outwit the police.
When he is leaving with two police officers, he says to the girl,
"Better not wait up for me." In the movie it was completely clear
that nothing had happened between the girl and the detective, and
that he used the phrase "wait up" to fool the police. But the Code
office was interested only in the words, "Wait up," not in the
meaning conveyed by the picture, and so asked for deletion of
the word "up."

In another picture in which two of the characters are much
attracted to each other and supposedly in love, the MPAA asked for
omission of the scene in which the couple's legs touched each
other under the table in a restaurant. Great care must be taken
with all kissing or embracing. No embrace can be made in a hori-
zontal position, and love-making is never supposed to take place
on a bed, even if the characters are both dressed and married. With
monotonous insistence the correspondence between studio and
MPAA on almost every picture includes the sentence, "There must
be no open-mouthed or lustful kissing," and the closed mouth in
kissing is one of the many technicalities rigidly insisted upon. The
Code also says, "In general, passion should be so treated that these
scenes do not stimulate the lower and baser elements." Any lines
suggesting deep sexual desire, such as "You wanted me so much,"
are supposed to arouse these "baser" elements and are accordingly
deleted.

Taboos on sex are extended to the sex organs of animals. In one
picture the Code office ordered that a scene showing the sex organs of an elephant be omitted. Close-up of the milking of cows
showing udders, or streams of milk from the udders used as comedy
gags, are regarded as violating the vulgarity clause and are usually
deleted by the Code office. It was even recommended for one picture that the action of an electric milking machine be suggested
rather than shown.

This emphasis on the negation of anything suggestive of sex is only one part of the Code's general taboo on the biological nature of man. Childbirth is another aspect. Not only are scenes of childbirth in fact or in silhouette cut out, but there can never be any dialogue about the dangers of childbirth. A woman moaning in childbirth is always deleted. Labor pains cannot be indicated, and producers are cautioned even about scenes which show a husband's distress during childbirth.

Pregnancy can never be treated with any sense of reality; here the taboos are carried to considerable length. In one picture, the Code office asked that the phrase "in trouble" be changed to "into this." It was completely clear from the context of the picture that "this" referred to pregnancy, but the MPAA had won its technical point. The phrase "wet nurse" is always deleted. Dialogue about diapers and scenes showing them are usually cut by the MPAA and any scene of a wet baby is unacceptable. Even a doll-wetting scene had to be deleted. The Code office questioned a scene in which a hot water bottle leaked and a woman, for a few minutes, mistakenly thought her baby was responsible for the water. This taboo extends to dogs and the MPAA recommended the deletion of a scene in which a dog merely sniffed at a fire plug. In one picture the remark of a colored maid to a dog, "If you gotta go, you gotta go," was deleted. Occasionaly such recommendations by the Code Office are not accepted by the studios and they remain in the films.

The showing of toilets is rigidly prohibited. They are always missing in any bathroom scene. Even the sound of an out-of-scene toilet being flushed is deleted. The reference to "toilets inside" and "outside stinkholes" had to be taken out of one picture, and in another, the reference to a character being a lavatory attendant was disapproved. In one film, the sign LADIES on the door of what was obviously a public ladies' room had to be changed to LADIES' LOUNGE.

Any reference to sexual perversions is completely ruled out, and words like "pansy" or gags which carry the connotation of perversion are always deleted. In one picture, the line "Because he's queer" was taken out.

Bigamy is, of course, considered a crime and must be punished. In a picture dealing with some Indians among whom bigamy was not considered a felony, the MPAA asked that dialogue which seemed to condone or accept bigamy among them be changed. In a film taken from an historical novel, there was a reference to an illegitimate birth which had happened six or seven generations before the events shown in the movie. For story purposes, it was necessary to keep this reference, which also happened to be a matter of record. The MPAA ruled that the only way they could keep it was to make a pointed reference to the mother's having died in childbirth. According to history, the mother did not die in childbirth.

The Code taboos on "vulgarity" are equally rigid. All burps and belching are considered vulgar and must be deleted. In one picture MPAA disapproved of the loud belch of an African chief, although this is not in the African concept of vulgarity. Sordidness is also considered vulgar, and so the Code office recommended that the locale of one film be changed from a dirty dive to a swanky night club and the same story was then told in a lush setting. Such commonly used words as "lousy," "punk," "nuts," "wolf," "damned" and "jerk" are considered vulgar and are deleted regardless of context, as are also interjections, such as "Oh God" and "Oh Lord." Over and over again, when a character is shown as drunk the point is made that he should not be "offensively" drunk, although just how "offensive" is defined is not clear.

All these and many more restrictions designed to maintain the technical appearance of virtue and to avoid the MPAA's concept of vulgarity are applied to all pictures, serious dramas, farces, Westerns, historical and contemporary movies. The same yardstick is used for two such different movies as *Duel in the Sun*, described by one columnist as "sex rampant" and as "lusty, lush, lascivious," and *Best Years of Our Lives*, a serious attempt to dramatize some of the problems of soldiers returning to their homes. Then, too, the Code office minutely censors dialogue for suggestions of sex, while studios continue to accent the sexiness of their stars.

Obviously, the Code has not been able to take sin, sexual or otherwise, out of the movies shown; but it insists that it be shown as punished. The MPAA rejected a script in which a woman who had had illicit sex relationships in her past was redeemed by falling in love with a decent man, and in which after much struggling and suffering she was eventually successful in living a happy and conventionally moral life with a man she loved. The Code office insisted that the woman must fail in her struggle for a decent, happy life. The age-old story of man's struggle with sin can never end in victory. Once man has sinned, there is no hope for him.

The successful Broadway play, *The Voice of the Turtle*, could not be made into a movie without changing its basic theme. The play was a quite moral tale about two young people who had "been around" and whose love life had been based on the principle of "love them and leave them." In the play, for the first time they find with each other a love that is lasting, and know happiness and life at its best. The moral of the play is that a permanent and monogamous love brings greater happiness than temporary, illicit affairs. In the movie, the whole point of the play and its moral theme is lost, and the picture has really no point beyond that of depicting a very immature and adolescent girl falling much in love with a returned soldier who is at first not attracted to her, but later falls for her and proposes marriage.

The MPAA presents the contradiction of insisting upon punishment for sin even when it will not permit the sin to be named. The Bible mentions the word "adultery," but it cannot occur in movie dialogue. In one film, the original script was about a girl of loose sexual conduct who falls in love with a decent man, but cannot marry him because of her past. When a character representing the voice of morality indicated what had been wrong with her past life, the MPAA said this should be spoken of in terms of general dissipation and shallowness, without any distinct reference to illicit sex. At the same time, she must be punished for the unnamed sin.

The emphasis on punishment for sin practically amounts to a fetish. A film about a woman who loses her mind because of a philandering boy friend, and murders him, is acceptable, because the woman becomes insane. In this picture the MPAA indicated deletions on the following points: the slapping of a woman, references to venereal disease and an illicit sex affair, and an undue exposure of a woman's leg. These, from the Code point of view, were more immoral and dangerous to an audience than murder, provided the murderer was punished by becoming insane.

Other taboos on crime are concerned primarily with preventing sympathy with it or inspiring imitation. The criminal must never be made heroic nor should his crime be justified, and the details of the crime must not be so explicit that anyone could learn from them. The treatment of guns is in the same class as passionate kisses or a naked baby. The Code says that there should be no display of machine guns or other illegal weapons in the hands of gangsters or other criminals. There can also be no off-stage sounds of the repercussions of these guns, just as there can be no off-stage sound of the flushing of a toilet. Nor can there be any new, unique or trick methods for concealing guns; and dialogue on the part of the gangsters regarding guns should be cut to the minimum. Suicide is discouraged in the same way that divorce is, and is particularly prohibited when used by a criminal to outwit the proper legal punishments. Nor is there supposed to be excessive brutality, unnecessary killings, or the motive of revenge.

The MPAA and the code of taboos which it implements attempt not only to safeguard audiences from sin, crime, sex and vulgarity, but also to protect the feelings of members of different nationality, religious, racial and occupational groups. No one must be offended. One studio feared that a picture that was supposed to open with several Mexicans embroiled in a street fight might be offensive to Mexicans. Since a fight was a necessary part of the plot, they kept it, but changed the fighting characters from Mexicans to gypsies. The studio representative blandly remarked that the gypsies had no country or organization to register a protest. Out of deference to the feelings of Cubans, the setting of one picture dealing with the underworld was changed from Cuba to New Orleans. Several times the MPAA has suggested that the character of a Negro maid be changed to a white one, because of protests from Negro organizations over the movie stereotype of the Negro as a menial. In one picture, the MPAA requested that a remark about "rattling the tambourine" be changed, to avoid giving offense to the Salvation Army. At another time the office considered the characterization of a juvenile court investigator unfair, and the producer agreed to change it. On one occasion, it cautioned against a jocular reference to the "Confederacy Dames." Stuttering is deleted from scripts and pictures because of a large number of protests from Parent-Teachers' Associations. In the case of the Spanish Revolution, the MPAA watches scripts and pictures having that Revolution as a background to see that leading characters are not identified with either side in the conflict, and in one film questioned the wisdom of depicting the Franco regime in a bad light. If the villain of the movie is a newspaperman, politician, lawyer, schoolteacher, doctor or member of any other profession, care must be taken to have other characters from the same profession portrayed sympathetically.

There are other taboos in the Code, but the more important ones and their manner of implementation have been described. How does Hollywood feel about its taboos? The Code is one of the most frequent targets for abuse in the community. Although the industry's own creation, no one loves it. The attitude of the studios is that the Code must be endured in order to ward off the threat of further censorship, but it is to be outwitted whenever possible. The staff which administers the Code resent being labeled "censors" or "bluenoses"; they earn their living on a routine job, painstakingly reading every script and looking at each film, conscientiously noting and warning the studio each time a taboo is not obeyed or a formula not maintained. No one — front office, producer, writer, director or publicity man — believes in the Code or takes seriously the values underlying the taboos. The attitude towards their implementation varies, but for the majority the tendency is to try to get around the matter. The MPAA censored the cleavage in the anatomy of Marjorie Lockwood and Patricia Roc, starring in the English picture *The Wicked Lady*, and the producers were therefore obliged to shoot several retakes of the film before it could be O.K.'d for United States release.

Universal, which is releasing the film in the U. S., however, apparently found there's more than one way to skin a cleavage. Trailer at the Winter Garden, N. Y., where the pic is slated to

open . . . is compiled of shots from the original British footage, giving wolves in the audience plenty to gape at and thereby
giving the film a hefty pre-opening boost. When the picture
opens, of course, it will have such shots deleted or retaken.[2]

A successful writer uses the strategy of putting a number of
things in the script to which he knows in advance the MPAA will
object and which he does not consider important to the story. He
then uses these as bargaining points to keep in others he regards
as essential. Quite a number of able writers think the Code is silly,
but they do not get excited about it. They regard it as a minor
annoyance, but say a good writer is sufficiently adroit to achieve
the desired meaning even if he does have to change a line or a
scene. They add that sometimes the necessary subtlety improves
the script.

Some producers say they have very very little difficulty with
the MPAA. They discuss each picture in advance with the administrator of the Code and are in constant contact on the necessary
changes as they go along. Out of the discussion of different points
of view a satisfactory compromise is reached. Perhaps they can
keep adultery, if they say divorce is bad.

Other producers and writers regard the Code as a serious limiting
condition. One mentioned that it was impossible during the war
to make a picture in which the hero killed a Nazi, because the
Code says all murder must be punished. One who is also a writer
complains that he tends to think in terms of the Code, and that his
imagination is restricted from going beyond its prohibitions. He
knows in advance that certain themes will be forbidden. On the
other hand, the MPAA may be used as an alibi by a producer
who tells a writer that he would like to do a story, but that the
MPAA will not O.K. it; actually the MPAA may not even have seen
the story. An occasional writer will likewise use the Code as an
excuse for his lack of success, saying he cannot write within its
limitations. Still others make the Code a scapegoat for all the ills
of Hollywood, and regard it as the villain of the piece.

*   *   *

[2] *Variety*, Dec. 4, 1946.

Whether the Code is outwitted, accepted philosophically as a necessary evil, railed against indignantly, or used as an alibi, no one connected with motion picture production believes in the system of morality it embodies. They do not think the words "nuts," "lousy," or "damn," vulgar or that the interjection "Oh, Lord" would corrupt Americans or any other people. Neither do they think a slight indication in a movie that a marriage has been consummated, or that a divorce occurs with no hell-fire and brimstone following, would contaminate even the teen-age members of the audience. Nor do they believe that the portrayal of a baby who needs diapering or the sign LADIES' ROOM would have an evil effect on anyone. Certainly, no one in Hollywood attempts to carry out the Code of taboos in his own life, or seriously believes them important for the audience. This is in sharp contrast to the way taboos are an integral part of the behavior and values of a primitive people.

On the other hand, much of the thinking of Hollywood people about taboos is quite similar to that of primitive peoples. The seal of approval given by the MPAA, when the taboos of the Code have been maintained, seems to have the quality of a magical spell designed to ward off the danger of hostile forces who would impose censorship. But in this case the would-be censors and critics are not always placated. A *Variety* headline proclaims **Pressure Groups in Pix Tug of War,** and the article says:

> Every organized political pressure group is aiming to pocket the pix field and then make it play its own tune. The drive on films sees Protestants whacking Catholics; vets' groups battling each other; the government moving in; and the left, all along the line, swapping potshots with the right. . . . And whenever Hollywood treats with any subject that has a glimmering of serious content, the same groups are hammer-and-tongs to boycott or cherish the theatre's playing the particular opus.[3]

The president of the MPAA comes forth from time to time with the awful threats of real censorship just around the corner, as when *Variety* reported:

[3] *Ibid.*, Jan. 21, 1948.

Unless Hollywood's individual film producers adhere to Production Code rules with more stringency, state censorship of motion pictures looms more than a likely possibility. State censorship bills are already before legislative bodies and can make Hollywood's problems tougher than ever, according to the message Eric Johnston will take around to individual producers. . . . Johnston will meet with producers on the various lots to give them a complete picture of the situation and the trouble looming ahead unless good taste and moral values are met more squarely. . . . The code, he believes, is still sound, but producers must be reminded of the seriousness of the situation.[4]

The National Legion of Decency, a militant Catholic organization, reviews all feature motion pictures and rates them as follows:

Class A: Approved.
Section I   Morally unobjectionable for general patronage.
Section II Morally unobjectionable for adults.
Class B: Morally objectionable, in part, for all.
Class C: Condemned.

In the thirteen years (1936 to 1949) in which the Legion of Decency has been reviewing pictures, the percentage of pictures to which they give their full approval, the A-I rating, has decreased from 61 per cent to 41.33 per cent. All other classifications have increased in the same period. A-II (morally unobjectionable for adults) increased from 30 per cent to 35.33 per cent. The B rating (morally objectionable, in part, for all) was 8 per cent in the first year of the Legion's operation and more than double, 20.56 per cent, in 1949. Class C (condemned) rose from 1 per cent in 1936 to 2.78 per cent in 1949.[5]

It appears that the Legion of Decency, one of the strongest organizations which Hollywood desires to placate, is not too well pleased.

However, the effectiveness of the Legion of Decency in keeping

[4] *Ibid.*, Jan. 19, 1947.
[5] *Feature Motion Pictures. Reviewed by the New York Office of the National Legion of Decency*, November 1948–November 1949, New York, p. 37.

people away from movies through the publication of their ratings is questionable.

> The more censorship trouble, the more b. o. [box office] for a picture, according to survey just completed by a California poll. Biggest group of filmgoers interviewed say picture's censorship difficulties has no effect on whether they will see the pic, but twice as many say they're likely to see a picture that has censor trouble as say they are less likely to see it.[6]

Forever Amber, Best Years of Our Lives and *Jolson Sings Again* received B ratings and at the same time drew large audiences and made profits for their studios. The publicity about censorship trouble often increases the audience for a movie as it does for a book.

While a B rating does not materially worry the industry, it is really frightened by a C (condemned) one, because then additional pressure is brought. The real reason behind Hollywood's taking on their moral "false face" is double-edged fear: of the political power of organized religious and civic groups to get restrictive legislation passed, and of their power in the community to boycott theaters showing condemned films. It never seems to occur to the industry that they could fight both. Take the case of the movie *Forever Amber* as an example, particularly as compared with the case of the book from which the movie was taken. The movie was originally given a C rating by the Legion of Decency. Cardinal Spellman then singled out the picture for special condemnation, and declared in a letter to all pastors in his diocese and read it at all masses, "I advise that Catholics may not see this production with a safe conscience."[7] However, the Catholic hierarchy went much further in their pressure. In Philadelphia, Cardinal Dougherty gave an ultimatum to the Fox theater to withdraw the picture in 48 hours, or he would throw a boycott at the house and any other in his diocese henceforth playing a product of the Twentieth Century-Fox studio. Similar situations existed in several cities. The

[6] *Variety*, June 4, 1947.
[7] *Ibid.*, Oct. 29, 1947.

studio capitulated from its original firm stand of no changes, and after many negotiations with the Legion officials, cut and revised the film. The studio president publicly made an apologetic statement. The picture's rating was then changed to B. Before this occurred, many bookings of the picture had been canceled because of the exhibitors' reluctance to incur the displeasure of the local church officials.[8]

The merit or demerit of the movie *Forever Amber* is not of interest in this context. What is significant is the contrast between Hollywood's attitude of appeasement and the fighting one of booksellers and publisher when the book, from which the movie was made, was censored in Boston. The publisher of *Forever Amber*, the Johnson Bookstore of Springfield and the Board of Trade of Boston Book Merchants all combined to take literary censorship out of the hands of the police, who had banned the book on the basis of obscenity. The prosecution, working very much in the manner of the MPAA, favored the court with a statistical analysis of *Forever Amber*, listing seventy references to sexual intercourse, thirty-nine illegitimate pregnancies, seven abortions, thirty-three bedroom scenes "more or less sexual." The result of this feat of literary criticism was a murmur of laughter from the courtroom. The Court cleared the book with the words, "While conducive to sleep, it is not conducive to a desire to sleep with a member of the opposite sex." [9]

It is almost impossible even to imagine an analogous combined action by the studio which made *Forever Amber* and an exhibitor or group of exhibitors when the showing of the movie was threatened.

The motion picture industry is an exception to the American pattern of resisting censorship through legal action. It does not even protest. Occasionally there is an anonymous murmur, such as that reported in *Life* [10] from a round table held in Hollywood: "As to the Legion of Decency, the mundane situation is that it holds the

[8] *Ibid.*, Dec. 10, 1947.
[9] Reported in *N. Y. Herald Tribune Weekly Book Review Section*, March 30, 1947.
[10] June 27, 1949.

whip-hand over Hollywood, and nothing can be done about it."

There are other critics besides the Legion of Decency. Complaints pile into the MPAA office from individuals and organizations. The Women's Christian Temperance Union complained bitterly in 1947 over the number of Oscars going to pictures or actors portraying alcoholics: Ray Milland, the alcoholic in *Lost Weekend;* Fredric March, a tipsy father in *Best Years of Our Lives;* Anne Baxter, a woman alcoholic in *The Razor's Edge.* The State Department, interested in carrying out a Good Neighbor policy with Mexico, asked that 152 feet of a film be reshot because it had shown some mass scenes with a number of Mexican children barefooted. That part of the film was reshot with the children wearing shoes. The burlesque of a United States senator in *The Senator Was Indiscreet* was taken seriously by many who protested to the studio making it.[11]

Negro organizations protest stereotyping. Jews protest the making of *Oliver Twist.* Protestants complain that Catholic portrayals are more favored than Protestant ones. Parent-Teachers' organizations protest violence. Members of various occupational groups, doctors, judges, lawyers, policemen and many others, remonstrate against the way they are portrayed. The only people who do not complain are rich tycoons, although they are almost uniformly portrayed as villains or heels without any redeeming qualities.

If the complaints from members of religious, professional, racial and national groups were all heeded, it would be impossible for Hollywood to make any picture with a villain in it. A much more fundamental criticism could be made of *all* the stereotypes which Hollywood offers as human beings. No one goes to bat for the human species; no one seems to care that mankind is presented falsely, and that the majority of movie portrayals are untrue. No worthy organization protests that human beings are shown as passive, unfeeling robots. Man, according to Hollywood, is either completely good, or bad. His personality is static, rarely showing any development either in growth or regression. The villain is a blackened sinner who can do no good and who cannot be saved; while the hero is a glamorous being, who can do no wrong of his own

[11] *Variety,* Jan. 28, 1948.

volition, and who is always rewarded. Missing is a realistic concept of the human personality, a complex being with potentialities for both kindliness and cruelty, who can love and hate, who has human frailties and virtues. The stereotyping of the Negro, the newspaper reporter, the politician, the rich businessman, the teacher, the Mexican, or anyone else is just a part of the larger stereotyping of mankind which prevails. If all movie characters were presented as part of the stream of humanity, good, bad and indifferent; if they were portrayed as thinking, feeling, human beings; if insight were given into their problems and their struggles, their victories and their defeats — then, whether a Mexican child was barefoot, or a Negro was a servant, or a politician corrupt, would not be important, and there would probably not be so many protests. I question if any individual salesman or organization of them objects to the popular Broadway play, *The Death of a Salesman*. This unheroic hero is a prototype for modern man's struggles, and the large audience responds to the play because it recognizes the truthfulness of the portrayal and gains understanding from it.

Only rarely does a movie-goer have the experience of seeing real human beings living in a complicated world. Instead, he is treated to static characters not unlike the symbolic personifications of sin and virtue in medieval miracle plays. It is only the exceptional movie which portrays any human being, member of majority or minority group, with truthfulness or understanding. The reality of most movies usually consists only in the photography, the setting, the curve of a star's leg, the friendly or handsome looks of the hero and heroine, and other surface characteristics. Seldom is anyone concerned with the reality of emotions and with truthfulness of meaning.

Many members of the audience, conditioned by years of such movies, do not expect anything different. And minority groups, insecure and fearful in general, pass over the usual Hollywood stereotyping of all peoples, noting only when one of their own group appears untruthfully portrayed.

The movies are an easy target, because Hollywood never fights back. Instead, it tries to please everyone; by using its formula, the MPAA in answering a protest can always point to figures which show a preponderance of sympathetic portrayals. That the sympathetic and unsympathetic characterizations may be equally untrue never occurs to anyone. The dazzling, beautiful young female psychoanalyst dressed in the most seductive manner who falls in love with her handsome patient and cures him in a hocus-pocus manner is just as false as the psychiatrist in another picture who misuses his profession to drive a patient insane and cover up his own crime. But Hollywood sticks to its formula.

Yet the Code of taboos not only fails to please the critics, but is also unsuccessful in its own terms. Although the staff of the Code office works conscientiously to enforce it, even the most casual movie-goer knows that movies are filled with sex, crime, cruelty, and violence. The word adultery is not mentioned, prostitutes are changed to dancing girls, and kisses are given with a closed rather than open mouth; but movies are openly sexy. The hero is a virile he-man, and the heroine has obvious sex appeal, enhanced by every device of make up, by accenting of bosoms with "falsies," by provocative clothes. An immediate and obvious sexual attraction between hero and heroine is part of the theme of most movies. Whether the story be a murder mystery, farce, musical, or serious drama, the sensual nature of the leading characters is always accented. This is carried still further in boldface type in the advertisements, such as *"Alluring, Seductive, Wicked!"* [12] One studio (Universal-International) wrote into its contracts with starlets a "cheesecake clause" to insure the showing off of their curves in publicity pictures.

"The clause requires that a suitably endowed feminine newcomer "shall for the first five years of the duration of her contract display said charms in publicity pictures as well as on the screen." . . . "Many young actresses begin screen careers by displaying their figures and later refuse to permit this type of exploitation, which seems unfair to their public and to themselves," a studio spokesman explained.[13]

[12] Advertisement for *The Bride of Vengeance.*
[13] UP release, *Santa Fe New Mexican,* July 6, 1949.

Certainly the taboos of the Production Code have not succeeded in making sex less attractive. Hollywood continues to be its symbol, and the movie industry continues to make a big profit by exploiting it.

Movies are likewise still filled with violence, crime and murder. As noted, punishment of the criminals and the taboos on details of the method or the loot supposedly preclude any effect on the audience, particularly young people. It is doubtful if anyone, young or old, who does not already have criminal tendencies, actually would be incited to crime, whether or not he saw loot or heard gangsters discussing their guns; it is also questionable whether the punishment of the criminal, pointing up the moral that "crime does not pay," prevents members of the audience from identifying themselves with him or her, particularly when the character is played by a glamorous star.

The MPAA gave its seal of approval to a picture in which the two leading characters committed adultery and then murder and, of course, were finally punished for all their sins. What the MPAA ignored were the implications of a sexy-looking, beautiful woman and a strong, handsome he-man, both popular stars, irresistibly drawn to each other, committing adultery, and finally murder. That they are punished at the end would not necessarily destroy the identification of the preceding sixty or eighty minutes.

In one small study of audience reaction, the results showed that a large number of the audience were able to identify with characters who transgressed conventional mores and of whose behavior they overtly disapproved. The identification was indicated by the informants saying that they could imagine themselves (or sometimes, friends) acting in the same way. That the exhibitors are well aware of this kind of identification is shown through advertisements — as, CAN YOU CONDEMN FREDRIC MARCH IN AN ACT OF MURDER? [14] The question of whether this kind of identification is psychologically good or bad is difficult to answer, and probably depends on both the kind of movie and the kind of individual. It might serve as a catharsis for unconscious or semiconscious aggressive impulses. It could also strengthen and give them a kind of permissiveness.

[14] Sign on movie theater in small Kansas town, June 1949.

However, what seems definitely harmful is the continuous portrayal of violent, aggressive and criminal behavior by actors who register no emotion. Murder is committed by passive robots without the flicker of an eyebrow or a change of inflection in the voice. Feeling of any kind, whether anxiety, guilt, or exhilaration, is lacking. Most of today's stars, particularly the younger ones, carefully cultivate a passivity of face and voice, giving the impression of complete callousness. The constant portrayal by admired stars of people without feelings, unconcernedly murdering their fellow human beings, leaves an impression of cold disregard for human life which remains even if the murderers are punished. The fact, too, that the solution of the problem comes about so often through murder or the convenient natural death of one of the characters, rather than through the individual's having to make a choice, may have a long-time corroding effect on the audience. Thus the distorted Hollywood picture of human nature and its unreal solutions to problems are probably more harmful than the showing of loot from a holdup or the dialogue of gangsters about their guns.

The Bribe may serve us as an example. It is an average feature picture, neither an Oscar winner nor a particularly poor movie. It stars Robert Taylor, Ava Gardner and Charles Laughton, and features Vincent Price and John Hodiak; it follows the Code's taboos, and has the MPAA seal of approval. It is advertised as a DANGER-FILLED PAYOFF, and is a story of crime, violence and murder with no particular point. It presents the following picture of human beings:

The hero, played by Robert Taylor, handsome and virile-looking, working for the United States Government as a detective, is sent to the Caribbean Islands to catch an unknown criminal who is illegally shipping airplane engines into the United States to avoid custom duties. The assignment is described as a patriotic one, in the interests of taxpayers. The hero is attracted to a beautiful girl (played by Ava Gardner) who, he thinks, is involved in the illegal operations through her husband, and there is a conflict between love and duty. Never does this conflict come through emotionally and instead the hero moves passively and without expression through his part. Love at first wins out over duty, and he is about to pass up the opportunity of catching the criminal; but duty triumphs finally, not because of the hero's strength of character or of his having thought through the problem, but because he finds out that the heroine is working against him and for her husband.

The first view of the beautiful heroine by the hero and the audience is as a singer, seductively dressed, singing and moving in a tantalizing manner among the tables in a café. Later, she appears as a serious and simply dressed young woman unhappily married to a drunkard husband, played by John Hodiak. She is still beautiful, and her very obvious, rounded and pointed bosom seems to be always strutting, whether she is in sorrow or happiness. She has fallen for the hero and has decided to leave her husband; he, however, has a heart attack and becomes very ill, and she decides to stick by him, even to the point of helping him evade the law and by giving sleeping potions to the hero whom she loves. Up to this point the heroine was innocent of even knowing about her husband's illegal activities. She shows a little more emotion and feelings in her conflict than does the hero, but she never becomes real.

Her husband is merely the tool of the real villain, who is played by Vincent Price in his usual, suave, cold-blooded manner. He is the completely stereotyped bad man, without a single redeeming feature, killing automatically whoever comes in his way. He tries unsuccessfully to murder the hero, and succeeds in killing the sick husband.

The only really human character is the payoff man, played by Charles Laughton, who is in the pay of the villain and trying unsuccessfully to bribe the hero. Laughton is shown as degenerate-looking and dirty, but he has feelings in his ugly face and squinting eyes, and while he plays one character off against another, he draws the line at murder. There is some human motivation for his being a payoff man — he is trying to get enough money for an operation on his continuously aching feet.

In the end, the hero, in self-defense, kills the villain, who as we have seen has first conveniently murdered the husband of the heroine. This now leaves her free to fall into the hero's arms. No so-called vulgar words have been used. Crime has been punished. There have been no extramarital relations, although the hero and married heroine have been obviously much attracted to each other. But the question might be raised of whether any movie with such a weak automaton hero and villain, with the solution of the so-called love relationship through murder, and with its only human character a degenerate payoff man, "improves the race," according to one of the stated aims of the Code. Its models of human relations and of solutions to their problems in this and many similar pictures may well be cumulatively injurious to regular movie-goers.

The many-sided failure of the Code of taboos can be explained by the complete lack of understanding which the industry, the would-be censors and pressure groups all appear to have of the problem. None of them seem to realize that good taste is never an arbitrary matter or subject to legislation. The taste, good or bad, of the men who make the movies will be inevitably stamped on them and will break through all rules and taboos.

"Vulgarity," as Henry Seidel Canby says, "is a quality of the mind. It is a baseness of the spirit." [15] The MPAA attempts the impossible when it tries to legislate on qualities of mind and spirit, and is accordingly doomed to failure.

Nor do the censors, apparently, understand that it is impossible to impose attitudes and values which are not representative of society or any considerable section of it. The nonbiological nature of man which is implicit and explicit in the Code is not part of our current thinking.

There is a basic absence of logic in the Code, since moral concepts are not distinguished from physical facts. Biology has a stubborn reality of its own which resists a political line about genetics and a moral one of a censor. The biological nature of man and other animals, whether it is expressed through a baby's need to have his diaper changed, a dog sniffing at a post, or a reference to the consummation of marriage, is rather widely recognized; and it is not necessarily vulgar or obscene. Most people take for granted that marriages are consummated, that toilets are in bathrooms, that cows have udders, that sexual perversions exist (even before the Kinsey report), and do not think that references to them are necessarily

[15] Footnotes to 1949, *Saturday Review of Literature*, August 6, 1949.

vulgar. They can be the subject of obscene jokes — part of the folk-lore of any society — but this is not their only use.

It is part of the routine of any urban apartment-dwelling family to walk the dog at required intervals to permit him to perform his natural functions. Diaper services in all our cities blatantly advertise their wares. That marriage is at least connected with sex is fairly generally recognized by fourteen-year-olders, and very few people would consider that a husband kissing the back of his wife's neck or giving an affectionate pinch to her posterior, necessarily arouses evil thoughts or passionate desire on the part of the young. That divorce is fairly widely condoned is proved by its present high rate. Words such as "lousy" and "nuts" are an accepted part of colloquial vocabulary, and even in the Bible Belt of the Deep South there are very few people who consider "damn" or the interjection "Oh, Lord!" either sinful or vulgar. The concept that the sinner cannot be saved is completely foreign to our society. All modern religions stress the theme of redemption through repentance and God's grace. Both the spirit and letter of the Code contradict the very core of Christianity, Christ dying to save erring mankind. The emphasis in modern penology and social work on redeeming the criminal, delinquent and others who break our fundamental mores, and on enabling them to become useful, normal members of society, is again foreign to the Code — which insists on its pound of flesh in punishment, and rules out the possibility of the sinner's ever coming back to society.

The Code simply does not belong to this world.

Neither morality nor taste is achieved through the mechanical following of taboos. They can be secured only through a positive set of values. In every society, from the most primitive to the most modern, these values form what the anthropologist Ralph Linton calls an inner core of culture radiating outward and influencing behavior.[16] However, many modern societies, including our own, are characterized by a conflict between competing and contradictory values. This is in marked contrast to the more unified value systems in primitive societies, among whom attitudes towards divorce, sui-

[16] Ralph Linton, *The Study of Man*, p. 358. New York: D. Appleton-Century.

cide, and ownership of property tend to be quite uniform. In our society, there is a wide divergence of opinion on many subjects, ranging from consumption of alcoholic liquor to philosophical concepts of the nature of man. It is therefore exceedingly difficult for any one group, no matter how sincere, to be the spokesman for our values.

Equally important is the question as to whether the nature of a kiss, the use of the word "damn," or the automatic punishment of sin are the most significant aspects of contemporary morality. Truthfulness might be equally important. Truthfulness in the portrayal of characters, in the solution of problems and in the meaning conveyed by the movie as a whole might conceivably have something to do with morality. Helping man understand himself and his complicated world, and thereby reducing his confusion and fear, could also be considered a moral matter. The struggle between the concept of man as a reasoning, free human being, responsible for his behavior, and the totalitarian opposite concept of a robotlike creature, trained to do as he is told, is a moral as well as a political issue. But a system of morals which includes truthfulness, understanding and a concept of freedom cannot be achieved by men whose idea of morality is limited to a set of taboos imposed out of fear. Only men who are themselves interested in truth, who consider mankind worthy of respect, can understand morality. That this kind of morality can and does occur in movies — whether in serious drama, melodrama, comedy, farce, pursuit-chase, or slapstick — is demonstrated by the early Chaplin pictures, by *Sullivan's Travels*, by *The Pride of the Marines*, by *To the Ends of the Earth*, *Gentleman's Agreement*, *The Farmer's Daughter*, *Best Years of Our Lives*, *Crossfire*, *Home of the Brave* and an increasing number of others. These pictures were profitable and good entertainment. They are not necessarily great pictures, but they are all exceptional to the general run of movies because in each case someone, with power enough to leave his stamp on the film, really cared for and respected mankind — someone who was truly moral. The presence or absence of the taboos was completely irrelevant. It is doubtful if through following taboos there is any more increase in morality in movies than there is in primitive man's catch of fish.

Hollywood, like any other business, is basically unconcerned with morality. But it has had to take on a moral system from powers outside and foreign to it. Again there is an analogy with primitive societies which have come in contact with modern ones and been subjugated by them. The South Sea Islander looks with awe and envy at the power of the white man, as demonstrated by his weapons, his tools, his boats and airplanes, his clothes and all his other wealth. Religion is a part of the white man's ways as much as his power and his material goods. Often they are interrelated in the mind of the primitive man: by his taking over the Christian God and following his rules, a heaven of material things in this life is expected to follow.

A Samoan chief has expressed it very well when he said: "Now I conclude that the god who has given his white worshipers these valuable things must be wiser than our gods, for they have not given the like to us. We want all these articles and my proposition is that the god who gave them should be our god." [17]

Hollywood has "got religion" — or more accurately, what it calls "morality." The motivation is not too different from that of the Samoans.

Very often when a primitive people are first missionized, Christian beliefs and ritual are reinterpreted in terms of native beliefs, or are followed mechanically while the Christian and native religions exist side by side. Just so in Hollywood, producers interpret the new religion so that there is the least possible damage done to their people's indigenous beliefs as they mechanically follow the new faith. They continue with their aboriginal custom, making pictures as sexy and violent as possible, while the MPAA makes sure that certain practices, like closed-mouth kisses and the omission of details of crime, are carried out. This fits in very well with the general studio atmosphere and behavior: one of meticulous attention to small details and very little emphasis on meaning. The research department or technical adviser will spend much time insuring that the uniform of a soldier or the hair-do of the star is correct for the historical period

[17] Felix W. Keesing, *The South Seas in the Modern World*, p. 230. London: Allen & Unwin.

of the film, but no one bothers to make sure that the mood of the picture is true for that era. So MPAA will mechanically count the number of sympathetic and unsympathetic portrayals of policemen, be on the lookout for certain words and expressions labeled vulgar, note the degree of coverage of a woman's bosom, make sure that anyone committing a crime is punished, but not bother about the real meaning of the picture. The Code office fits very well into the larger system in which movies are made.

Many people in and out of Hollywood have made the Code, the Legion of Decency and other pressure groups into the stereotyped villains. Perhaps they are not so much villainous as unintelligent and ineffectual in dealing with the important problem of morality. Neither they nor Hollywood would appear aware that the biggest taboo in the making of movies is an unwritten one. It is a taboo against man.

CHAPTER IV

Front Office

THE MAKING OF MOVIES is even more strongly influenced by the power situation in Hollywood than by the Code of taboos. Power resides in the front office of each studio and the executive in charge of production wields it, which is similar to the situation in most large industries.

Among the crucial problems of modern society are those which center around power, as it functions in both economic and political areas of living. Its foundations are not necessarily the same. Power can spring from ability, as when a man wields authority over others and has the responsibility of making important decisions, because of his acknowledged competence, training, experience or talent. Or another person may have the same position, and power, not because he has any greater ability than the people under him but because through aggression, cleverness, or luck he fulfills a drive to dominate others. In each case the basis on which the power rests determines the type of relation between the headman and his followers. On "my" South Seas island, the chief in one village had been chosen by the people because of his courage and ability, and was respected by all. A few miles away, in a neighboring village, the chief had ingratiated himself, mainly through lies and flattery, with a representative of the white man's government who had then appointed him as chief. Since he had no special skills and was known to be a liar, the natives did not take him very seriously.

Naturally all those who wield any power, big or little, whether Stone Age savages, chairmen of college departments, or tycoons of industry, would like to believe and to have others believe that they achieved it through their special ability. But only the followers can speak with any objectivity on this.

In Hollywood, it is rare to hear anyone talk in a complimentary fashion of front-office executives. Most studio people, whether well-known directors, producers, stars, or writers, or the lesser known assistant directors and publicity men, have no respect for the big boss, who they say owes his position to luck, to smart maneuvering, or both. Rarely do they think he knows anything about how to make movies. Yet the same people are quick to recognize ability when they see it. They speak in both admiring and respectful terms of the exceptional executive whose power is based on ability and talent.

The front office, with occasional exceptions, rests on a combination of various types of influence which are associated with the big business executive, the political boss and the medieval lord. Like other businessmen, front office executives are concerned with attaining large profits, but the profit motive is not always primary, and rarely the only one. For many executives, power is even more important; and Lord Bryce's description of the political boss fits many Hollywood executives. He writes: "The aim of a Boss is not so much fame as power, and power not so much over the conduct of affairs as over persons." [1] This type of boss often displays his power in the most obvious manner.

One Hollywood executive, now dead, kept a hundred-dollar gold piece in his pocket and while talking to a producer or director would continuously throw it up in the air and catch it after it had bounced back on his desk. The metallic ring of the coin on the glass-topped desk did not make conversation easy. The symbolism was clear. The same man enjoyed having conferences with a director in the studio barbershop. The executive would recline in the barber's chair, and while his face was covered with lather and the barber shaved him, and a manicurist filed his nails, and a bootblack shined his shoes, the director stood nearby, listening with respectful attention to his boss's discussion of the movie on which he was working. This man often showed kindness and affection towards his underlings, even if he did not respect them.

Another characteristic of power in Hollywood is seen in the

[1] James Bryce, *The American Commonwealth*, Vol. II, p. 115 3rd Ed. New York: The Macmillan Company.

prevailing attitude toward people as property. Every individual has his price and this attitude exists straight down the line from top executive to least important employee. Everyone is a piece of property with a specific price, for whom negotiations are carried on through an agent. A producer frequently asks for "a $750 [a week] writer" or "a $2000" one. Actors are often loaned by one studio to another without their consent and most of the time without any advance knowledge of the deal. The studio profits by getting more from the deal than it pays as salary. The publicity departments regard actors as property whose value they are responsible for, or at least have increased. One star who reluctantly refrained from giving out details of a forthcoming marriage because the studio was embarrassed by some of the attendant circumstances, said to the reporter, "I'm their property. If they tell me not to talk, I don't talk." [2] The attitude of being able to buy anything or anyone is reflected in one of the folk tales circulating around Hollywood. A producer who sent his daughter to college was informed that she was being sent home because she was not doing well in her classes. The father, much concerned, asked what was the matter and was told that the daughter did not have the capacity to do college work. The producer's answer was, "I'll buy her a capacity."

The feudal characteristic of the power situation lies in the option contract which legally binds directors, actors and others to the studio for a period of seven years. The employee is not permitted to break his contract for any reason. If he refuses a role the studio suspends him without pay, and formerly the number of weeks of suspension was added to the duration of the contract. This last provision is no longer legal. If an actor receives another and better offer while he is under contract, he is not allowed to take it. Court cases in which the actors and directors try to break their contracts usually end in victory for the studio.

The cases coming to court are the exception but the problem comes up frequently when an actor or director has unusual and unexpected success during the life of the contract. The studio then often gives him a bonus and raises the salary check, but rarely as much as if he were in a bargaining position. For many, the problem

[2] *New York Times*, March 14, 1948.

is, of course, not to get out of the contract but the ever-present anxiety of whether the studio will take up their option at the end of a six months' period. But, no matter what the problem, the option contract which binds the employee to the studio for seven years and permits the studio to dismiss him at the end of six months or one year, without having to show cause, smacks more of medieval power relations between lord and serf, than of employer and employee in the modern world of industry. It is interesting that the guilds have never fought to change the option contract although the Actors' Guild has tried to reduce the time limit. They fight for higher and higher salaries, which they seem to regard as sufficient compensation for servile and undignified conditions of work. At least they sell their freedom for a high price. Of course, everyone does not work under a contract. Some take their chance and free-lance, making a separate contract for each picture. Relatively few stars and leading actors are in this latter group.

Although the relationship between the powerful and the power-less in any situation follows well-formalized patterns of dominance and submission, there is usually some flexibility and manipulation on a personal level. In the Deep South before the Civil War, relationship between house slaves and their masters were frequently quite personal and could be manipulated through wheedling, tact and the sex relations which sometimes existed between the master and his female slave. In Hollywood, while the relationship between the powerful and the powerless is determined by the contract and the well-established mores, it too can be manipulated by social ties, flattery, gifts and sex relations. Every conversation is filled with blandishing phrases such as "You're wonderful," "You're mag-nificent," "You're perfect." Expensive gifts are exchanged between stars and their directors, producers and executives, and often given by stars to their cameraman. Social ties and sex relations flourish between the important people engaged in a production, but are not confined to production time. Both are constantly used in "playing the game" by those ambitious to succeed and by the successful to demonstrate their power. The men with power usually have no respect for the people so controlled, and the latter are resentful.

They, in turn, frequently manipulate people beneath them and so exchange roles. The concept of people as property, valued at a certain price, who can be bought and sold and managed so as to do one's bidding is not unique to Hollywood, but is exaggerated there to such a degree that it becomes an outstanding characteristic.

The structuring of power varies a bit from studio to studio, as it did in the Old South from one plantation to another. It may be divided between several men or be held almost completely by one. However, a top executive is always responsible for the major decisions, one of which is to pass on what stories and scripts are acceptable for production. Some executives have the reputation of making their decisions not on reading a story treatment, or the novel or play from which the latter may be taken, but on listening to someone telling the story. Their judgment must of necessity be colored by the skill and enthusiasm of the storyteller. The final script must also receive the O.K. of the front office. In one major studio, where power is delegated and divided among four or five executives, the finished script is sent to all of them to be read. It usually ends rather emasculated, with only the weakest portions, which offend no one, remaining. Most of the strong parts will have worried or irritated one of the executives and will therefore have been eliminated. Sometimes an executive feels he must cut or demand changes merely to prove that he has a critical mind or to demonstrate his authority.

Whether the executive reads or listens, acts singly or with others, he usually projects his own taste onto the public. His attitude is, "If I don't like a picture, nobody else will." The mechanism of projection, that is, ascribing one's own feelings to others, can be considered a normal process, underlying our understanding of other human beings. However, it becomes abnormal when the need to project is so strong that it has a defensive function and the individual uses partial and superficial data to attach meanings taken from his own experience, but which do not correspond to the real behavior of the other person.[3] The question is raised of whether the

[3] Ernest G. Schachtel, "Projection and Its Relation to Character Attitudes and Creativity in the Kinesthetic Responses," *Psychiatry*, February 1950, pp. 75-6.

usual executive's projection of his image of himself onto the audience is normal and realistically true. In any case, the important decisions on scripts are conditioned by the taste, judgment and personality of executives. Decisions about casting and cutting or on shooting a picture on location or in the studio, on the production's budget, and the settlement of disputes which may arise between any of the important people involved in the movie are likewise the responsibility of the production executive.

All power has its perquisites. Among the aborigines of Central Australia the old men, with knowledge of totemic ceremonies, are the most powerful; they have their pick of women and the choice food, in a society characterized by scarcity. In our culture a traditional prize for the powerful is wealth; and Hollywood executives, many of whom set their own salaries, follow the tradition. The Treasury list of big money-makers in 1946 was dominated by movie people (executives and actors) and the best anyone outside of the movies could do was to tie for sixth place.[4] Unlike the custom in most industries the heads of studios earn, on the average, more than the presidents of companies of which the studios are a part. For the fiscal year 1945 (except in the case of Metro and Warner Brothers, when the totals for 1946 were available) the salaries of the heads of the major Hollywood studios ranged from $500,000 to $182,100 as compared to a range of from $255,273 to $115,970 for the presidents of the companies.[5] An executive, Louis B. Mayer, with his salary of $502,571 for the fiscal year 1945–1946, topped all the Hollywood earnings including those of the highest paid stars.[6]

It was easy to get data on salaries and on returns to stockholders, which are about the same as those on other stocks. But it was practically impossible to get accurate information about the net profits of individual pictures, which is what remains to the studio after salaries have been paid to all those connected with the film, deductions made for all costs such as sets, music, costumes, raw film, laboratory costs, exploitation, and subtraction of from 25 to 55 per

[4] New York Post, February 21, 1948.
[5] Variety, February 5, 1947.
[6] Ibid., March 25, 1948.

cent for overhead. The amount of net profit was the holy of holies in Hollywood.

In all field work there is usually one piece of esoteric data which is hidden by the natives. Among the Melanesians in the Southwest Pacific it is black magic. Among the Hollywood executives it is net profits. Even producers rarely know this about their own pictures. A general suspicion prevails that much of the profit is siphoned off in overhead expenses and executive bonuses.

Automatically from 25 to 55 per cent of the cost of production is charged to overhead expenses. If a Broadway play is purchased, one studio immediately adds 50 per cent to the original cost for overhead. This is done for each item, such as writers' and actors' salaries, although it is for the same overhead. There are other more devious techniques. An actor's salary for the period of his contract has been charged against the costs of the movies in which he plays. During his contract he goes on some kind of publicity junket and his salary is charged a second time to "overhead for junket." A couple of studio people go out to look for a location which serves three pictures, but the expense of finding it may be charged separately to each one. The cost of dismantling the set may be charged to a picture, although the same set may be kept and used again with a few minor changes in another film. A producer may work on several pictures at one time, but his salary will not be equally divided among them — instead, more may be charged to each picture than is warranted. Laboratory processing offers another place for concealment. The laboratory is owned by the studio but a bill for the work is sent to it.

All these and many more devices are common knowledge in Hollywood and regarded as customary. Independent producers and others who work on a percentage basis have to be on the alert against these "paper" expenses, and are constantly inquiring why another $200,000 has just been tacked onto overhead. Some raise objections to the amount of overhead charged against their films. It was reported in *Variety* of September 29, 1948, that the president of the Hal Wallis Independent Unit was trying to get a reduction of the overhead figure, or the right to move out of the Paramount Studio to a rental lot.

Mr. N. Peter Rathvon, formerly president of RKO, formed a company for financing independent movies, and in the description of his new activities it was said:

> As an investor he is able to call the tune on spending and keeping costs down by helping a producer avoid credit deals for studio and laboratory facilities which involve ruinous overhead and "padded" charges.[7]

Mr. David O. Selznick was very outspoken on this matter in a newspaper interview:

> "The whole industry, as a matter of fact, is built on phony accounting." . . . He declared it was entirely fallacious to burden all categories of films and all expenditures with the same percentage for overhead.
>
> Illustrating his point with a studio that used a 50% overhead figure, Selznick declared it was misleading its own executives.
>
> What happened, he said, was that $250,000 was added for overhead to a $500,000 film and $1,000,000 to a $2,000,000 one, while actually there was nothing like that difference in the overhead cost between the two films. For instance, he pointed out, if it was decided to bolster the big film with an extra star at $200,000, that added an additional $100,000 to the picture's overhead cost. Actually, it didn't cost the studio an extra cent in overhead. Result is, Selznick declared, that when the two films go into distribution, the phony bookkeeping makes the $750,000 one appear to show a profit, while the $3,000,000 production appears to suffer a loss.
>
> "Actually that may not be true at all," Selznick pointed out. "Nevertheless, seeing the figures, the boys in the front office decide that what they need is more $750,000 films. The result is that they have completely misled themselves."[8]

There are a number of reasons for concealing the amount of net profit, which practice is, of course, not limited to the movie industry, although one wonders if executives in other industries actually mislead themselves. Concealment is desirable because of taxes,

[7] *New York Times*, July 24, 1949.
[8] *Variety*, June 2, 1948.

fear that employees will ask for a raise if profits are high, and because some directors, actors and producers work on a percentage basis of net profits. In the New York theater the playwright receives a percentage of the gross intake against an advance payment.

When the question is asked, "Has a picture made money?" it usually means "during the first six months." A top A hit may bring back its cost in two months, a medium successful picture in one year, but full profits are not in until after a three-year run, and in the case of revivals, longer. In the past nothing less than 100 per cent net profit was considered good and on top successes it was much more, sometimes as high as 300 per cent. It is rare for a picture not to bring back its costs; when a picture is said to be "unsuccessful," it usually means that it did not bring in a big profit. Unless a profit is "sensational" or "terrific," it is not considered a profit in Hollywood; and according to *Fortune*,[9] the movie industry has reached the end of its era of fortunes on films.

The domestic box office rose steadily to a peak in 1946, but began to decline in 1947. There was then much discussion on the need for economy in the studios because of the falling markets, foreign competition and dwindling box-office receipts. It was even rumored that there would be some reductions in the salaries of the top people. It is part of the mores of Hollywood always to begin their "drastic" reduction with the lowest-paid employees. The following paragraph from *Variety* of November 19, 1947, bears this out (italics ours):

> Moskowitz huddled with studio toppers on his arrival last week and held several sessions with an eye toward determining how to effect further payroll economies. On Friday (14) he is reported to have advised various department heads that their departments must be cut by 40%. Cutting is already under way, it's understood, with 10 dropped from *contract department, eight girl messengers discharged and 20 janitors swept out in the shuffle.*

Most of the executives justify their enormous earnings because they say they are showmen who know by "instinct" what makes a good picture. Many of them can point to their long years of experience

[9] April, 1949.

since the days of the old silent "flickers," and they take credit to themselves for the financial success of the industry.

The description of their business practices indicates the degree to which this belief is based on myth or reality. The reliance of the executives on a series of well-known formulas has already been described. Behind the lack of faith in their own judgment about doing something different from the hackneyed rules may be the fact that most of the top executives seem to be men without real understanding of what makes a good movie. When they have an unexpected success or failure, they appear unable to analyze the reasons for either, but attribute it to the fickle public or to luck. In other businesses, successful designers of clothes, hats, jewelry and architecture launch new styles and take chances on their success. Theater and publishing, which are taking on more and more characteristics of big business, still constantly take chances with new ideas. But the motion picture industry only rarely has this courage, and its system of production discourages originality. This is not only detrimental to the artists who work in Hollywood, but also bad business practice.

It is also uneconomical for any industry to buy twice as much raw material as is used. A conservative estimate by story editors of major studios is that not more than half of the story properties purchased are filmed. Other people outside the story departments estimate the ratio as twenty-five to one rather than two to one. Behind each picture produced is, at least, the cost of two properties. The reasons given for this unusual business practice are several. The reading and buying of the stories is done very hurriedly by the story-editing department, because of the fear that some other studio may buy. Unlike the practice in the publishing world, a writer submits a story, script, or book to a number of studios at one time and hence the need for speed in the competitive buying. After the story is purchased, presumably with the intention of production, there are many reasons why it may remain on the shelf. What was first seen in it does not, on more serious consideration, have enough possibilities to make production worth while; or the star for whom the picture was originally bought does not like it, or is tied up with other pictures; or the producer who liked the story has gone to another studio. To the additional cost of the story bought by the studio and not used may also be added the salaries of writers and producers who have tried to develop a script from it. Production on a picture is sometimes postponed or shelved even after sets and costumes have been designed.

The general hostility to planning is seen not only in the extravagant buying of story properties, but comes out in many other parts of the industry. Any executive will talk about how essential stars are, and yet there is no long-range plan to develop them — instead, training is a hit-or-miss affair. Almost every producer will hold forth at great length on how few good script writers there are; but there is little analysis of the problem or plans to improve the situation: In most businesses the decision to hire or fire a $500-a-week employee would be made after considerable thought and consultation between a number of executives; but in Hollywood a $3500-a-week writer is fired without consultation with anyone and, if he is not on contract, on a week's or less notice. One such writer was told to quit when his week was up, but when the time arrived the producer had changed his mind and he was told to stay. Whims and personal desires often override business interests. It is reported that one executive insisted on being accompanied by a star to the opening of her picture in New York, even though she was working in another film at the time. This meant that the whole company had to be laid off, at a cost of $50,000, while the actress was at the New York opening with her boss.

Instead of relying on carefully thought-out plans the Hollywood executives pride themselves in working on "instinct." The editor of the *Hollywood Reporter* (September 26, 1947) writes:

> Motion pictures are not an assembly-line mass-production enterprise like automobiles or prefabricated houses. The motion picture industry was not built by mechanical geniuses or financial wizards. It was built, and built well, by showmen — showmen with an instinctive feeling for what the public enjoys, and with the same instinct for delivering just that kind of entertainment.

The use of the word "instinct," a biological term, is incorrect; but if we accept the trade paper's colloquial use, what the editor implies is that these Hollywood executives are showmen gifted with special intuitive powers, who do not need to plan, and think, and work hard, as presumably do the heads of factories turning out automobiles and prefabricated houses. There is a circular process here, for even when executives do plan and work hard, they credit the results to instinct and luck. Both these qualities are considered more fashionable in Hollywood than thinking and working. Yet these same showmen, with their "instinctive feeling for what the public enjoys," are repeatedly surprised by "sleepers" (pictures not expected to be very successful which turn out to be box-office hits) and by others, made to be top hits, which do not come off.

There is one executive, an independent, who does have what seems to be an intuitive feeling for picking a box-office hit. But what he actually has is sound judgment on what makes a good movie, the courage to try something new and very high standards. He knows also how to select able people to carry out his ideas. But for most of the showmen to whom the editorial refers, their "instinct" may cover up poor business judgment and an actual lack of knowledge about movies. Theaters must have movies, and until the present time Hollywood has had a monopoly on the product.

This inefficiency and wastefulness are not unknown to Wall Street, which is continuously wary about film stocks in spite of the record profits by the major studios. According to *Variety* (December 25, 1946):

> . . . New York Exchange quotations on majors' common is from 25% to 50% below what it ordinarily should be. . . .
>
> Number of other stocks such as steel, oil, automobiles and chemicals, Wall Street concedes, are computed on a basis from 10 to 15 times their equivalent earnings. Only those considered more speculative are down to the eight times earnings tabulation, they say.
>
> What has film execs further puzzled is demonstration as far back as 1929 of profit-taking power of film companies.

Industry did not feel full brunt of stock crash until a number of years later and was one of the first to stage a phenomenal recovery when conditions picked up. Staying power of film biz plus record profits ordinarily would warrant much higher prices, execs say.

Only real factor weighting prices, it's believed, is idea among financial circles that Hollywood throws big money around and out the window on caprice. Prejudice has been of long standing, and such items as junking of first takes on 20th's "Forever Amber" which reputedly cost the company some $350,000 hasn't helped to diminish it. Production costs, notoriously ballooned by hard working flacks, has also taken Wall Street in film trade believes.

Although the studio executives seem puzzled and hurt at Wall Street's suspicions, yet they themselves continuously say that each big picture is a gamble. For most everyone in the industry, Hollywood is regarded as a place where one plays for big stakes — where chance, luck, the breaks, are among the determining factors. Executives and producers appear never to have any certainty of success, and profits, but instead are always and continuously fearful of failure and losses.

There is, of course, some uncertainty about profits and losses in any business. Book publishing is very much a gamble. No publisher is always turning out best sellers and there are many tales of how a best seller was turned down by seven or eight publishers before someone took a chance on it. Indeed, no publisher feels that every book must be a best seller and most firms are satisfied with a few a year which they regard as a means of paying off the small returns or losses from other books.

Movie executives and most producers, however, think that every picture must be a top box-office hit and bring in from 100 to 300 per cent net profit. This attitude is probably conditioned by two factors, one historical and the other psychological. As we have seen, one reason movie makers do not think in terms of ordinary business profits of 20 or 25 per cent is because of their exceedingly high returns in times past, when a 100 per cent profit was considered only normal, and when returns were sometimes as high as 300 per cent. The studio heads cannot bring themselves to believe that the end of that era of fortunes made overnight has actually come.

The constant fear of failure and the need for excessive profits on every picture may also be conditioned by the very high personal insecurity of most executives and producers. Dramatic financial success, gained mostly through a set of fortuitous circumstances, such as that movie going is a popular habit and fills a real need and that Hollywood until recently had a monopoly on the product, is, however, looked upon as a sign of genius, or at least, greatness. The executives therefore *need* a box-office hit every time — not just for profit, but also to convince themselves of their greatness. This problem is not confined to the executives but pervades all of Hollywood and is the logical psychological result of a situation in which most everyone wants to think he is a genius, or at least unusually gifted — whether it be as showman, actor or writer — and is constantly being told that he is "great," "terrific," or "wonderful." In any industry, profession or art, the proportion of outstanding ability or talent is very small. It is no smaller in Hollywood than anywhere else, and may be larger among the artists, but the pretensions to it are much greater.

Yet, as is well known, it is rarely possible to fool oneself completely. Always there is some lurking doubt, ready to come to light at the first sign; and of the signs, that shown in profits is the most symbolic for the executives. The discrepancy between the idea of himself which the executive wants to believe and to present to the world, and the one he really is, is rather wide. In the former, he is a great showman who can unerringly spot a good movie through listening to a proposed story treatment, who "instinctively" knows just what the public wants, and who, in addition, has great business acumen. In the latter he is an aggressive man, lucky in getting into the industry when it was young, possessing sufficient clever business sense to take advantage of opportunities, with little taste or understanding of the ingredients of good drama, and whose knowledge of the audience is limited to a projection of himself or to meaningless polls. Most people engage in some self-deception, but that practiced by executives, and a large number of other important people in Hollywood, appears to be much greater. The hypothesis is that this covering-up of inner uncertainties about ability is sometimes projected onto the market. The question — *Will the public think my picture wonderful and give the sign of approval by a big box office?* — may hide the more basic anxiety: *Am I really good, or do I owe my position only to luck?*

A psychological explanation of the industry's fears of hard times has been noted even by a trade paper:

> Rather than being a year of recession for films, 1947 may well turn out to be the greatest or close to the greatest b.o. year in industry history. While talk is widespread of a drop in film grosses, a careful check by *Variety* makes it appear the recession is considerably more *psychological than economic*.
>
> Survey of major distribs, affiliated circuits, independent circuits and scattered indie houses reveals the average of gross income — at both the b.o. and in film rentals — on a par with or better than the comparative first nine weeks of last year. Unless there should be serious adverse changes in the present general economic picture next summer and fall, profits should come close to the phenomenal figures of 1946.[10]

Many actors, writers, directors, producers and others have the same problem. Adjectives of superlative praise are not limited to the movie advertisements but are part of the small talk exchanged between Hollywood people and pervade all conversation. The employers want to believe these laudatory words about their $3000-a-week employees, and the latter want to believe them, too. The very heights of such standards must inevitably lead to great emotional insecurities for mediocre or average people. The most psychologically secure people in Hollywood were those who did not think they were geniuses, but who had proved ability and a real knowledge of the medium, and those whose goals were commensurate with their ability.

Since success is so important to the executive for deep personal reasons as well as the usual economic ones, he does what he can to

[10] *Variety*, March 26, 1947. Italics ours.

insure it. His use of polling techniques, his employment of the highest paid writers, directors, actors, and others, his following of taboos and superstitions, are his insurance against uncertainty. Of course, a well-written script, ably directed with talented actors, might also be regarded as an insurance for success; but it could be used only by a man who had the necessary ability to recognize it.

In Hollywood the causes for success or failure are still considered luck and breaks, comparable to primitive man's thinking. For him, the causes of illness are in the realm of the supernatural; cures are therefore of a magical nature. When he first comes into contact with Western society he is glad to have the white man's medicine even though he is still as ignorant as ever of the nature of the disease. He soon has two kinds of magic instead of one, which he uses without discrimination. Later, as he takes on the cultural heritage of Western society, disease moves out of the supernatural world and into that of reality. His magical practices then tend to disappear and be replaced by whatever understanding medical science provides for prevention and therapy. A highly paid writer is only another kind of magic. Front-office executives, as well as most other Hollywood people, are in various stages of emerging from magical thinking and replacing it with realistic knowledge of their medium and their audience.

The fears involved in the gambling and magical attitudes are only part of the blanket of anxiety which overhangs Hollywood. Some executives live in fear that people are ganging up on them. In one studio, if an actor asks for a particular director the executive immediately fears the latter. On the other hand, if it is known that the actor does not want that director, then the executive is more confident of the director. Some executives are jealous of their own employees who have been outstanding. There is a whole collection of folk tales about one producer who won an "Oscar" for a picture and so incurred the jealousy of the executive head of his studio. The latter according to the tale did not want to fire the producer outright immediately after he had won the "Oscar," but did everything possible to annoy and irritate him. Of course the producer quit after a short time. Among the stories of the executive's techniques of annoyance are that he had the plants dug up around the studio in which the producer worked and substituted fertilizer in their place; that he caused the interoffice telephone in the producer's department to be cut off, or to work very poorly; that he forbade the studio publicity staff to give the producer any publicity.

One cannot vouch for the exactness of the above tales, but they are heard over and over again. Their significance lies not in the degree of veracity to be attributed to them but in their reflection of the executive's attitude toward an unusually gifted employee who brought both prestige and profits to the studio.

The roots of such fear can only be speculated on. One hypothesis is that executives are not completely satisfied with their roles, and, although they pretend to look down on artists and creative people, are at the same time jealous and resentful of them. Another possibility is that their insecurity and strong drive for power causes them to fear anyone, artist or not, who receives so much prestige that he may become a threat to the executive's power. Neither explanation excludes the other, and there are probably still more.

Fears are not limited to the studio and are even greater toward anything which threatens from the outside world — such as pressure groups, whether religious, racial, business or political. Toward all the pressure groups the answer has been uniformly appeasement; again, these are opposing forces that appear to be in the world of the supernatural and therefore impossible to oppose successfully. Publishers, newspaper owners, and theaters may take a stand, and fight any attempted censorship; they do not think defeat inevitable. But the aggression of the movie showmen evaporates at the first sign of any threatening forces from outside their little bailiwick. They can only appease and try to retreat further into their safe cocoon on the West Coast, cushioned by isolation, large bank accounts and the flattery of an incestuous back-slapping.

Another characteristic of executive existence, not unrelated to the blanket of fear, is the frenzied tempo in which the important people live. After they have made their millions, the same mad pace continues for a prestige picture, for one which will win an Oscar, for one which will be sensational over and above all other sensations. There is no sitting back on laurels, no rest for even the most successful. They carry on in an atmosphere of excitement, flying back and forth to New York and Europe and continuing to meet one crisis after another. One man, with a beautiful home and swimming pool, says he likes to swim but that he hasn't had time to go into his pool more than four times during the past year.

Always there is a fear of being outdistanced by competitors. Lewis Carroll in *Alice in Wonderland* might have been describing Hollywood executives: it takes all the running you can do to stay in the same place. Always there is that struggle, for more and more of something, whether money, prestige, power, sensations, or what not, until the man drops dead. The game becomes the end, and is played compulsively.

CHAPTER V

Men Who Play God

THE PERSONALITIES of the men who sit in the front office are of interest as much as their customs, because their own natures influence the content of the movies and mold the human relations in the whole system of movie production. Also it is the executives (and producers) who have the greatest power to stamp the movies with their personal daydreams and fantasies. Then, too, the tendency of executives to see the movie audience in their own image results in a rather high correlation between the executives' personality and their opinions of the audience.

Apart from this situation, peculiar to movie making, a knowledge of the personalities of any men who wield power is always important, because power concentrated in the hands of one man or a few becomes personalized. An extreme example is the way the abnormal personality of Hitler helped to give Nazi Germany its particular character. Even in quite simple situations, where power is not highly concentrated, such as on a relatively democratic college campus, it is still personalized. The type of president who sits in the front office will influence the behavior and attitudes of both faculty and students. In Hollywood, too, the man who sits in the front office sets the tone of the whole studio, influencing and shaping attitudes and behavior of everyone in it; even more important, he leaves his stamp on the movie.

To understand these men it is necessary to know their backgrounds. Most of them have been with the industry since its beginning, and there are many folk tales about how they started.

The tale of Mr. Smart Guy, now dead, goes back to the early pioneer days of California when he and a partner sold soap to gold miners and pioneers. Mr. Smart Guy double-crossed his partner by secretly cutting each cake of soap in half, selling it for the price of the whole cake, and keeping the additional money for himself. He soon became wealthy and began buying up vaudeville and other show houses in the West. Soon a competitor came on the scene, and also began buying up the same kind of show houses. The competition between the two men was extremely keen. It was carried to such length that if anyone worked for Mr. Smart Guy he could not work for his competitor and vice versa. Mr. Smart Guy, however, managed the situation in his usual clever way and married his daughter to his competitor, thus merging the business interests.

When the movies began he bought up a circuit and later a studio bought him out. In the deal Mr. Smart Guy agreed to take less money than the original price on the condition that his son have a permanent job with them as a producer. The son was an alcoholic and finally the studio pensioned him off because it was impossible to get any work from him.

Another and more recent story concerns a top executive whose background was that of a poor New York boy who started out as an office worker, and through a chance meeting on the beach in Coney Island with the president of a movie company, received a job as secretary in the New York office of the company. Soon he was on the way to bigger and better jobs. He eventually became engaged to the boss's daughter and was given an executive's job. Then he received a better offer from another studio, which he promptly accepted. He broke his engagement.

Like other executives with similar backgrounds, he surrounded himself with assistants who had also been poor boys whom he had known in his childhood and youth. Very few had any training or special gifts in the medium of the movies, but they seemed to be the only kind of men he could trust. It happens frequently, and not only in the motion picture industry, that men who have attained great success by being "smart" and by getting the "breaks" are jealous and distrustful of men with training or with special abilities.

* * *

Not all in charge of production are poor boys without training. Mr. Intelligent, a very exceptional front-office person, is from a middle-class background and began with the ambition of becoming a playwright. He wrote plays for which he was unable to get Broadway production and supported himself by doing all kinds of odd jobs, some related to the theater and some unrelated. He spent his summers in the traditional way of many unsuccessful theater people, in charge of entertainment at summer camps. Eventually he came out to Hollywood as a writer and had considerable success; he went on to being a producer, where he was again successful. Recently he became the executive head in charge of production for a major studio. He is the first man, starting as a playwright and movie writer, to achieve this position. Unlike the previous executive described, he tends to surround himself with men of training, of proven intelligence and ability. His personality and functioning are each quite different from the other top executives.

The personalities of the front-office executives are more complicated than their backgrounds. Mr. Big Shot, the head of a large studio, has a reputation for imposing his will and authority on everyone in the studio. And yet his desire for power over people is not the whole story, for he has a deep and strong interest in the production of movies and the output of his studio includes some unusual and excellent pictures as well as the run-of-the-mill.

Mr. Big Shot brooks no interference, and wants to have his finger in every pie. Firsthand accounts of his treatment of employees from producers to costume designers are legion. He had a discussion with an able director who said he did not think the sound effects in a picture they were making were good. Mr. Big Shot turned to him and shouted belligerently, "Who said *you* were any good? You stink!" The director said no more about sound effects. He did not, however, remain much longer at the studio.

Another time Mr. Big Shot did not impose his will quite so easily. He ordered a scene which gave the psychological motivation for the picture cut out. Both the producer and director wanted it in, and fought with him on the issue; but of course, in the end, lost.

The producer withdrew his name from the picture. Another time Mr. Big Shot enforced his will on a trifling detail when he told a costumer who had been in business for thirty years that the collar of an actor's costume was one quarter of an inch too high. The costumer changed the height of the collar.

Mr. Big Shot's desire for domination is so strong that he keeps people in a position of subservience even if it means a loss to the studio. A gifted director objected to doing a certain picture because he thought the story was false and that the movie could not possibly be anything but a flop. He would not enjoy doing a bad picture and he knew his reputation as a director would suffer if he turned out one. He tried to explain all this to Mr. Big Shot — who, however, insisted that the script was O.K. and that it must be done. The director attempted to hold his own, but in the end lost out. Mr. Big Shot told some other people that he *wanted* this director to have a "flop," because he had enjoyed three box-office successes in a row and was becoming too independent. A flop would bring him to heel and keep him more under control.

Many actors and directors find it difficult to work for Mr. Big Shot because of the drastic changes which he introduces into the script. The actors complain that the directors never seem to know from day to day what they are doing. The former come to the studio prepared to do their parts, only to find them changed. Mr. Big Shot may have ordered five pages of the script replaced by new ones on short notice. They can never trust the director or the producer, because both are completely subject to Mr. Big Shot's orders which keep on coming in during the entire making of a film.

Typical of the atmosphere which surrounds this executive is a scene in the cutting room. When Mr. Big Shot sees the first run of a picture which has just been put together, his own projection man runs the machine. Gathered in the room for this first running will be a number of people: the producer, the director, the cutters, the leading stars and others who have been concerned with making the picture. They all wait for Mr. Big Shot to appear. When the projection man hears his footsteps in the hall, he lowers the lights and immediately everyone becomes quiet. The great man then enters and the picture is run.

The situation is reversed when a banker on the Board of Directors visits the studio. Then Mr. Big Shot, like many others of this personality type, becomes subservient before a higher authority. The studio was doing a picture based on a successful Broadway play. At the first running of the picture in the projecting room, Mr. Big Shot indicated that he liked it except for one sequence containing a dream; he said to the director: "That dream sequence stinks. Cut it out." So it was cut out. A day later the picture was run again without the dream sequence before Mr. Big Shot and the banker on the Board of Directors, who happened to be visiting the studio. The banker had seen the Broadway play from which the picture was made, and after the film was run, turned to Mr. Big Shot and said, "What happened to the dream sequence?" Mr. Big Shot was silent for a minute or two and then replied, "We're working on it." As soon as the banker left the room, Mr. Big Shot told the director to put the dream sequence back. The interesting point is that Mr. Big Shot originally took the dream sequence out because it was not well done and not really essential to the picture. He preferred omitting it rather than incurring the expense of doing over a sequence which could be removed without affecting the story. But when the banker questioned him, he could no more dissent that he could allow an employee to differ with him. This kind of behavior is common to most people of the sadomasochistic type, or more colloquially, the bully.

Mr. Big Shot, however, is not an executive who lacks understanding of movies. His suggestions for cutting are sometimes, but not always, good and for the improvement of the picture. But frequently the point at issue is not the good of the movie, not even profits; it is simply the imposing of one man's will on his employees.

Big Shot has the desire to say, "I did it," regardless of how many other people have contributed to the picture, and is personally concerned with almost every picture that comes out of the studio. These vary a great deal, from light musical comedies to important, serious films. He appears to enjoy doing a serious film, perhaps one with social implications, because it presents a challenge. Other executives have said that this kind of picture is impossible and cannot make money. He responds: "There is nothing impossible for me. I'll show that it can be done." He appears to have no social or political principles, conservative, radical or liberal, and from his studio have come pictures with social implications on both sides of the political fence.

Although many people who have worked for Mr. Big Shot spend much time taking cracks at his egocentric behavior, most of them agree that he has at times shown real understanding of films (particularly in the cutting), and that his consuming interest in life is movies. At least, they say, he spends his time in the studio. The fact that this point is made very spontaneously and frequently, and a comparison drawn with other executives whose major interests lie outside of the studio, is not without significance.

A number of executives give the impression that their only concern in the studio is profits, that they have no particular interest in movies, that they would have been equally happy in any other profitable industry, and that their major interests lie in their hobbies — such as horse racing, aviation, yachting or women. When the head of one studio sold his horses, it was the topic for every columnist connected with Hollywood and reams of words were turned out, some designed to be taken seriously and others facetiously. That racing was not just a pastime for this executive, but also a source of his wealth, is indicated when it was reported in the Hollywood *Citizen News* [1] that his horses were reputed to have won, over a nine-year period, $1,732,036, and that the auction price for his stable was $1,553,500.

Mr. Intelligent, whose background as a playwright and script writer has been described, is a new type of front-office executive. He stands out from the typical ones because of his personality, ideas, and manner of functioning. He thinks the content of a movie is at least as, if not more, important than its star and that the best pictures are those on which one man, a producer, a director or a writer, leaves his mark. He is frankly interested in seeing that there will be among the annual output of the studio — which includes musical

[1] March 27, 1947.

comedies, farces, serials and Westerns — several serious pictures which attempt to illuminate a section of contemporary life. He knows he must make a profit for the studio if he is to continue in his high-salaried job. But neither studio profit nor personal earnings have been able to eliminate his serious interest in producing good movies. He is an intelligent man with broad interests and knowledge, and yet at the same time he is probably the most unpretentious person in the top ranks. He is able to take the intellect for granted and is not under any compulsion to show off as is one executive who mistakenly prides himself on being an intellectual. Mr. Intelligent does not regard himself as a genius, but seems to have realistic knowledge and a capacity for planned intelligent work. He is not a-political as is Mr. Big Shot but has, in a number of situations, been outspoken on the liberal side of social issues, and again he differs from others who pride themselves on being socially minded but whose liberalness is limited to being on innumerable committees and making lofty pronouncements. Mr. Intelligent has never gone in for racing, for gambling, yachting, night-clubbing, and all the other aspects of "playing the game" in Hollywood. This does not mean that he has paid no attention to personal relationships. His own personality is unique among Hollywood executives in that he is even-tempered, without obvious tensions, and with a faculty for getting along easily with large numbers of different kinds of people. He is even more unique in that he respects the people he works with. He is not surrounded with the usual pomp and ritual of the front office and makes a direct contact with practically everyone in the studio. If a writer or director argues with him, the argument does not become a struggle for domination with the victory going, of necessity, to the executive because of his power. Instead, it is a rational discussion on basic issues connected with the film, and the outcome is not predetermined.

A distinguished character actor who has been playing second leads for the past twelve years in Hollywood says his experience at Mr. Intelligent's studio was unique. At Mr. Big Shot's studio, where he did a number of pictures, he saw the executive walk through the set occasionally saying "Hello" to the actors, and this was the limit of the relationship. At another large studio where he worked for five or six years, he saw the top executive only twice and never spoke to or was spoken to by him. At the studio headed by Mr. Intelligent he and all the male actors in the cast received a personal letter and a tie clasp from him wishing them well, and the girls received flowers with the same good wishes when the shooting of a picture began. When it was ended Mr. Intelligent sent him a bound copy of the script personally inscribed. During the shooting Mr. Intelligent came on the set, making helpful and intelligent suggestions, always in a "soft-spoken and gentlemanly manner," rather than in the browbeating tone of so many others. This actor, successful and with prestige, talks about the incident in great detail, stressing its uniqueness, and ending with the statement, "I would love to work at that studio again."

Mr. Intelligent was the only top executive of a major studio who received such spontaneous and sincere loyalty from the able and talented people of his studio. The genuine respect and admiration in which he was held by producers, directors, writers, actors and publicity men and many others, is in sharp contrast to the face-to-face false flattery and behind-the-back derisive disparagement, amounting many times to contempt, accorded most other executives. The atmosphere of his studio was very different from those ruled by an authoritarian head dominating through fear. In one such studio everyone, from heads of departments, big producers, $3000-a-week writers and actors to bit players, was affected by the fear which pervaded the studio even when its "master" was away for long periods of time. They talked in whispers when saying the most innocent things.

Mr. Intelligent not only respects the people who work for him but is again unusual in that he respects the audience. He confirms the hypothesis that executives and producers tend to see the audiences in their own reflection. He is unorthodox enough to believe that a function of the movies is to raise the taste of the audience rather than to cater to its lowest point, and he thinks that a sufficiently large section of it appreciates good pictures to make them profitable.

Mr. Intelligent does not think he is a genius or the greatest showman on earth. He seems to have a realistic concept of himself, of the motion picture industry, and of a world beyond that. There is no other top executive in the major studios like him, and his significance lies in the fact that a man of his sort can and did become successful. It is too early to know whether he represents an aberration or a new trend. The hypothesis is the latter.

A much clearer picture of the way the front office functions and its influence in the studio and on the movies is revealed in the day-by-day relationships of the executives with producers, directors, writers, and actors. Here, it must be emphasized, Mr. Intelligent is unusual; his background, personality and behavior highlight, by contrast, the norm among executives. The majority of them are in their present positions of power because they were lucky in getting in on the ground floor of an industry which meets a popular need and for whose products, good or bad, there has been up to now a continuous demand. They do not seem to have the planning ability, acumen, and common sense of executives of other industries such as pre-fabricated houses or automobiles. Unlike many other business executives they have little knowledge of the actual consumers of their product, and none of the potential ones. Nor do they truly compre-hend the nature of movies as a popular art. They are in positions of great power in one of the major mass communications, and although there are many lofty pronouncements — such as one studio's slogan, COMBINING GOOD PICTURES WITH GOOD CITIZENSHIP — it is only the very exceptional executive who demonstrates any responsibility, social or aesthetic. Most of them are a-social and a-political rather than antisocial or antipolitical. They are opportunists ready to exploit the latest sensation or any popular attitude. A studio executive will favor making a pro-Russian picture at a time when it will bring in profits, and at another time an anti-Russian film when that will be profitable.

The god is profits, and opportunism the ritual of worship. To the average executive any picture with a "message," unless it is one fitting into the latest sensation, is condemned. The point that re-sponsibility might be concerned not with messages but with whether the picture has inner truthfulness, whether it offers a refreshing or deteriorating form of escape, has not even occurred to most of them. They talk naïvely in terms of "pure entertainment," without any knowledge of the many-sided functions of all entertainment.

In the best of times, these experienced showmen are anxious and they are in a panic when the demand for the product ceases to function automatically because of restrictions on foreign markets, an inflation reduces the money people can afford to spend on movies, foreign films become popular in urban centers, and government prohibitions threaten monopolistic control of the industry. A visitor to Hollywood remarked that, "Hollywood is the only town in this booming country which has managed to manufacture its own private depression." [2]

The showmen's instinct seems to have failed. For otherwise they might know that there has been a constant trend to more and more diversification in the audience since its early days. Yet an important executive of a major studio looks to the past when he thinks of its future policy. In 1949, "viewing the industry's future, Louis B. Mayer says, 'I am reminded of the late Marcus Loew always pounding home to Nick Schenck, Bob Rubin, myself and others that the picture business was a Woolworth business where they can bring the entire family." [3] This may have been true once. But, today, even a casual glance of any movie audience would indicate that it does not consist of family units. In most families, ten-year-olds, teen-age adolescents, and their parents do not feel that they should necessarily go to the movies together or even see the same one. They take for granted that the same picture will not please all of them, and usually each one has more fun going with his own age group. The potential audience for movies is as diversified as is that for books, for magazines and for newspapers.

The showman's instinct seems also to have failed to indicate the improvement and changes in popular tastes that are due in part to a rising educational level. Hollywood has consistently prepared fare suited to a young and relatively uneducated audience; yet it is surprised when surveys of audiences show that the majority are under

[2] Thomas F. Brady, "Opinion from the West," in *New York Times*, August 15, 1948.

[3] *Variety*, February 9, 1949.

thirty years, and when educated people are critical of the average movie fare. Perhaps the executive is no longer correct in saying, "If I don't like this picture, no one will." Perhaps his instinct is not such a sure guide. Perhaps the present "hard times" may in the end be beneficial if a custom known in other businesses as "thinking" is substituted for instinct. Perhaps a new type of executive is needed.

It is only the men who have an understanding of drama who can integrate in any meaningful way the art of storytelling with mass production. It is apparently easier for these entrepreneurs of early movie days to learn about the business end of mass production than it is for them to learn about storytelling. The problem remains essentially one of knowing how to achieve the best conditions for creative storytelling in a mass-production system. This cannot be done by men whose drive is for domination rather than creativity, who think in formulas and in clichés, and who have no realistic concept of the audience.

CHAPTER VI

Lesser Gods, but Colossal

NEXT TO THE FRONT-OFFICE bosses at the studios are the producers, one of the very important controls in Hollywood. The contrast between the producer's power and role with his ability is rather marked in most cases.

The producer usually selects the kind of story he wants to film. He may suggest to the front office the purchase of a certain book or play (called a property) in which he is interested, or offer his own idea to be worked out by a writer. Or, he may follow a formula currently successful at the box office. Or, the picture may be assigned to him by the front office. However the story is initiated, the producer then controls in greatest detail the writing of the script. He works closely with the writer, reading what he writes, and continuously criticizing, suggesting and commanding during the entire process. It is the producer who decides if and when other writers should be brought in, and the producer's O.K. is necessary before the picture passes to the front office for final approval.

The producer's power is not limited to control of the writer and the contents of the script. He has authority over the casting, and his judgment in cutting, one of the most important aspects of movie making, supersedes that of the director. It is the producer's O.K. which is necessary for the work of the composer, scene designer and everyone else connected with the production of the movie.

Producers have been compared to foremen, since they tie together and supervise the diverse ends of production. But the foremen in most factories have technical knowledge and understanding of the processes which they supervise, and they never control the engineers and designers. Most producers know nothing or very little about writing, acting, directing, composing, or painting, but they control others who do, and set the boundaries within which they all work.

The explanation of this paradox lies in the past. The producer's role in the movies began humbly. In the days of the silent films there were no producers. The head of the studio directly supervised all its output and the director carried many of the present producer's functions. Toward the end of the "silent" era and the beginning of the talkies, the industry grew rapidly and each studio multiplied its production many times. The studio head could no longer directly supervise everything and delegated authority to assistants called "supervisors" — the predecessors of the producers, who in the beginning had little status. Then various departments became increasingly more efficient and the supervision therefore more mechanical. But the producer, instead of becoming less important, as would have been the natural evolution, became more powerful and took on the function of representing the front office in the never-ending struggle between the business and creative aspects of production.

The producers do not always see themselves in this light. Many of them seem not to be completely satisfied with the typical business goal of wealth for themselves and profits for the studio. They talk also about being creative. One told how he sneaks anonymously into a theater to see one of his movies, and as he sits there in the darkness he feels like God. He thinks to himself, "In three minutes I will cause this audience to laugh; in ten minutes they will cry." He is the one who has produced the magic to which the men and women in the theater are responding.

The creativity of most producers is rather debatable. But it is interesting that they, as well as the executives, are often not content to be businessmen controlling artists. They want to be artists, too. Because they have so little understanding of the creative role it is easy for them to think they are playing it. The producer may mistake his power, to control the content of the movie and the people who work on it, for creativity. This situation creates more problems than would a clear-cut struggle between artists and businessmen, each sticking to his own role.

Although the producers are in positions of power, they are at the same time scared employees, which is another part of the Hollywood paradox. Most of them work under the prevailing option contracts, by which the studio can drop them at the end of six months or a year, and they cannot leave of their own accord for the seven years' duration of the contract. A few have straight contracts without option clause. The range of salary varies from $350 to $4000 or more a week, determined by ability, prestige, bargaining power, and all the tricks of playing the game. Their income is, however, not always limited to the salaries paid by the studio. Many are entre-preneurs on their own. It is part of the Hollywood mores for some producers to have actors directly under contract to them personally at one salary, "farm" them out to the studio at a higher salary, and pocket the difference. The actor is a piece of property which the producer, in these cases, rents out on a profit basis.

Thus, producers likewise know all the insecurities of everyone else in Hollywood. The studio may not renew the option on their contract and they will be unemployed. They shift from one studio to another as do other Hollywood workers. Of the seventy-two pro-ducers employed in the seven major studios in 1936, only eleven, 15 per cent, were still in the same studios in 1947. Seventeen were unemployed, fourteen were producing at other studios, and fourteen were independent producers. The remainder had gone into other businesses, disappeared, or died. Only thirty-nine of the original seventy-two were working as producers.

The producers' insecurities are not purely economic. They are ex-tremely sensitive to public and to Hollywood reactions and are fear-ful if they are not continuously having box-office hits. Unless they are successful in every picture, they are apprehensive that the big stars may not be willing to appear in their pictures or that the studio will not take up their options. Like the executives, they usually fol-low formulas or rely on their "instinct," in the selection of a story to be filmed. When the "instinct" goes wrong, as it often does, there is an attempt to shift the blame or conceal the mistake in compli-cated bookkeeping.

They follow the Hollywood pattern of being carried away by enthusiasm which often later turns out to have been unwarranted.

Many go "all out" for a story or idea which someone sells them. They sink so much money into trying to get a movie out of it that they are compelled to go ahead, even after it is obvious that the story is no good or not suitable for a movie. In one case a producer made a mistake in purchasing a bad story, and then asked a writer to do the impossible, that is, do a good script by making changes completely inconsistent with each other and with the original story. Another writer was later called in to "doctor" this script. She was a person of considerable skill and realized immediately that the original story with the revisions was impossible, and so rewrote the whole thing, changing the story completely. All that was left of the original purchase was the title. Many times even that is lost.

In spite of the producers' paradoxical position they belong with the front-office executives to the in-group, while most of the writers, actors and other artists are members of the out-group. Some form of in-group–out-group division prevails in all societies. Naturally, most people want to belong to the in-group, and each society has its own ways of becoming a member of it.

Among the Maori, a Polynesian people living in New Zealand, the in-group is an aristocracy dependent, in part, on biological relationships. In Hollywood, kinship is also important. Since producers do not need to have technical knowledge, it is the easiest position into which the head of the studio can put a relative or friend, and the charge of nepotism is fairly common in the industry. However, cultural kinship is as important as biological. Executives can trust and feel at home with relatives, old boyhood friends, and others who speak their language and who concentrate on profits and power. There is one tale of how a man who had been a production manager, a kind of super-bookkeeper, became a producer. He had a big fight with a director over costs, and the front office was so pleased with the way he put money before the creative needs of the movie that he was promoted to producer. This happened a number of years ago; but the man is still a producer, and of A pictures.

Another way of becoming and remaining a producer is through the prevailing Hollywood pattern, "playing the game." Producers appear to participate in this practice more than most of the other occupational groups. If the front-office executives go in for horse racing, the producer does likewise. If the executive likes bumming around the town in night clubs and getting drunk, the producer goes along. Becoming "pals" with the boss is a kind of social security. If a picture is not a box-office hit, or if the studio releases a number of people through a reorganization, a producer is not so apt to be fired or to have his option dropped if he and the boss are pals.

Another technique for holding on to a job is playing cards for high stakes with the front-office executive, so skillfully that he loses a lot of money. The producer is very tactful and does not mention the gambling debt, and his job is safe as long as the boss continues to owe him money. The debt may never be paid but the producer considers it insurance for keeping his position. There is a story about a man who attained the position of producer through gambling. His background was not even remotely connected with making movies. He came to Hollywood about twenty years ago anxious to break into the industry. He managed to get himself invited to a week-end cruise on the private yacht of an executive of a major studio. The week end was spent mostly in gambling with high stakes, and the would-be movie maker lost several thousand dollars to the executive. On Monday he showed up at the latter's office and said he regretted that he could not pay the gambling debt because he was unemployed. He then told the executive that he was a talented man in movie pro-duction and that if he could be given a job as producer he would pay the executive three hundred dollars a week until the gambling debt was paid. He got the job and is still a producer.

Others have acquired their positions because they have been around Hollywood for a long time. These came during the period of "silent" films and more or less accidentally fell into producers' berths. They may have begun in a humble capacity and become producers at the time the job was primarily that of supervisor. Some of them are conscientious, hard workers, but only a few appear to be men with real knowledge and ability. There is today a rather strong trend for a writer, director or actor to take on the producer's role. Most of them do so in order to gain at least partial control over their own creative work. These men always belittle their producing role, saying that there is nothing to it.

One writer-director-producer said that if he were asked how much he should earn for his three functions, he would reply: "Twenty-five hundred dollars [a week] for being director, twenty-five hundred as a writer, and twenty-five dollars for being a producer." This expressed the attitude of most of the men I met who combined being producers with another function. They did not have to pretend to themselves or anyone else that the producing job was of itself creative. They viewed it as purely administrative and not difficult to handle, and had their creative satisfaction in writing, directing or acting.

Much of the producer's power is similar to that of the front-office executive. Both tend to project onto the movies their own personalities, their ideas of love and sex, their attitude to mankind, and their "solutions" to social problems. If the producer thinks that every dame is a pushover, then the dame in the picture, whether she be a dancing girl or a doctor, is a pushover — of course, within the tricky limits of the Production Code. If his idea of love is that of an adolescent boy, that concept will most likely emerge in the film. If he is interested in social problems they too will be reflected in the films. One producer interested in those that make newspaper headlines makes many a picture involving a social problem, but always with an unrealistic and overeasy solution. Another producer's warm humanitarian interests, on the sentimental side, are regularly reflected in his pictures. The satirist's outlook on life is part of another producer-director's personality and reflected in his films. Another producer-director, a rather sadistic person, is at his best when he produces and directs a picture dealing with cruelty and violence. There are other films on which mature and intelligent men leave their stamp of honesty and understanding, not only of the film medium, but of human beings.

Mr. Rough-and-Ready is a successful producer-director of Westerns and serials, who has his own independent unit at a major studio, through which his pictures are released. He refers with a matter-of-fact honesty to his background, that of a poor New York boy with little formal education. His first movie job, back in the days of the silent films, was as an office boy in a New York studio. From that he went on to property man, cutter, and a little acting, all before the days of the talkies. He now functions efficiently as a producer and director of Westerns and serials whose budgets range from $200,000 to $500,000. He completely controls and dominates his pictures, which are concerned with heroic escapes from danger and an exciting rescue at the end. A boy and girl are in the film but rarely any romance. The characters are all clear-cut. The hero is pure white and the villain pure black, in old melodramatic style. The formulas he uses are almost unchanged since the silent movies, but the locales are different. Today the setting may have something to do with aviation or electronics — anything which appeals to the youth who make up most of his audience.

On each serial there are four writers, one of whom is a supervisor of the team. The characters are definitely set and each writer works on certain incidents which the supervisor ties together. After the supervisor has done his job, the script is handed to Mr. Rough-and-Ready, who edits and suggests changes to the supervisor, who carries them out. On the set Mr. Rough-and-Ready works very quickly and is all activity. There is none of the slowness and the many retakes of the big productions. The rapidity of the shooting resembles the tempo in his films. He knows exactly what he wants and is able to verbalize to the actors. He once played some minor roles in the old, silent days and still considers himself an actor, although he has no ambitions along that line. However, he still has his superstitions. On each picture he walks across the set at least once taking a very minor part. This, he thinks, insures the picture's success.

He does not live in the usual Hollywood manner. His home is unpretentious and furnished in a mail-order catalogue style. He belongs to no social circle. There are a number of relatives to whom he has given minor jobs and he has a number of business associates, but he appears to have no group of friends. Mr. Rough-and-Ready rarely reads anything outside of the scripts for his movies. He says frankly that movies are for him good business, and that he knows and cares nothing about the "art" of the films. He regards his Westerns and serials as the "bread and butter" of the industry, saying that there is always a demand for them, while the A pictures have their ups and downs. Among producers he is unique in that he has none of the gambler's attitude, for he asserts that he has never lost any money and that his profits are always good.

However, serials and Westerns are not just good business for him. He loves them. He does the kind of picture he would like to see if he were a member of the audience. Excitement and fast action are his "meat" and he projects himself completely into his movies and has a grand time. He is not a man of subtlety nor has he any artistic pretensions. He knows what he wants and how to get it efficiently. He is independent, producing a staple product for which there is always a demand. He appears to be both economically and psychologically secure. He has no ambition to compete with the big-time A producers, is unworried about prestige, and his working life stands out in Hollywood for its relative lack of conflict and frustration. There are no discrepancies between his goals, achievements and abilities.

Mr. Mediocre, an elderly man, had been a producer of B pictures before he was given A ones. His quiet personality is in sharp contrast to Mr. Rough-and-Ready's boisterous one, which communicated the excitement he was continuously feeling on the job. Mr. Mediocre has a long unpretentious role in show business. Both his parents were in vaudeville, and when he was still young his first job was to take tickets at the box offices of vaudeville houses. Later he wrote skits, did publicity work for shows, and many other odd jobs. After the "talkies" came in, vaudeville declined and he had to look around for some other field of work. He knew no world except the theatrical one and he thought the movies had a good future. Besides, he had always wanted to live in California; so he came to Hollywood, where he had a few friends and acquaintances. One of them gave him the opportunity to write scripts for B pictures. The producer for whom he worked took Mr. Mediocre along when he went to a major studio. For a while Mr. Mediocre assisted this producer in making B pictures. When the producer left the studio Mr. Mediocre was given his job. After a number of years, he was promoted to A pictures.

Mr. Mediocre says that his choice for a new picture is influenced by the theme of whatever movies are currently successful. If the psychological murder thrillers are enjoying box-office success, then he decides to do one of them. Of course, many times he simply does whatever is suggested by the head of the studio.

In one case the studio purchased the rights to a novel, and a script which had been written from it, and assigned him to that. He worked in the following manner. He thought the script needed considerable change, so assigned Writer Number 1 to the job, indicating the kind of changes he wanted; when Writer Number 1 had finished, Mr. Mediocre showed the script to the director, who thought there should be more romance in it. Writer Number 2 was then called in to put in the romance. Writer Number 3 was called in after that, to sharpen and polish the dialogue. Mr. Mediocre then decided that the script needed comedy gags and Writers Number 4 and Number 5, who worked separately and not as a team, were employed to give it comedy touches. Mr. Mediocre suggested the lifting of gags and other funny incidents from successful movies, which were not always relevant to this one. The writers did as they were told. It took about six months to complete the script. This movie, like some of his others, was less than mediocre.

He thinks of himself as born to the show business. His enjoyment of the job is rather passive, and while he does not talk pretentiously about art or say that he is an artist he does talk about the "thrill of creation" he experiences when he sees his movies on the screen. He has no definite opinions about anything and is reluctant to commit himself to anyone's point of view, for fear of being held responsible if it should fail. He works rather mechanically with a number of people, in an assembly-line manner and within a well-established frame of tried formulas and gags. He is happy if his picture has success at the box office. He tells of one time suddenly thinking, at a preview, when it was too late, that the ending of the picture was all wrong; for a while he felt quite badly. A bit later the front office congratulated him on the success the picture was having at the box office — and he says he felt badly no longer.

Mr. Kowtow, in his middle thirties, with some success already although not yet in the big producer class, is clever and intelligent, and has great ability for compromise. He knows his way around and has made a point of getting along with people and having them like him. He is particularly quick to seize any opportunity presented.

He too started his movie career when he was fourteen by selling tickets at a movie house and had a number of lowly jobs such as that of "prop boy." Later he worked on some of the trade papers and has had miscellaneous jobs at various studios. His last one before becoming a producer was as assistant to an executive producer and his functions included supervising the work of writers and directors, the casting of actors and serving as a liaison person between the executive head and all the people who were working on a picture.

In this capacity he learned a great deal. He saw that one picture which the executive head planned to produce was headed for failure. He knew that the script on which several writers were working was coming to a dead end and that it would be impossible to film. He foresaw this several weeks before it actually happened; he knew in advance that the executive would have to turn down the script and would then be left "holding the bag" and in an anxious position. For the executive had commitments to a producer, to a director, and to two stars for a certain type of picture, for which studio space had been reserved at a definite time.

Mr. Kowtow, however, gave the executive no advance notice that the picture was going to fizzle out, but instead used the time so that he would be prepared to save the situation when it occurred. He took a property which the studio owned, in which he thought were the possibilities of a good picture, and immediately began making a script from it. He worked on this at night and at home.

Everything happened as planned. The executive saw the first script when it was finished, knew immediately that it was no good and that it would be better to write off the expense incurred as a loss and start with something different However, he did not have the "something different" ready. He was in the usual panic which prevails at such a time.

This was the cue for Mr. Kowtow to step in and show the script he had been working on. The producer liked it, was naturally grateful to his assistant for saving the situation, and promoted Mr. Kowtow to the position of associate producer. From that he quickly rose to producer.

Mr. Kowtow says that the pictures he likes best to do are those with a great deal of feeling and somewhat on the sentimental side. But he does many different kinds. The executive head of his studio is known as a very arbitrary and dictatorial person and Mr. Kowtow has the reputation of getting along well with him — that is, giving in. However, he has a picture of himself in which he would like to be the kind of person who can say "no" and fight, if necessary, for the picture he wants to make. He says he thinks it necessary to do this for his own self-respect, that one cannot give in all the time. In the same breath, he adds that most of the time he knows he cannot win and there is nothing to do but obey — or get out. He is not willing to do the latter.

Mr. Kowtow is the kind of person who is described as having "needled" his way into his present position. He has the reputation for never getting mad at anyone and always keeping his temper. No one at the studio ever speaks badly of him, and this is unusual. Of course, no one speaks very highly of him either.

He has no particular flair for new ideas, and even if he should have one he would not have the strength of character to forge ahead with it in the face of opposition. His is the ability of handling people and compromising. One sees him becoming more and more successful, not doing anything spectacular and always in the middle of the road, yet slightly wistful that he has not done something better. At the present time his attitude is a combination of being pleased with his success and at the same time disappointed that he cannot respect the mediocre films he produces.

Mr. Persistence is another middle-of-the-road producer, considered a bit better than the ordinary, whose career, particularly in its beginning, illustrates some of the difficulties which come from the front office. His first jobs were on newspapers and magazines, and he more or less drifted into pictures through a close relative. He started his movie career in one of the smaller studios, producing "shorts," and finally landed a job at a major studio as a writer, with the understanding that he would be given an opportunity at production. The executive kept his word and, after Mr. Persistence had been there a while, told him to read the studio properties and see if there was anything among them he cared to produce. He picked out the one he liked best, a rather sentimental love story, which represented his own fantasy of love. The executive approved of his choice and told him to go ahead on the treatment. He worked hard and the boss liked the result.

A writer was assigned and work on the script began. It went along satisfactorily until, to Mr. Persistence's great disappointment, the front office took the whole thing away from him because they decided it was too big to give to a new and untried producer. It was handed to another one, more experienced and with a record of box-office successes. A bit later Mr. Persistence was given another picture and again worked on it with a writer. Then, within two weeks of the shooting date, when it was practically ready, a deal was made with a Broadway producer to put it on as a play first. Again nothing had come from all his hard work. Although discouraged, he accepted it as part of the general situation and wrote it off as good experience.

Then, the first picture, which he had so wanted to do, was handed back to him. The other producer had not been able to lick the script. Finally, he and the writer got the script ready. Then came the question of casting. They had made a "package deal" with another studio for the loan of two actors, in which they got one they wanted; and another, whom they had to take in the package, was assigned to the male lead, although not appropriate for that part. Fortunately he became sick and had to leave the picture; they were then able to get the actor originally desired, who had not been free earlier. The picture was a box-office success and a bit better than the average. Mr. Persistence was "made" as a producer.

In discussing it, he feels that his success was entirely due to lucky breaks. He did have a couple, such as getting a good male star after starting with a poor one. Yet he had also worked very hard, had done his best, and had suffered many disappointments. These he discounts, and is startled at a question as to whether they too might have counted. Like so many Hollywood people he is accustomed to thinking of success only in terms of breaks, and has not confidence in his own hard work and ability. He is happy in his job as a producer although he has many headaches in connection with it. His aim is to do pictures which are good entertainment, and which "lift people up a bit." He says he is not interested in messages or social implications, and what he likes best is a good sentimental film. That also is the kind of novel he selects when he reads for pleasure. He regards production as a creative job because he says the idea to do a particular picture is his, and he stays with it until the final product is on the screen. He is in constant huddles over the problems which come up during production, and it is he who ties together the innumerable details. This job of supervision makes him feel creative.

Mr. Scoop is one of the top successful producers at a major studio, with a long list of box-office hits to his credit, among which are some regarded as decidedly very good and others more or less run-of-the-mill. He began as a hack writer, first for newspapers and radio, then for the movies, without any particular success. But as a producer his progress has been consistent. However, his standards and thinking are still close to those of the newspaper, with its interest in headlines. His goal is to do a movie involving a problem of current interest and with social implications, and to do it quickly before anyone else does. His method of getting ideas is through an omnivorous reading of newspapers and popular magazines, listening to radios, and keeping a very careful record of all ideas with any possible appropriateness for a movie, gleaned from any of these sources. The ideas are filed in hundreds of folders, filling a number of cabinets, which he constantly consults.

His technique of work is to give the idea for a movie and something of a story line to a writer, who then develops a treatment and a script from it. Mr. Scoop says he regards his relationship with a writer as a "marriage of brain, heart and soul," and he usually picks able, skilled authors who share his interests. He gives them considerable freedom, relatively speaking, although there are frequent story conferences in which, of course, his is the final word if there is disagreement. The director usually is in on these conferences from the beginning, and the principals of the cast and the set designer may participate in later ones. He tries to give his pictures an integration frequently lacking in the assembly-line type of production. He thinks of his job as that of guidance and of himself as a kind of pilot, giving direction to talent. He regards the script as the one most important element in production, since, he says, without a skilled one, a good picture cannot possibly result.

Mr. Scoop works all the time and very hard. He lives and breathes movies. They seem to ooze from his pores. They are his god, whom he continuously serves. Everything he sees, reads or hears is possible material for his pictures. He has great persistence and argues at great length with the executive head of the studio about a picture he wants to make. He may lose out, but he does not give up. He returns six months or a year or two later, if he still thinks his idea good, and this time he may win. In conversation he gives the impression that he listens to other people only as long as they are saying something which might be useful to him for a movie. This single, wholehearted, almost fanatical concentration, combined with intelligence, has produced results. He has attained a position of prestige, with sufficient power to carry out many of his ideas.

Yet his pictures, although rather well constructed and smoothly produced, and decidedly better than the average, are for the most part limited to reflecting his standard of the newspaper "scoop." He is more concerned with being the first to do a picture on some social problem previously considered taboo to the movies than in illuminating the problem with understanding. He sees himself as a courageous person, "sticking his neck out." Yet in most of his movies the problems are so oversimplified as to become phony. Their implications are rarely treated with insight, and his solutions do not ring true.

His pictures reflect him as Westerns reflect Mr. Rough-and-

Ready's personality. Mr. Scoop is a man of mildly humanitarian ideals but with apparently limited knowledge and understanding of the social problem which he is so eager to be the first to present in a movie. He is a strong man with an earnestness and concentration on the medium which transcends that of the usual producer, whose concentration is mostly on himself. At the same time he is still a newspaperman with the goal of being first with his story. He resembles Mr. Rough-and-Ready in being relatively unfrustrated. Each knows what he wants and how to get it, and each one enjoys enormous personal satisfaction in achieving his goal.

Mr. Schizo differs from both these men in that he suffers from a real and obvious conflict in goals. He is in his thirties, from a New York, middle-class background. He had literary ambitions, but was never able to write anything which achieved recognition. His work was limited to that of an unknown newspaper reporter. He came to Hollywood with a rather minor job and immediately began playing the social "game." He met the right people, was invited to the big parties and seen at the best night clubs and restaurants. He has considerable charm and people liked him. He was a great success, and made a "good" marriage to a wealthy girl with studio connections.

And so Mr. Schizo became a producer. But he had been too busy with his social activities to learn anything about how movies are made, and he never seems to have acquired the knowledge since.

He did not lose his old ideas and continued to think of himself as a literary person. He can hold an interesting and intelligent conversation about contemporary authors, discussing their virtues and faults from the point of view of a writer. At the same time he is intensely ambitious to be an important person in the industry. He wants money, but even more the power that comes with it, and he sees himself as a kind of major general dominating the situation and everyone in it. The rival pictures of himself as a literary artist and big business executive appear to be in constant conflict. Neither goal wins out sufficiently to provide direction, and the result is the appearance of impotency in his work.

He rarely knows what he wants. While one picture was in production, he discussed a particular scene with the director, making the point that he thought it should be more involved. So the two men worked all morning on adding complications to the scene. At the end of the morning's work, when it was time to go out for lunch, Mr. Schizo walked from the desk to the door, turned around and said, "You know, this scene was all right, but now it is complicated."

Although he has his own independent unit, his reputation is of giving in very easily to the head of the studio or to the star, or to anyone else with power. He will talk to a gifted writer or director about a picture he plans, the idea of which may be sufficiently different from the run-of-the-mill to get them excited, and to make them promise to work on it. But when the time comes, it invariably turns out differently because drastic changes have been made. Many times he is caught with studio space assigned to him and no story. Then he buys one in great haste though it offers no possibilities for a good movie. He appears completely unable to plan ahead, and the few weeks before shooting is scheduled to begin are characterized by hectic, frenzied inefficiency. He seems to have a need to get himself into a panic situation, which he communicates to all those who work for him. He is always "on the neck" of his writers, never leaving them alone at the studio or away from it, constantly interfering and interrupting them. The harassed writer may want to "bow out" of the whole situation. Then Mr. Schizo implores him not to leave, not to "desert" him in this crisis; and the writer, out of a sense of personal obligation to the men and in accordance with the obligation of "not walking out on a picture," remains. Schizo usually picks able writers with prestige, in the high-salary brackets — probably the kind he would have liked to be — and establishes a personal, friendly relationship, the underlying tone of which is his dependency on them. What Mr. Schizo projects on to his pictures are not his fantasies but rather the state of confusion and conflict that exists between them and in his personality. As might be expected, none of his pictures has been very successful, either from the point of view of box office or in receiving critical approval.

*   *   *

Mr. Good Judgment is different from any of the producers yet described. He is in his early forties and has been a producer for the last four or five years. He is a college graduate and majored in the theater arts, doing all kinds of things — acting, directing, writing, producing. His ambition then was to become a Broadway producer. After college he came to New York and earned a meager living in a number of jobs connected, some way or other, with the theater.

About nine or ten years ago, Mr. Good Judgment came to Hollywood and wrote original stories which he tried to sell to the studios but with no success. Sometimes he almost made a sale, but for some reason or other it always fell through. During the first year and a half he lived mostly on borrowed money. Eventually, through a writer friend who was working at a big studio, he got a job at the same place for $50 a week. He worked there for nine weeks, teaming up with another writer on B and Western scripts, and at the end of that time they offered him a contract at $50. He refused because the salary was so low. In the beginning he had been willing to work as an apprentice writer at this figure, with the assumption that if he stayed he would get more. (The Screen Writers' Guild has since set $75 a week for an apprentice; if promoted, they must get the minimum of $187.)

For a number of years Mr. Good Judgment then earned his living on free-lance writing jobs on Westerns and B pictures. He had considerable success, and his salary went up first to $150 a week, later to $350 and eventually to $750. His reputation was that of a skilled writer on B pictures.

He never considered himself a particularly good writer and his ambition was still to become a producer. Eventually he was offered a producer's job on B pictures. He hesitated in accepting it because he wanted to get out of the B classification. However, no one was offering him anything in the A group, and the executive who was offering the job said that the studio wanted to do better B pictures, which he thought could be accomplished if an intelligent and skilled writer handled the entire picture.

Mr. Good Judgment accepted the job and looked over the properties owned by the studio. He found a novel from which he thought an excellent melodrama could be made. He asked the producer if he could put on an old New York friend with whom he had worked on a magazine, as a writer at $150 a week. This man had not written any movie scripts but Mr. Good Judgment was convinced that he could and that they would work well together. The salary of $150 was considered so low that Mr. Good Judgment had his way. The two men worked hard together and in three weeks they had an eighty-five page treatment which the front office O.K.'d. They started on the script, working night and day. Mr. Good Judgment helped the writer on the structure and on many technical movie points.

In the meantime, a producer of A pictures from another studio wanted to buy the novel on which the script was based. The front office knew nothing about this novel except that it was in their B department and that Mr. Good Judgment was working on it. However, when a prestige A producer became interested, they sent for Mr. Good Judgment and asked him about the script he was doing. He was very enthusiastic about it and talked in glowing terms of the picture which would come from it. The executive was impressed, particularly since someone else wanted to buy the novel, and asked him why he had not put on a better writer. Following the stereotyped executive way of thinking, he could not see how a $150-a-week writer could possibly be any good. The producer managed to satisfy him by saying that the writer was worth at least $3000, that they were just lucky in getting a bargain. The producer had confidence in the script based on a real knowledge of movie writing which is unusual in Hollywood, and he was able to communicate this confidence to the front-office executive, who otherwise might have cold feet. Instead, the executive permitted the producer to go ahead in his own way. The script was finished in nine weeks, and when the front office read it, they were enthusiastic and refused to sell the novel on which it was based. They gave the writer all the time he wanted for polishing, which took three months. The picture was made on a bigger budget than first anticipated, not that of an A picture, but halfway between A and B. It was a smash hit, and with a known net profit of several hundred per cent.

Mr. Good Judgment now became an A producer. He kept the writer with him, and they worked together continuously as a team. They have similar tastes and ideas and mutual respect for each other. The writer is shy and inarticulate verbally, while the producer has enough aggression to stand up to the front office when necessary, and the two make an effective team. Mr. Good Judgment has had a number of big box-office hits to his credit, and therefore now enjoys considerable power in the choice of pictures. Among his box-office hits are those which have received critical acclaim not only for their presentation of dramatic conflict but also for their honesty.

He does not think of himself as a creative genius, but has confidence that he knows a good story when he sees one, and that he has the ability to pick people, such as writers and directors, who can carry it through. He is one of the very few people who do not emphasize the breaks. He is an intelligent person with the technical skill and the dramatic knowledge necessary for the production of movies. He has a point of view about life, an interest in it which goes deeper than headlines. He has known what he wanted to do for a long time, plowing steadily ahead towards his goal, and achieved it without playing the usual Hollywood game. Even though he has given up his former role of writer, he agrees with other writers, and the directors and actors who have become producers, on the relative unimportance of the producer's role. He, however, enjoys it, and brings to it both skill and knowledge gained from his previous experience.

Producers, like other people, get their jobs in different ways, and there are various kinds, some typical and others exceptional. Mr. Good Judgment, the college graduate of good taste and confidence in it, is most exceptional. Mr. Scoop, with his fanatical devotion to movies and humanitarianism, even though limited by his standards of the newspaper scoop, is not typical. The majority of producers of A pictures are well represented by Mr. Mediocre, who has been a Hollywood producer for a long time and who works completely according to the formula; by Mr. Kowtow, clever and intelligent but lacking in self-confidence and courage;

by Mr. Persistence, conscientious and a hard worker but with no unusual talent; and Mr. Schizo, a man in conflict, who works in a constant state of panic and without direction. Mr. Rough-and-Ready, who gets so much genuine enjoyment out of producing Westerns and serials, is partially typical of his group, although here too one finds pretentious and frustrated men.

The fundamental question of whether producers in general are really necessary can be raised. It would be possible to produce movies in which the director would have the power the producer now enjoys, and in which financial details would be handled, as they are now, by the budget director, who at least usually sticks to his last and rarely thinks of himself as being creative. But if the structure in which the producers are important is accepted, then it seems not unreasonable that the producer should know how to pick a good story and how to select the proper men to help carry it through. These capacities must, however, come from something besides the desire to "make a buck," for they depend on a knowledge and understanding of theater, literature, people, and the movie medium, and on good judgment and understanding. It likewise should be important for the producer to be able to plan thoughtfully in advance in a more or less businesslike manner.

Very few producers have those qualities, which are important for an administrator in any field. A man cannot be a good college president if he does not have some knowledge of the ingredients of good teaching and scholarship. On the other hand, an effective college president is content to be an administrator and does not dictate in detail how each member of the faculty should pursue his particular academic interests.

The problem in Hollywood is that while the producer's is basically an administrative job, the people who play his part are often neither good administrators nor content to limit themselves to that role.

CHAPTER VII

The Scribes

WRITERS, as well as producers, are part of the *mésalliance* which eventually gives birth to a script. What kind of people are the writers? Although they differ as do all members of any occupational group, certain uniformities appear; and as usual, the exceptions as well as the norm contribute to our understanding.

The best way to understand writers, or any other people, is through their motivations. The primary one for Hollywood writers is the same as it is for everyone else there, namely, the inflated salaries for which the industry is famous. Mediocre writers with no particular ability swarm there with the expectation of earning up to a thousand or more dollars a week. Gifted and talented writers come when they are broke, or are attracted by the idea of getting rich quickly. Usually they do not plan to remain, but many stay and are sucked into the system. Only a few struggle against it. These are the ones who, in addition to the desire for big salaries, have a genuine interest in making movies, a special facility for seeing stories in film imagery, and who are hopeful of utilizing some of the potentialities of the powerful medium. For some, also, the traditional fascination of anything connected with theater or movies acts as an added spur. Diverse motives are blended but underlying all is the basic one of easy and big money, which few writers, gifted or ungifted, can earn outside of Hollywood.

Most of them before coming to Hollywood made only a precarious living. They were newspaper reporters, sold an occasional radio script, did play reading in the offices of Broadway producers, read manuscripts or proof in publishing houses, or wrote advertising copy. Some had won a one-act play writing contest in college or the local Y. A number had written unproduced plays which an agent or producer said showed promise. Others were white-collar workers, salesmen, or businessmen. A few were established novelists and playwrights.

Some writers came "on their own" to take their chances in getting Hollywood "gold." Others arrived at the suggestion of a friend or relative who promised to help them. Many were brought out by producers on a contract with the usual six months' option clause, often given little or nothing to do, and then dropped at the end of the six months. But the writers stayed on hoping to get a break. Some became successful; others are still waiting for their chance.

Of the slightly more than a thousand members of the Screen Writers' Guild, which includes practically all the writers, only a relatively small proportion achieve their goal of big money. Probably not more than two hundred earn their living by writing exclusively for the movies, and even in a period of prosperity less than half are employed at any one time. During unemployment periods in script writing, many of them go back to their former occupations of writing for radio, newspapers or magazines.

Their salaries range from $187.50 to $4500 or more a week. In what was considered the last relatively prosperous year, from November 1, 1945, to October 31, 1946, 57 per cent of the members of the Screen Writers' Guild earned more than $5000 in the industry and 22 per cent less than $5000. The remaining 21 per cent were not employed in movie writing that year. In the first half of the same year, 150, or slightly more than 25 per cent, worked full-time. During the same half-year, weekly earnings were:

Less than $500	a week	248 writers
$500–$1000	a week	163 writers
$1000–$2500	a week	124 writers
Over $2500	a week	12 writers

More than half were thus earning over $500 a week. Slightly more than a year later, July 21, 1947, fewer writers were employed, but more were in the upper-salary brackets. There were 114 who were earning over $1250 a week as compared to the 86 of the year before.[1] This increase in top-salary brackets points to one of the business anomalies of Hollywood, that in times of increasing

[1] All figures from the Screen Writers' Guild.

unemployment and layoffs the writers in the lower brackets suffer more than those in the upper ones. When the producers are most worried about the market and their profits, they employ the highest-paid writers, whose salaries then go up because they are in such demand. The average producer's idea of insuring success and profits is to spend more money. This strong belief in the magical efficacy of money is common to our society. But while there is the general assumption by the studio that the more a person earns the better he is, neither writers nor producers always think that everyone in the top-bracket class is necessarily gifted.

Although no one would expect all members of any group to be equally able, it is not easy to evaluate writers (or actors, directors, or others) according to their ability. Two methods, however, can be used for a general appraisal. One is to take the studios' judgments in terms of their own value system: salaries; and the other, to consider the informal opinions of producers and of writers. Presumably anyone in the salary bracket between $1250 and $4500 a week would be considered "tops" by the industry. By "tops" is meant creative people with ideas and the ability to write a finished script. There were 114 writers in this salary bracket on July 21, 1947. But neither the writers themselves nor the producers thought there were 114 gifted writers then in Hollywood. The estimates of the actual number of really talented writers were much lower and ranged from 25 to 50. The same and sometimes greater discrepancy occurred between the number in the high-salary class and those estimated by their own groups to be gifted, among actors, directors and producers. If competent writers are considered, it might be assumed, again in the studio's scale of values, that anyone earning between $500 and $1250 a week would be so regarded. For the six months preceding April 30, 1946, there were 213 people in this salary bracket, or about 20 per cent of the Guild membership. The informal estimate of a large number of writers and producers ranged between 10 and 20 per cent, averaging about 14 or 15 per cent. It is not that there are fewer gifted and competent writers in Hollywood than anywhere else. There are probably more. But the salaries of all writers, with and without talent, competent and incompetent, far exceed what they could earn elsewhere. This situation is not unique to the writers, but applies to everyone concerned with the production of movies. There is no other field, except radio, where a writer or anyone else on the lower rungs of the success ladder earns $500 a week and where such a salary is described as "peanuts."

It is for this reason that many writers (and others) are willing to sit it out and wait for the breaks. The stakes for which they play are high.

While waiting, they have lower expenses than if they were living in New York or Chicago, since it is not necessary to buy winter clothing and, in the past, rent and food have been less than in Eastern cities. Another advantage is that since there are so many other writers in the "same boat" they do not feel lonely.

But neither the structure nor the atmosphere of Hollywood is conducive to helping writers broaden their experiences, sharpen their insights and become good movie writers, either as they wait for good fortune or after they get it. Their private life away from the studio does little to offset the disadvantages of the assembly line on which they work. The isolated suburban quality of most of the areas in which Hollywood people live has been mentioned. The writer's social life is usually with other writers, occasionally with producers and directors, but almost always confined to people connected with the making of motion pictures. This means a withdrawal from the everyday life which might provide experiences and new ideas for movies. Of course, this is important only for those who are writers in the literary sense of the word. The large number of mediocrities would not be creative in any situation.

Writers vary in how much they play the Hollywood game. Some cultivate important people, entertaining and being seen at big parties and popular night clubs. A few employ a publicity man to keep their names in the trade press. But those doing this and extensively playing the game seem to be considerably fewer than actors, producers and directors who do so. There are successful writers who live unostentatiously, picking their friends on the basis of congeniality. In one small group are three or four such men whose friendships date back to many years ago when they were all struggling in New York. The settings for their parties are now more comfortable and the liquor a better brand, but conversation is a bit dull — although there may be some critical conversation about books and events of interest in the writers' world.

More typical of a successful writer's party is one with a dozen or more people present when conversation opens on the latest bit of Hollywood scandal, with each one vying with the other to say something clever about it. Then there may be some superficial talk about a new book or movie or politics. After this the men may separate for gin rummy or poker, leaving the women alone to their gossip. Or if they all remain together, the discussion turns to their troubles with a producer or the MPAA office which enforces the Code and to boasting about how much money they are making. Rarely is there serious discussion about writing or movies.

For only a few writers is participation in Guild affairs and politics a major activity. But — whether they play the "game" or politics, give small unostentatious parties or big lavish ones — the lives of most writers, like everyone else in Hollywood, are limited to the movie world.

The general atmosphere tends to make people soft. Most of the writers, good and bad, have never previously known financial security. Now for the first time, if they have any success, they have money. Instead of living in dingy apartments, they have homes, gardens, a servant and enough money in the bank to pay the doctor's bills, and those in the higher salary brackets have luxury. The much-heralded Southern California climate contributes to the softening process. There is a natural temptation to spend a considerable amount of time out of doors; and for many writers, as well as for other people, one of the major advantages is the ease with which children can be brought up in Los Angeles.

The perpetuation of this pleasant, comfortable life, therefore, becomes the goal for which writers — gifted and ungifted — are willing to be a producer's "lead pencil."

There are the exceptional men and women who do not become soft. One consistently refuses Hollywood offers on a contractual

basis but comes instead for one picture a year; the rest of the time
he is in New York. He admits that Southern California is a very
good place for bringing up children and that the weather is most
enjoyable, but his main drive happens to be creative, and he says
that for him the best place to write is a small hotel room, and
whether or not there is sunshine is irrelevant. There are others who
do not have to be quite so drastic in their efforts to resist the
California sunshine.

Of course, there is nothing "wrong" about enjoying the Southern
Californian life. It is merely that the creative person who functions
as such has to make some sacrifices. Creation has its price, too.
Writers outside of Hollywood have likewise been known to suc-
cumb to the ease brought on by returns from their first best seller.
But the temptations in Hollywood are much greater.

This abstract picture of writers, like that of the producers, becomes clearer through specific examples of the different kinds of
individuals and the manner in which they work and live.

Mr. Hopeful, in his late twenties, is one of those waiting for the
breaks. Back East he had written four or five plays, none of which
had been produced. A New York producer who thought he had
promise went to Hollywood and took him along on the usual
six months' option contract. Mr. Hopeful thought "heaven had
opened" and was sure that his days of poverty were over. During
the six months at the studio he was given the opportunity to do
only a few small bits on different scripts, not enough to earn a
screen credit or to give any indication of whether he had ability.
At the end of the six months his option was not taken up. The
producer who had sponsored his coming had gone to another
studio and no one was particularly interested in Mr. Hopeful. He
now began working on original scripts. After several years of no
success in selling them, he is working with a more successful col-
laborator, who, he feels, has no more ability, but whose name is
better known. Mr. Hopeful has also begun to write a novel.

After a couple of years in Hollywood he does not seem particularly worried. He feels that any moment his luck will change,
and that he will sell a screen play and be made as a writer. He

and his wife, who is employed, live very modestly in a one-room furnished apartment. Although he has no screen credit and has been unemployed except for the first six months, he thinks of himself as a movie writer and part of the motion picture industry. He is an active member of the Screen Writers' Guild and is in constant social contact with a large number of other movie writers, some in the same class as himself and others more successful. His life is a pleasant contrast to the lonely one in New York, where he was simply an unsuccessful playwright with little or no contact with other playwrights. Although he talks a great deal about the play and novel he wants to do after he has hit the jack pot in Hollywood, he nevertheless gives the impression that he could settle quite comfortably for becoming a movie writer in the $750-a-week class.

Hollywood is filled with young people (writers, actors and others) who in their home communities stood out as being different from the average. The very desire to write or act set them apart from their neighbors. Success on an amateur level encouraged them to think of this difference as talent. Every big city is filled with them. Outside of Hollywood they tend to come to terms with reality more often and settle for less. But in the movie world they see other mediocre people in prestige jobs, earning big money. So they too wait for the breaks.

Miss Sanguine is one of these. In college she won a prize in a playwriting competition and after graduation came to Hollywood "cold," that is, completely on her own. For two years she wrote screen originals, which she took around to story editors and producers, without the help of an agent. At the end of two years a producer who had read some of her originals and with whom she was friendly, had a story he could not lick and gave Miss Sanguine a job. She was employed by the studio for twenty weeks at $150 a week, writing the treatment and then the screen play. On the latter she had a collaborator with a prominent name, and with whom she shared the credit. When the picture was finished Miss Sanguine was not given another job. Everyone, according to Miss Sanguine, thought the "name" writer was responsible for the screen

play. She went back to writing original stories in the hope of selling one of them and getting a chance to do a screen play from it,
but this has not yet happened. She is now thirty years old and
has been in Hollywood three and a half years. She feels successful,
since she has succeeded in getting one credit, and she is opti-
mistically waiting for the chance to get more.

Mr. Pretentious is one of those who thinks of himself as a "real"
writer, though frustrated, and blames his low status on not getting the breaks. He majored in playwriting at an Eastern University and came straight to Hollywood upon graduation about ten
years ago. For a number of years he wrote originals for B pictures, receiving about $500 for each one. He never sold more than
seven in any one year and only once succeeded in selling a script
for which he was paid $2500. That year he sold nothing else. When
the number of B pictures was drastically reduced by many studios,
he had no income at all. He was quite desperate and finally secured a job on a small Los Angeles newspaper.

Mr. Pretentious speaks bitterly about others who, he says, have
achieved their positions only because they got the breaks. Yet,
there is nothing to justify his claim to be a real writer. He always
works through a card catalogue, in which he keeps an analysis
of every movie he has seen, giving its plot and characters. One of
his methods of doing an original, particularly when he is in a
hurry, is to run through his file and pull out a movie he has
analyzed; he changes the characters, keeping much of the same
plot; sometimes he keeps the characters and makes a small change
in the plot. He says that the story analysts, the first readers of these
originals, like a certain opening; so he uses the same paragraph
with slight modifications over and over again. He adds that this
is a common practice among writers of originals for B movies.
One such writer, who was getting his story ready, mislaid his
traditional first paragraph and, hurriedly going through his papers
looking for it, asked, "What did I do with my paragraph?"

Mr. Pretentious has never written anything for the movies or for
any other medium which indicates talent or even a minimum of
creative ability. But he continues to think of himself as the "real

thing" and is jealous of successful writers. When he mentions a prestige literary person, also successful in movies, who came to Hollywood about the same time as Mr. Pretentious, he insists that the successful writer has no more ability than he, but knew how to play politics and was lucky. It is far easier in Hollywood than elsewhere for a person like Mr. Pretentious to believe that his lack of success is due only to not getting the breaks; because almost everyone, successful and unsuccessful, talented and mediocre, regards those same breaks as the most important factor in success.

Mr. Modest started as a newspaperman and short-story writer, without too much success, and came to Hollywood when he was about thirty-five years old as a $75-a-week writer. Before the war he worked up to $250 a week on B pictures and Westerns at one of the smaller studios. Then he was away for the duration of the war. When he returned, he had no job, but a good friend, with a well-established reputation as both playwright and screen writer, suggested him to a producer for a particular script. The producer gave Mr. Modest a short story he had purchased and asked him to do a treatment. He took the story and thought about it very carefully, came back to the producer and said that he did not think it was possible to do a script from it. He added that if the producer would permit him to make certain changes, which he then described, he might be able to do something. The producer, impressed with his ideas and honesty, told him to work along the suggested lines, and liked the story treatment which Mr. Modest then did. The executive head of the studio then O.K.'d it, making suggestions which were passed on to Mr. Modest. He incorporated them in the script and a gifted director who had been assigned to the job sat in on the story conferences. Upon the producer's and director's recommendation the front-office executive agreed to let the writer go with the director to do any rewriting on location that might be necessary. Since Mr. Modest was earning only $450 a week, the executive did not think his salary would unduly increase the budget. Mr. Modest says he learned a great deal by working closely with the director, the cutter and the cameraman on location. The picture, produced on a relatively low budget, turned out highly successful from the points of view of both box office and critics.

After the picture was finished Mr. Modest was raised to $600 a week. Although not in the upper brackets, he is happy, and is now working with the same director and producer on another picture which he thinks is good. If it turns out successfully he will get a substantial raise. Also, it is likely that some other studio will bid for his services and his value will be increased. Mr. Modest says that the writing of Westerns and B melodramas was good training on how to build up suspense, which he now uses in A pictures. His outstanding qualities are his honesty, unpretentiousness and ability as a good craftsman.

Mr. Cynic is one of the many who once hoped to write the great American novel. He started as a newspaperman in the East and came to Hollywood, when a friend, well-established in the movie industry, secured him a writer's job at two and a half times his newspaper salary. Today he is a successful writer of B pictures and over the last five years he has earned from the movie industry approximately $100,000, or an average of $20,000 a year. He considers this very good, and much in advance of what he would have earned if he had stayed in the newspaper world.

Now he is in his early forties, has an attractive home, and is seemingly content with his life. However, he opened a conversation with the statement, "I am a hack writer," in a rather bitter tone, and then mentioned that he had no respect for anything that he had written in Hollywood. He never goes to see any of the movies on which he has worked, because, he says, all the original meaning has been taken out and he cannot stand looking at them. He has likewise no respect for any of the producers for whom he has worked and very little for other writers. He seems to have accepted the limitations of the medium, but his acceptance is bitter. He tells a number of funny stories which always show the producers as inferior to the writers. He enjoys the fact that the producers, who are his bosses, are also employees who might be fired tomorrow, and that they are more insecure than he is, because it would be more difficult for them to get another job. Mr. Cynic disparages his own work, jeers at his employers, but enjoys his comfortable home and a substantial bank account.

Not all successful writers are frustrated. Mr. Acquiesce has been in Hollywood about fifteen years and before that he, too, was a newspaperman doing publicity also, and advertising, but he never succeeded in making a good living for his family. Today he is in a high-salary bracket — over $1200 a week — owns a very attractive home, has steady work and a large number of screen credits. He thoroughly enjoys the medium and seems to feel no frustration about working on someone else's ideas or having other people follow him on his script. He appears to have completely accepted all the limitations of writing in Hollywood, and says that these are the conditions which writers must expect and that he is prepared to take them in his stride. He feels the same way about the censorship Code, most of which he considers "rather silly," but he obeys it without getting upset and indignant. He stresses the large movie audience as one of the major compensations and talks about getting a message across. Since his pictures are all the most conventional stock melodramas and mysteries devoid of any message, this appears to be wishful thinking or rationalization. It is interesting, however, that Mr. Acquiesce has to have that, in spite of all his talk about accepting the limitations of the medium and enjoying his work and his life.

All who become part of the Hollywood pool of writers have not started with literary ambitions. The idea of writing had never occurred to Mr. Coincidence. He was a resident of Los Angeles and his chief interest was aviation. He happened to know a big-name writer doing a script based on an aviation story, who asked him to help with the technical details, for which he was paid $75 a week. When the big-name writer moved to another studio he took Mr. Coincidence along, paying part of his salary. Mr. Coincidence learned the game and started writing originals, selling them under an assumed name, since he did not want the studio to know about it. In a couple of years he was averaging between ten and twenty thousand dollars, more than he had ever earned before.

For Mr. Coincidence movies provide an exciting life. He has always been susceptible to beautiful women and he finds more of them in the movie industry than in any other one place. In addition there is always the chance of making big money. He lives gregariously, going to many parties and drinking fairly heavily, partly because he enjoys it and partly also because he considers it necessary to getting along. His becoming a movie writer was accidental; he was intelligent and developed a certain knack or craftsmanship, and then, by playing the game, he managed to achieve some success.

None of the people so far described are especially gifted. Mr. Literary, however, before coming to Hollywood, was well known for his novels, short stories and essays, some of which had appeared in anthologies of distinguished writing. But he had been poor, insecure and living a "hand-to-mouth" existence; and so he too jumped at the opportunity of coming to Hollywood when it was offered him. Today he is a successful writer of A scripts, in the over-$1250-a-week bracket, and with steady employment.

He has the sensitive literary person's knowledge of people and of their motivations. He is highly intelligent and his background is rich in experience and knowledge of literature. He can also write very well. Without many screen credits, he was much in demand and fortunate in working for more than a year with a producer who had originally come from the theater and whose goals were still influenced by it. The two men became close friends; and the writer, having the stronger personality, dominated the relationship and had more than usual freedom in the choice of story and the conditions under which he worked.

He regards his work at the studio as a form of play and rather enjoys it as such. He uses the word "play" because he says that he cannot take it seriously. He and some of the others pretend to themselves and each other that it is serious. Each day there is a crisis; a crisis about getting the star to interpret her lines in such a way as to bring out their meaning; a crisis in the front office which lays down the law in a way contrary to what he and the producer regard as the best interest of the picture; a crisis because someone gets sick or they cannot get the proper actor for a part. Although he gets excited about all these "crises," deep down he knows that they are not really important and that the film will be made one way or another.

It will be made, and in the end it will not please him. It will not have the integrity that any work of his own would possess. He has never worked on any movie which has even moderately satisfied him. Each time he starts with high hopes that this one will be different, but each time it is the same: so many interferences, so many changes, that the final script is not his, although he has far more influence over it than do most writers. He does not have this attitude of "play" toward writing a novel or a short story. That is deadly earnest. Then he is concerned with working out a real problem and any interference with it he would regard as a real crisis.

His attitude of "play" may well be a defense mechanism. If he took the script as seriously as he takes a novel, he would suffer too much. This way he manages to "get by" and even to enjoy it. He lives comfortably, but not luxuriously, and saves about $500 a week toward his goal of a quarter of a million, when he plans to retire and write as he pleases. He does not play the usual social Hollywood game, but chooses his own friends discriminatingly on the basis of congeniality. On the surface it would seem that he had made a good accommodation to the situation. But — he has ulcers.

Mr. Gifted has an even more distinguished literary reputation. Before coming to Hollywood he was well known for several novels and short stories, and a play. None of them, however, had been sufficiently popular to enable him to support his family in even modest comfort. After a protracted period of family illness he was broke, and a writer friend in Hollywood suggested that he come there. Mr. Gifted traveled on a bus because it was cheaper than the train, and left his family with relatives, until he could earn sufficient money to send for them. When he arrived his friend talked to the story editor about him, and it so happened that at this studio a producer had read some of Mr. Gifted's short stories, and thought highly of them. Because of this combination Mr.

Gifted was employed on a contract basis. But he was assigned not to the producer who had appreciated his writings, but to another one who made only fast-action B pictures and Westerns. Mr. Gifted was known through his novels for subtle insight and understanding delineation of characters and their motivations. Westerns obviously did not call for these qualities. Nor did he have the particular abilities or training required for these action pictures. His work was not successful. The producer was displeased and Mr. Gifted was unhappy. The studio was about to drop him. The first producer, who had known his work and his potentialities, saved him by having him loaned to another studio.

Here he was given a chance to work on a good script, more in line with his particular ability, on which he could use his knowledge of people and his skill in dialogue. The movie was successful, and he went on to another script of the same type; again the picture was successful. Now he was made as an A writer in the upper-salary brackets and in great demand. As soon as his reputation was established he refused to work on a contractual basis and became a free-lance writer at over $3000 a week. He has enough prestige to make his own terms and to exercise a certain amount of choice on the scripts he works on. He does a sufficient number to give him the financial backlog necessary for taking time to write novels. He regards himself primarily as a novelist, and his creative satisfaction comes in functioning as such. He and his family live modestly, but comfortably, in an unfashionable neighborhood. He saves a considerable portion of his income from movie writing and for at least six months out of a year works on a novel.

He plays none of the usual Hollywood games. He has, however, a very good relationship with most of the producers and directors with whom he works. He uses the same understanding of people which comes out in his novels and stories in his working relationships. Instead of giving the producers fulsome flattery, he is aware of their little foibles in an understanding way. He also has confidence in his own taste and judgment and says "no" rather frequently to producers. This increases their respect and confidence in his judgment.

Mr. Gifted is exceptional in a number of ways. He has continued his writing of novels and at the same time become a movie writer in the top-salary bracket, so sought after by studios that he can work whenever he wants to. He lives in the present rather than in some mythical future, has the satisfactions of doing his own creative work and at the same time being regarded as one of the top movie writers. Unlike most writers, he has almost no bitterness, but is tolerantly amused by Hollywood and defends it if necessary.

Mr. Truly Interested is another successful and gifted movie writer, understanding Hollywood and aware of his own goal, which differs from those of the community. His accommodation to the situation is, however, different from that of Mr. Gifted. Mr. Truly Interested passionately cares about movies and persists in trying to reach his goals through this medium. He came to Hollywood ten years ago from New York where he had been a playwright with some minor prestige but no financial success. The year before he left New York his net earnings had been between $2000 and $2500 a year. On his last job there, a temporary one, he earned $150 a week, which he regarded as exceptionally good. He came to Hollywood on a contract at "only" $300 a week — now, ten years later, he uses that term to describe a salary which was twice what he had in New York.

His first job was at a big studio, where he worked with a producer who had more than average ability and knowledge. The first story given to Mr. Truly Interested was not particularly good, but he thought it had possibilities. The theme was laid in the past. Without anyone's suggesting it, he began to read widely about the historical period in that part of the country, and got a number of new and interesting ideas for the picture. The research enabled him to do what he considered a good script from a story which had not been much to start with. The producer liked it, particularly because it was different from the run-of-the-mill picture in this category. It was then given to the executive head of the studio, who, when he had finished reading it, called the producer and writer in for a conference. This was the first time that Mr. Truly Interested had ever been in the front office; he was quite excited about meeting the executive. He was confident that the latter would like the script, since the producer was enthusiastic and since he himself had a real faith in it. He was therefore surprised and angry when, at the opening of the conference, the executive, without any preparation, lashed angrily out at him saying, "We did not hire you to write a new script," and then criticized it from beginning to end. He gave no praise at all.

Mr. Truly Interested was mad. The producer, who was present, surreptitiously motioned him not to give vent to his anger. He obeyed and said very little. Later he followed a few of the executive's injunctions, but retained a great deal of the material which the latter had criticized, and kept his original story line relatively intact. The script was again sent to the front office, and this time it was O.K.'d.

The picture then went into production and Mr. Truly Interested was put to work on another script in the same studio. However, again without anyone's suggesting it, and without asking permissions, he took time off to go on the set where his first script was being shot. He talked to the director and the actors, trying to get them to understand the meaning. Finally, the front-office executive heard about the strange phenomenon of a young and inexperienced writer in the $300-a-week class going on the set and trying to influence the shooting of the picture. He did not think a $300 writer important enough to call in for a reprimand, but instead called in the producer and asked whether Mr. Truly Interested did not know that a writer is forbidden to go on the set and that his job on the picture was finished when he wrote the end of the script? The sympathetic producer, instead of telling Mr. Truly Interested to stop going on the set merely cautioned him to be "careful." There was one amusing incident when the writer hurriedly made an exit from the set just as the executive entered from the other side. Mr. Truly Interested continued struggling with the director, winning on some points and losing on others. He is a diplomatic person, and his fight was carried on subtly, trying to instill ideas into the director's mind. He won the director over to his side about a long speech which was delivered by one of the characters at the end of the film, and which was planned to tie the picture together and to point up its theme. However, after the picture was shot the front-office executive looked at the rushes and did not like this final speech, and so ordered it cut out. Mr. Truly Interested was extremely angry, because he thought the speech necessary to the picture. The director did not feel strongly on the matter and was the type of person inclined to do as he is told. The producer was a weak man, and although he thought the speech good, he had resigned himself many times to giving in to front-office demands. He explained his resigned attitude to the writer by saying that no picture was important enough to make a big fuss over. Then Mr. Truly Interested, without realizing its unconventionality, wrote a long letter to the executive, spending an entire Sunday typing and revising it so it would express his ideas as clearly as possible. In this letter he gave, in considerable detail, his reasons for thinking the final speech should be retained; he ended by hoping that the executive would understand them and change his mind about cutting it. An answer came very promptly. It was, "This picture cost $1,500,000. If you decide to buy this picture you can have any ending you like."

Mr. Truly Interested continued writing scripts and not only went on the sets but into the cutting room, watching the cutter at his work. In every way possible he learned as many details as he could. All of this he did on his own initiative, which seems to have sprung out of a sincere interest and curiosity about the medium in which he was working. It seemed natural to him to find out as much as possible about it.

During his early years at the studio he was suspended a couple of times for refusing to work on scripts which he insisted could not be made into good pictures. Suspension meant, of course, that he lost financially, because under the terms of his contract he could not work at any other studio and his salary stopped. It then became a question of how long he could hold out. It is most unusual for a young writer without financial assets to refuse to work on a script simply because he does not think it is good.

Today, Mr. Truly Interested is now in the top bracket of the writers' group and works only in those situations where he has some control. At present he has an arrangement whereby he does one picture a year with a director whom he regards as one of the best in Hollywood. Within his contract, he has the freedom to refuse to work on a picture if he chooses. He sees the movies as his major medium of expression. He respects them and is fascinated by their potentialities, many of which have not yet been realized. What set him apart from most other writers of equal ability are his personal honesty and courage, his passionate interest in carrying through his ideas and his ability to fight diplomatically. He carries over the standards of a functioning artist into a situation where they are strange and unusual.

He is an exception; he has been successful in spite of the Hollywood structure, rather than because of it.

There are very few writers in Hollywood for whom the satisfaction is not primarily limited to the pay checks. Of course, salaries are important to all people who have to earn their living, in and outside of Hollywood, and for the majority of workers may be the only or major compensation. But for writers, artists and scientists, the satisfactions inherent in their work have always been primary. It is questionable whether money ever can be the only satisfaction for any of them. The essence of a writer's drive is his interest and curiosity about his fellow men and a desire to communicate the results of his observations to an audience. It so happens that if the latter is large, financial rewards follow almost automatically. In Hollywood the situation is reversed. The financial rewards come first, in weekly pay checks. The script on which he works is apt to be a confused jumble of many people's ideas and unrelated notions. The occupational satisfactions, traditionally a part of the writer's craft, are lacking. Even though the script writer's name may be among the list of credits for a movie, it is rare — unless he has taken on functions other than writing, or is in an exceptional position — for him honestly to feel that he has communicated anything of his own to an audience. He has ceased to be a writer in the real sense of the word. Instead, he takes dictation. For men who have known the satisfactions of creation out of their own experiences and imagination, this must inevitably cause frustration.

Many writers rationalize the situation by saying that they were frustrated also when they were newspaper hacks and that they were not free then, either. They compare that position to the prostitute and identify the Hollywood situation with that of the "kept" woman in a New York Park Avenue penthouse. In Hollywood they maintain they are merely paid more highly for "selling out" as writers. This reasoning is, however, deceptively simple. There is a large quantitative difference of money returns from the sellout to the tabloid press, and to Hollywood. This quantitative difference is so great that it frequently results in a qualitative difference in attitude. Many of the writers who work on the tabloid press for a small salary are not satisfied with their jobs, employers or wages, and never fully accept the situation. They are always looking for a way out and planning an escape, and sometimes succeed. But in Hollywood the money rewards are so great that the average individual tends to become satisfied, and not only to accept the system, but even to defend it and build up a set of rationalizations.

Writing for the movies becomes the means to wealth or comfort, which eventually becomes the goal. The writers take over the executive and producers' values more successfully than the latter take over the artists' goals.

CHAPTER VIII

Assembling the Script

Wʀɪᴛɪɴɢ in Hollywood can be compared to an assembly line, but one in which the assertion of an individual's ego, usually the producer's, is generally more important than the quality of the script. Since the Hollywood structure is somewhat fluid, a star or director may also dominate the script, but rarely does a writer. As we have seen, the front-office executive is always in the background ready to wield his authority, too.

The script is the basic raw material from which a movie is made. If it is weak or shoddy, a good picture cannot be made from it, any more than a strong bridge could be constructed with poor steel. The importance of the script to the finished movie cannot be overestimated. Therefore, how scripts are written is significant not only in understanding Hollywood, but also in answering the question of why movies are good or bad entertainment.

While many people engaged in the production of movies realize the script's importance, they take for granted the system in which it is turned out. The anthropologist, of course, takes nothing for granted, but analyzes the way any part of a system functions in relation to the whole.

To make clear the nature of movie writing, it is necessary to replace the usual connotation of the word "writer" by its meaning in Hollywood. There, writers are part of the production of pictures rather than authors. A *bon mot* in the community is that "writers in Hollywood do not have works, but are workers." In the customary and literary sense, a writer is a person who has the desire and ability to write about his experiences and observations, for others to read. These observations reflect his philosophy or point of view about life.

In Hollywood the writer does not write to be read. Nor do most writers write because they have something to say, or to express a point of view, but rather in order to earn large weekly salaries. If an occasional one does have something to say the structure is such as to make it difficult for him to say it with any force or vigor. Only an exceptionally gifted and strong writer, working in an unusual combination of favorable circumstances, can leave his stamp on a movie.

The position of writers becomes intelligible only through historical perspective. They became a part of the production of movies rather late. The first "flickers," consisting of one and two reels which exploited the novelty of movement, did not need them. The high point of these early movies was a train moving through space, a fire engine dashing down the street, or people running down a road. When they lengthened to four or five reels, writers began to trickle into the industry. They assisted the director in getting a story and wrote titles to accompany the action.

The "talkies" obviously made writers more necessary. Today they are an accepted part of the production of every picture, from a low-budget Western to the high-budget A film. They came, however, into a medium in which the essentials were still movement and action and their main job was the creation of plots. Characters were secondary and important primarily as mannikins to keep the plot moving. In both melodrama and farce, which comprise the majority of contemporary movies, plot is always more important than characterization. Tragedy and comedy, more concerned with the unfolding of characters from whom the plot stems, are just beginning to appear in the movies.

The cinematographic muse to which both producer and writer bow is the "gimmick." This is a kind of trick, an unconventional device: something different — particularly useful in the beginning of a picture. An example of a gimmick is to have the hero and heroine meet in a way different from the conventional introduction by a mutual friend. One such device is to have them both running for the same taxi, entering it from opposite doors, and colliding in the middle. Many a writer and producer sit at the feet of their muse, waiting for inspiration for a gimmick. A man to whom inspiration comes frequently is invaluable.

It is taken for granted in Hollywood that there be a symbiotic relationship between producer and writer — that is, a very close union — and that the producer is in authority. The producer picks his writer, which they say is like picking a wife. They explain that they want someone who will laugh at the same jokes, smile at the same innuendo, cry at the same misfortune. This is essential because the role of the writer is to transfer the ideas and fantasies of the producer onto paper. Actually he is looking for an *alter ego*, rather than a wife. (An *alter ego* may be the producer's concept of an ideal wife.) In the producer-writer situation, it might be more accurate to say that the producer *buys* his wife. However, in parts of Africa where the bride-price, or *lobolo*, is customary, the bride has far more freedom and rights than the average Hollywood writer. The producer may really believe he is only "guiding" or "helping" the writer. But if the writer puts something in the script which displeases the producer, or which does not fit into his fantasies, or which he does not understand, then it comes out and is replaced with the producer's idea, obediently inserted by the writer.

Writing in Hollywood frequently begins with talking. Going back to prehistoric times, before the invention of writing, all story-telling was oral. In Hollywood many producers seem very much more at home on the verbal level than on the written one. In assembling the script at least as much time, and frequently more, is spent in talking as in writing. At the end of a day a writer and producer may be quite exhausted from talking.

The producer may start by outlining his ideas of the kind of movie he wants. Perhaps his idea comes from a sensational newspaper story, a radio skit, or another movie. He may become quite histrionic in the telling, walking up and down the room acting out his ideas. The writer later transcribes them to paper in a "treatment." This is limited to the "story line," ranging from twenty to eighty pages, and done for the inspection of the producer to see if he likes it. If it is accepted, it forms the basis for a script. The story line consists of a series of events which have a logical relationship to each other, but often little to the characters, who may be merely pegs on which to string the incidents. The logic of the story line usually takes precedence over the logic of the characters, or of life.

Sometimes it is the writer who, in the beginning, does the talking, selling his idea to the producer. There are some writers whose only ability lies in being able to talk dramatically about their ideas and who have never written a screen play. Gifted writers, too, may become talking salesmen for their ideas. One had an original idea for a movie which a producer thought so highly of that he called together several of the studio's top men, an executive, a director, a story editor, to listen to the writer describe his idea. The writer, quite verbal, was carried away by his own eloquence as he dramatized his recital for an hour and a half to this group. He was so effective that he fired their imagination and at the end they sat with their mouths open, convinced that this was a "great" story. Having a sense of humor and suddenly seeing the whole performance objectively, the writer, when leaving, said ironically, "Now get someone to write it."

The original source may be a novel or play the studio has purchased, and the writer is employed to do an adaptation from it. He makes the changes necessary for dramatic effect in another medium, those required to conform to the producer's personal fantasies and his notions of what the public wants, and to meet the taboos of the Production Code, and tailors it all to the screen personalities of the actors who will play the star roles. Sometimes only the title of the original novel or play is left.

This "adaptation" then becomes the source for the "screen play" — probably done by another writer.

It is part of Hollywood movies for the writer to give the pages he has written each week to the producer. There are long story conferences in which the producer suggests, criticizes, and argues with him. He then tries to implement the producer's suggestions. When he is finished, if the script is still not to the liking of the producer, or the front office, or the star, or the director, another writer is called in. Rarely is the previous one called back. The general idea seems to be that he has given his all, and so if the script is not right another one is put on. If the producer is inarticulate the new writer may be told only that the script is no good or that it stinks and that he should make it better. He will go to the producer's secretary and ask to see some scripts which her boss considers successful and he may then ask for a showing of some of his pictures. All this is to try to find out what the producer wants, what will please him. The demands of the story are secondary.

There is a highly developed specialization in the writing. If a more articulate producer decides that the script needs humor, a gag writer is put on. If the plot needs tighter construction, or romantic touches are required, or the characters must be made more human, or the dialogue polished — there is an expert for each need.

The script continues down the line as the gag man, the dialogue polisher, or just another writer make their contribution and pass on to another picture, another studio, or to unemployment. Even if the writer remains at the same studio, at this point it is customary for his contact with the picture to be finished.[1]

At the end the producer decides to whom the screen credits go and, following the rules of the Screen Writers' Guild, he is under obligation to notify each writer who has worked on the picture. Any one of them has the right to object to the studio's award of credit, and in that case the Screen Writers' Guild, or rather a committee of three members chosen from a rotating panel, acts as arbitrator and its decision is accepted by studio and writers as final. Of the approximately 500 pictures produced a year, about 50 are arbitrated for writers' credits; these are the important movies for which credit brings high prestige. The studio awarding of credits is changed by the arbitration committee on about two thirds of the cases.

The arbitration of credits is a highly technical and not an easy problem for the committee. It reads first the final script, then all the

[1] This description refers to the scripts of the large-budget A pictures and not to small-budget ones and Westerns. There are also exceptions to this pattern for A pictures, when one writer stays with the picture and when the director is part of story conferences.

preceding ones, and any communications from the writers involved and from any other studio person concerned with the matter. There are no oral hearings. To receive major credit for the screen play, an individual writer must have contributed at least 33⅓ per cent; a team of two, 40 per cent; and a writer-producer 50 per cent. The number of writers who can be included in the screen credits are three individuals or two writing teams. The various possibilities in the awarding of credits include *Screen Play by* . . . ; *Adaptation by* . . . ; *Additional Scenes by* . . . ; *Additional Dialogue by* . . . ; *Original Story by* . . . ; *Suggested by a Story, Novel or Play by* . . . ; *Based on a Character from a Play by* . . .

The battle for credits is important to the writer because his jobs, prestige and amount of salary are largely dependent on them. It is his work record, and he is typed according to it, not only quantitatively but qualitatively. A writer who has only one credit for a psychological murder film may be chosen by a producer to do another script of that type, as against another writer with more credits but none on this type of film. There are exceptions — writers with no screen credits but with excellent reputations outside of Hollywood, or a few without reputations but in whose ability some producer has great confidence — who have prestige writing jobs. There is also the occasional writer who refuses credit because he is ashamed of the script which is filmed and thinks it would hurt his reputation. But for most writers credits are important and the members of the Guild's Arbitration Committee have to use all their wisdom to arrive at approximately just decisions. Obviously it is impossible for them to please everyone, and in the past one man resigned from the Guild because he did not like the decision on his case. But in general the members respect the work of their committee as fair. It is an interesting example of a group of workers settling their own jurisdictional problems; and the producers seem relieved at not having to handle them.

Obviously writing in Hollywood cannot be described on any abstract level. Its setting is in a complex set of power relationships of a highly personal as well as business nature, functioning outside of the studio as well as in it. They involve not only producers and writers.

but also front office, directors and stars. The intricacies, rivalries and confusion can be appreciated only through concrete examples.

On one film, fifteen writers were assigned at one time or another; six of them were designated by the producer as substantial contributors. The film was based on an original story by writer Mr. One, employed by the studio to do it. After writer Mr. One finished the story, writers Two and Three, working as a team, wrote the script. The producer wished to test out every conceivable character and scene, and was so prolific in his suggestions that the two writers working as a team produced sixteen versions, not all of them complete. Between seven and eight months were spent on this phase of the work.

A director then came on the job with a shooting date, and also with a definite viewpoint on what could and could not be included in the story. The period of discussion and experimentation was therefore ended and the script was now rewritten according to the director's ideas, which differed considerably from those of the producer. Mr. Four, who had previously done some writing with Two and Three's team, was called in to help. While they were working, another writer, Mr. Five, had been sitting in at all the story conferences. Later, when the producer and director decided that writers Two, Three and Four could not bring the script to a satisfactory conclusion, Five began doing the final version. Later, Mr. Six was called in to help him. These six were the major contributors but nine other writers had also worked on the script. Eventually a very mediocre script emerged which was the basis of an A picture – no better, of course, than its script.

For another film a story by a well-known author had been purchased at a high price by the studio. Mr. One was asked to read the story to see if he could do a script from it. He thought it impossible and refused the assignment. The producer then said that he was not particularly interested in using the story and that he would prefer an original one with a similar theme. (The question of why he bought the story never seemed to occur to him or to anyone else.) Writer One and the producer then discussed various possibilities and finally agreed on a theme, which was approved by the executive head of the studio. The writer was then employed to do an original script, although the title of the already purchased story by the famous author was kept for "studio convenience." This enabled the studio to allocate the price of the original story to the new film and thus to make it seem that the purchase of the original story was not wasted.

After the script was finished the international status of the foreign country in which the picture had been set changed and the director and star refused to do the picture unless it was revised accordingly. There was no apparent reason why the first writer could not have done this, but according to the Hollywood system a second one was called in to "develop" a script which would be approved by the director and the star and be in accordance with the international situation. The major story elements were retained, but much of the actual dramatization was discarded for reasons of political expediency. Writer Two was given credit for the screen play; writer One was credited with the story and the adaptation.

On one movie, based on a novel from which another country had already made a film, there were eighteen writers working over a period of slightly more than two years. Details on the contributions of all eighteen are not available, but enough have been obtained to give an idea of how the script was done. One writer claimed that the scripts written subsequently to his were based on his script, rather than on the book, and pointed to a particular character he had developed who was not in the book. Another writer says that he was called in by the producer after the previous ones had failed to create a dramatic ending, and that he did not read any of the other scripts. He claims that he wrote a long treatment which was almost a screen play, inventing material and indicating dialogue and special treatment. He thinks that he created the broad pattern and mood of the final film. Still another writer, the last one, says that he read the novel and two of the scripts which had been written and looked at the foreign picture. He then decided to deviate completely from the two scripts and from the foreign film, and he turned out something quite different, for which he received credit. The work of the seventeen men who had preceded him was practically wasted and this unnecessary expense might have been avoided if someone in authority had known what he wanted or had understood the medium sufficiently to know what was possible.

Sometimes the struggle for credit is not for the script but for the adaptation. Writers One and Two acquired the screen rights to a published novel and on their own time wrote a screen play based on it. They sold this and rights to the novel to a studio. Writer Three was employed by the studio to do a second screen play, based on the first, under the supervision of a producer. Subsequently writers Four, Five, Six and Seven worked on this material, the last two as a team. Writer Seven said that he wrote two complete adaptations based only slightly on the novel before he worked on the screen play, and also did a half-dozen outlines and sequence developments. Adaptation credit was given to writers Seven and One. Credit for the screen play was given to writers Six and Seven. Of the seven writers employed on this film only three apparently made substantial contributions.

Confusion in the writing of a script may be caused by the change of producers and directors. Writer One was given an assignment to do a screen play based on a story purchased by the studio. During the six months he was working on this assignment, two different producers and three different directors were assigned to the script. Writer One was continually doing, under pressure and in a great rush, different versions in accordance with each new producer's and new director's ideas. Each one asked the writer to carry out his idea "just to see what it looks like." During these six months writer One wrote five scripts, all done in a hurry, and he always assumed that he would eventually have time to polish and smooth the final one.

For some unknown reason the film was suddenly taken away from the second producer and reassigned to the original one, who had to start production in two weeks. Accordingly, a script was hurriedly prepared in accordance with the original producer's ideas. It was admittedly a hodgepodge. It was at this point that the third director was assigned and the writer worked for four days and nights continuously with him, discussing and changing the script. When the director finally O.K.'d it, the writer began the final draft. He was told two days later that writer Two would follow him to polish the dialogue, and that the latter would get dialogue credit. Writer One felt pressed for time and agreed to this arrangement.

In the meantime, a star had objected to the script and refused to act in it unless more changes were made. Writer One made the changes suggested by the star, with writer Two working behind him and polishing the dialogue. Credit for the screen play was given to One and for additional dialogue to Two. The final film was a confused jumble but produced on a large A budget. It reflected the lack of planning by the front office and the fact that there had been no one authority over the script.

The competition between writers for credits sometimes degenerates to the point where a writer will accuse another of playing a trick on him. In one such dispute, a writer claimed that his rival had pages remimeographed to make it falsely appear that changes had been made. When changes are made the pages are remimeographed and the new ones are in a different color from the preceding ones. The ritual is the following: Yellow pages are temporary and white pages are final. First corrections are made on pink paper, and corrections on them are made on green; and further corrections on green are on blue.

In another case the final script was written by a well-known author, writer One, whose short stories a studio had purchased. But before this final script three other writers had been involved. When the studio purchased the stories, they had employed writer Two to outline a screen play from them and develop the story structure. This story outline was turned over to writers Three and Four, who developed a script from it. Considerable time elapsed before the studio was ready to put the picture into production; and it was then that the original author of the short stories, writer One, was engaged to polish and make revisions in the script. However, he did a complete rewrite, not using the script at all. Since writer One, the author of the original stories, was also a practiced screen writer, the question might be raised of why the studio did not employ him to do the script in the beginning, instead of using three other people.

Front-office executives may likewise exert their authority over the script as in one case after a producer had assigned writer One to develop an original story. Writer One prepared the story, which was in effect an outline for a screen play, each scene dramatized to establish action and characterization, with some dialogue indicated. This outline was taken by the producer to the executive head of the studio, who approved it, and the cast was decided on. Writer One then began the first draft of the script, slanting it to the particular cast. When he finished the producer was satisfied and pleased with it. However, the executive head did not agree with him and said that he had many new ideas for the film, but that he did not want writer One to carry them out. He gave no particular reason. The executive then assigned writers Two and Three, who worked as a team, to carry out his ideas.

Sometimes it is the director who has sufficient power to dominate. Writer One, a man with an established reputation in literature as well as in movies, wrote a script more or less alone, and when it was finished the producer liked it very much and gave it his O.K. Then it was turned over to the director, who did not like it. He called in writer Two to make changes. The second writer did not quite please the director either, who then assigned writer Three to "write behind" writer Two. The final picture was very different from the original script, and although writer One received credit, he was not proud of the movie.

The problem of power and credits becomes particularly involved when a producer or a front-office executive is engaged in the actual writing. In one case the source was a movie made several years ago by the studio. Writer One made a new story line from the old film, which he told to the executive head of the studio. The latter gave his approval and writer One proceeded to write the screen play, turning in copy from time to time to writer Two, who was writing behind him. There were frequent conferences with the executive head of the studio and with the director who had been assigned to the picture, at which time changes, revisions and cuts were suggested. These were all incorporated by the same method, that is, with writer One working on them and writer Two working behind him. The two writers discussed each sequence and then the first one wrote it and sent it to the second, who would rewrite. Then the two went over the last version and together did the final script. It then turned out that writer Two was also the producer of the film but that writer One had not been told this at the time of their collaboration. The producer claimed credit for the screen play. The Screen Writers' Guild has since adopted the rule that when a producer intends to claim collaboration credit as a writer he must so signify to the Guild and to any other writer assigned to the script, at the time he starts work on writing.

In another case the executive head of the studio became the writer, although he did not start in this capacity. He purchased from another studio a novel, two treatments and the screen play which had already been done from it. He then employed writer One to do another screen play conforming to his ideas. While this script was being prepared an experienced director was sitting in on the story conferences, giving suggestions. Later, writer Two was added to contribute ideas and dialogue. However, after the script was finished the executive was still dissatisfied and he then proceeded to rewrite the entire film. He received screen credit, and writer One credit only for adaptation. Writers One and Two were experienced and in the upper-salary brackets. The executive had had no previous experience in writing and this was his first screen play. The film from it has been generally described as "hammy." However, a small fortune was spent on its exploitation, considerably above the usual amount allotted for this purpose.

Quite a few producers appear to have mixed feelings of respect, envy and contempt for the functions of the writer. One employed a skilled writer at $3000 a week to polish the dialogue of a script. After he had finished, the producer, a powerful but insecure person with no writing ability, changed all the dialogue. That the final dialogue is hackneyed and trite and that the money paid to the high-salaried writer was wasted seemed irrelevant to the studio. The producer had the satisfaction of having dominated the writer and of having taken over his creative function.

Another writer with a literary background, earning $2500 a week, had the good fortune to work alone on a script. But he had a long argument with the producer about the nature of one of the main characters. The writer tried very hard to convince the producer that this kind of character was essential to the story. The producer did not attempt to answer the argument, but kept repeating what he wanted, and ended with: "Well, you write it as you please; but I will change it after you leave." He did, and the result is a movie in which there is no motivation for one of the leading character's behavior.

The writer is constantly at the beck and call of the producer even after the day at the studio is finished. One successful writer had a producer who continuously phoned him at home about his latest idea for a script. Once the producer, very drunk, phoned at three A.M. to describe his latest notions about a movie they were working on. This kind of thing happened a number of times and the writer, weary of it all, decided to take a vacation for a couple of weeks in a remote place without a phone. However, through special messenger and at considerable expense, the producer managed to reach the writer in his hide-out.

Another producer interrupted a family Christmas party a $3500-a-week writer was giving. The producer phoned and said he had to have a conference immediately; the writer left the party to attend it. This kind of relationship indicates both the dependency of the producer on the writer and also the slavelike position of the writer.

The personal aspect of the producer-writer relationship is exemplified in further detail by the description of how the Producer, Mr. Schizo, described in a preceding chapter as always in conflict between his different goals, worked with a writer. He had bought a story for $50,000, consisting only of a series of plot incidents which were not particularly good. Characters were completely lacking but he thought the story lent itself to quick adaptation. It had been purchased in a hurry because, as usual, Mr. Schizo was caught un-prepared with studio space allotted to him for an A picture. He picked a writer he liked and whose ability he respected, and handed him the story and a script which had already been written from it. He did not mention that he was the author of the script, which turned out to be completely unusable even as a first draft. Writer One was told that he must have something ready for shooting in six weeks' time.

The first two weeks at the studio Mr. Schizo was "on his neck" all the time and it was very difficult for the writer to accomplish anything. The producer then suggested that the writer go with him for two weeks to a desert resort where, together, they could work. The writer preferred to remain at home and work alone while the producer was away, but the latter prevailed on him to go. He found himself on a train with not only the Mr. Schizo but Mr. Schizo's wife, children and several friends: he was part of a house party. They had a pleasant social time which included gambling, drinking and dancing. The producer and writer were in the same age group, and between them was a vague liking: the writer does not respect him, but says he is a "nice man." However, the writer worried about the script and every once in a while asked the producer if he didn't think they, or at least he, should do some work. Then they would come in from some gay place at two A.M. and talk for a couple of hours about the film. During this time they were staying at an expensive hotel ($20 a day for room and meals) and the writer was the producer's guest. At the end of two weeks, they returned to the studio and there remained — now only two more weeks before the scheduled shooting date.

Mr. Schizo frantically called in writer Two and divided the script in half, writer Two taking the first half and writer One the second part on which the most work had to be done. The two writers worked separately, each on his own half, without knowing what the other one was doing — because the producer told them they should not lose time with story conferences. Writer One was disgusted and had no faith in the outcome. He wanted to leave but felt that the producer, to whom he was now under obligation for an expensive two weeks' vacation, was in a hole and that he should not desert him. In the end the script was a bad mess from which only an equally poor movie was made. In this and in other situations, the producer's inefficiency and lack of planning seem compulsive. He starts with big ideas which never come through. He picks able writers and then puts them in a situation where it is impossible for them to function. He makes each working relationship into a personal one which usually ends in his begging the writers not to desert him in the crisis.

A similar type of producer asked a distinguished writer to do a script which had excellent possibilities. The latter worked alone and it was understood that there would be sufficient time to do a good job. Suddenly the production date was changed because the star had to start earlier in order to finish in time for another contract. Just at this time the producer decided, in conference with the executive head of the studio, that the picture should be much more conventional than had originally been anticipated and that the story line should be drastically changed. The writer found himself in a situation quite different from what he had anticipated. He had only three weeks and the story line had been so altered that it seemed impossible to him. He told the producer that he could not do a good job in three weeks and that he did not think the changed story line would work out regardless of the time factor. The producer begged him to stay on because he felt that the success of the picture depended on this writer and he wanted a prestige picture. He did not seem to realize that a prestige writer could not magically bring a prestige picture out of a story line and approach, basically hackneyed and untrue. The writer, who stayed, later regarded his decision as a mistake and thought he had let his sympathy for the producer's piteous cry "Don't let me down!" outrun his better judgment. He is ashamed that his name is attached to the movie and thinks his reputation has been hurt. However, he does not worry over it unduly. He banks the money he earned — $3500 a week — and goes back to writing his novel.

It is not only executives, producers and directors who claim the prerogatives of dictating to writers: after the script is finished stars often demand alterations, and usually get their way. While one film was being shot the star insisted on changes sufficient to distort the meaning of the film. The writer of the script was a man of prestige and the producer a "big name" who agreed with the writer's version of how the film should be done. Together they opposed the star's demand. They thought they had won their point. However, the star still had the ace up her sleeve. She became "sick" and stayed home for the day. This caused such a big financial loss that the producer gave in and permitted the changes in order to keep his star "well."

In dramatic contrast to the usual disorganized way of assembling a script which represents the norm in Hollywood, is the occasional example of intelligent planning and real collaboration. There is one team of producer and writer who have been working together for the last four or five years, and their relationships with each other, with a director and with an unusually intelligent front-office executive are unique. All four are men of ability and what is more important, they respect each other and have similar goals which include high standards for a movie as well as big profits.

The history of one of their successful pictures began with the desire of the producer to do a dramatic presentation of a social problem which interested him. He persuaded the studio to buy a novel which, while not concerned with the problem, lent itself to adaptation. He and the writer talked out all the points involved in it and together did an outline and treatment. Before they started the script they discussed the general approach and construction with the director, who had worked with both men before. The writer then did the first draft of the screen play working closely with the producer. This was given to the head of the studio and to the director to read. Both made a number of good suggestions which were incorporated in the rewriting of the script by the writer, with some help from the producer. The writer received full credit for the script and the producer thinks he only played his legitimate role in initiating and guiding it. A finished and polished script was turned over to the director, who was able to shoot it in record time, twenty-two days, because he and the others had planned everything so well in advance.

Ironically, this picture, made by the men whose goals and motivations were not limited to profits, was a big box-office hit and had far larger net profits than many films with only financial gains for goal. It also was praised as an exceptionally good movie. The economies of production which contributed to the net profits are obvious: the careful planning in advance; a producer, executive, director and writer acting rationally and towards the same end which was well defined in the beginning; the use of the story property purchased for the movie; the salary of one writer instead of seventeen; the saving on actors' salaries due to the speed of shooting, made possible by advance planning and by the absence of major changes in the script on the set.

The thought, common sense and economy in the production of this picture highlight the weaknesses, business and esthetic, in the production of the majority of movies. None of the men involved in the picture just described were geniuses. But all were men of ability who knew what they wanted to do and how to do it. They had also an interest in and understanding of the world outside of Hollywood and felt strongly that a movie could be used to illuminate a segment of contemporary life. For all of them, front-office executive, producer, director and writer, the movie was more important than the assertion of their ego.

The making of this picture indicates that there is nothing inherent in the production of movies which necessitates the confusion, wastefulness and lack of planning which underlies the assembling of most scripts and which is taken for granted in Hollywood.

In a relationship as close as that of producer-writer, their attitudes to each other are very important. It is rare to find a writer who respects the producer. Part of this may be due to the unpopularity inherent in any supervisory role. Part seems to be due also to the type of men who so frequently have the producer's job and to their lack of either creative or business ability. Over and over again it is said that most producers spend their days on the phone with agents, playing politics to get a star away from another studio, talking to their brokers about buying and selling stocks; or in concern about their stables and races. That many producers do not give their writers cause for respect is obvious from the illustrations of their relationships. The writer's resentment against the total situation is also apt to be vented on the producer — his immediate boss, the person with whom he has the most contact.

Producers have likewise little respect for the writers. If someone would invent a gadget to replace the writer, the producers would pay millions for it. The producers know that almost no writer ever stands up for his own ideas, that they have accepted their position as employees on the assembly line, as the producer's lead pencil, for the sake of the large amount of money they receive. This is just what the producer wants and is the system he has helped build, but at the same time it does not encourage him to respect the writer as an artist.

There is an apocryphal story about a writer who was not a producer's lead pencil. This man had been getting $75 a week working on a newspaper. He was brought to Hollywood at $150 a week, very low as Hollywood salaries go, to write a script. When he had finished it the producer suggested a change in one of the characters. The writer refused to make this change, saying that it would injure the basic theme of the story. The producer asked him again to make the change, and offered him a contract at $450 per week. However, in spite of the advice from agent and friends, who told him that with such a contract he would be on his way to success, he still refused to make the change. He said that he had been happy at his previous $75-a-week job, and would be glad to go back to it; and anyway he didn't care much about working in the studio. He left. The producer then yelled to the story editor: "Don't give me any more of these $150-a-week geniuses. I want a $2500-a-week writer who has a swimming pool and is paying alimony."

Many producers feel that the large majority of writers are "phony." By phony they mean men of no ability, or very little, who are overpaid and who stretch out their work longer than is necessary to get more weeks of salary. They also vaguely feel that the good writers do not give themselves fully to their jobs, but hold back some of their creative ability. One producer complains that these writers are not enjoying themselves or the situation in which they work, and he attributes this to some kind of innate perversity in the writer's temperament. It seems not to have occurred to him that a situation in which the producer regards the writer's territory as his own property, which he is constantly plowing up, may not be conducive to bringing out a writer's creative ability or to permitting him to function with enjoyment. It is difficult for the producers to see the situation objectively. Some feel that they are only "helping" and "advising" the writer and do not face the fact that the writer has to take the advice, whatever he thinks of it. Part of the confusion in producers' thinking comes from their ignorance about the nature of writing.

A writer who is a distinguished novelist and in demand as a script writer, describing the difference between writing a novel and a movie, says that when he works on a novel it comes from his "guts," from his innermost being. It is almost as if the novel is physically born out of his entrails. On the other hand, when he works on a script it is from his head up, and purely intellectual. In the script he follows the logic of a story line which comes from his brain while the novel involves all his emotions. Even if he is working on a movie which he happens to like very much, he knows, after he finishes, that the whole thing may be completely changed, or that it may never be produced. Over the years he has learned that it is wiser, psychologically, not to identify with any script, and so he avoids disappointment and frustration. This is what some of the producers vaguely mean when they say writers do not "give" themselves wholly to the job and when they think the writers are cheating on them. In a sense this is true, but the producers unfortunately do not look for the causes. These, to others, obviously lie in the system under which scripts are assembled, and the kind of relationship which exists between producers and writers.

The atmosphere of Hollywood which emphasizes working by instinct and attaining success through breaks is not conducive to thoughtful analysis of the system. Objectively, the structure of any system, or any part of it, should have some relationship to its function, what it is supposed to do. The assembly line in an automobile factory is planned to turn out cars, and college courses are organized towards certain ends, such as a liberal arts education, a vocational objective, and so on. The function of a movie is to tell a story, and the script is the basis for the story which director and actors will interpret.

All storytelling, whether in folk tales, drama, literature or movies, is based on a projection of fantasies. In the movies, as contrasted to the other mediums, the fantasies are for the most part those of foremen and their bosses, or controlled by them, rather than of the writers whose business is storytelling. The writers sell only their craftsmanship in writing gags and dialogue, thinking up gimmicks, and their sufficient knowledge of how to incorporate the producer's ideas. If one writer does not give him something he likes, he thinks another one may. The general idea is that if one writer is good, five are better. It is only an occasional producer who has sufficient knowledge of drama, of storytelling, and of people to warrant his authority. The Hollywood assembly line has no relationship to either the usual factory one or to the needs of movie writing. On the Hollywood line, more workers are used than necessary, raw material is thrown away, highly skilled men are employed and then not permitted to function with any degree of efficiency; foremen, bosses, and others are constantly asserting their will, without regard to the effect on the product — and all this in an extremely personal atmosphere. All move within an orbit of love and hostility, competitiveness and dependency, and are together in card playing, horse racing, drinking, week-ending, and other sociability. A pseudo-friendliness and show of affection cover hostility and lack of respect. No co-operative venture could function well on that basis. In any such system, whether it is making a canoe on an island in the Pacific, the functioning of a college department, or the making of movies in Hollywood, the human relations are as important as is the more formal structure. In Hollywood, neither are designed for storytelling. Any system which employs men of talent, whether artists or scientists, and does not recognize that certain conditions of freedom are necessary for their effective functioning, is destined to destroy their usefulness and value.

CHAPTER IX
The Answers

It is part of man's nature to try and find answers to his problems, and, in Hollywood as in any society, the answers are conditioned by the culture. If a primitive agricultural people are faced with a shortage of rain, their culture prescribes the making of appropriate magic to meet the situation. The answers to the writers' problems are likewise conditioned by the Hollywood social system.

The nature of any particular writer's problem depends, in part, on his position in the success hierarchy. For the young and inexperienced, the question is, How can they learn the craft of movie writing, get jobs and screen credits, and rise in the salary scale? For the successful writers, particularly those with talent, the problem is, How can they gain more control over their material and so increase their personal satisfactions?

There is, of course, more than one answer to each problem.

For the first group, there are the traditional Hollywood techniques: "playing the game" and "knowing the right people." However, although the community emphasizes the breaks for everyone, there is more recognition of the necessity of the writer's having some skill than there is for the actor or producer. Most people think the writer should be, at least, a good craftsman.

But the industry as a whole sponsors very little formal training. Two of the major studios had, at different times in the past and for limited periods, an apprenticeship system for young, promising writers. One selected twelve such writers on the basis of something they had written which seemed to show talent, and gave them six weeks' training, during which time they were paid $75 a week. The group met one night a week with three of the producers. They were given assignments, such as writing a scene to show conflict between two characters, or one which would bring the two together. The scenes would then be discussed and criticized by the producers and the members of the class. After that the students did original story treatments which were discussed in the same way. At the end of the six weeks, the studio employed a few of the writers who had done usable story treatments or who showed promise. The apprenticeship plan was abandoned after a short time, but even when it was in effect, it was unimportant because it involved so few individuals. Outside of this formal apprenticeship, studios have sometimes given contracts to promising writers and kept them on the payroll for a year or more in the hope that they would produce something good. But during the year the writer often sat alone in his office and it was only rarely that he received anything resembling training or experience.

The writers themselves are not in agreement about training. While all recognize that telling a story in the movies differs from telling it in a novel or on the stage, there is considerable disagreement on the importance of these differences and on techniques of learning about the movie medium. One group, which emphasizes the differences, believes very strongly that a script writer should learn everything about how a movie is made, by being on the set, watching director and cameraman, going into the cutting room, seeing the daily rushes, and listening to discussions of why some are better than others. In this way, they say, the writer would know the potentialities of the camera and learn, for instance, that a glance indicating anything from love to hate may be more expressive than any dialogue.

Most of the young, ambitious writers with no previous success as novelists or playwrights complain that they are not allowed to get this kind of training while they are working in a studio. Some say that they are prevented from going onto the set, that they are told they are hired to write and that they should remain in their own offices writing, and not roam around poking their noses into other people's business. On the other hand, some producers and directors say that the writers are too lazy to do anything not required of them and that they would rather play gin rummy or gossip than go into the cutting room to learn how things are done there.

The situation varies from one studio to another and from one individual to another. There were a number of writers who had access to sets and cutting rooms who took full advantage of it; there were others who did not. And there were still others who were prevented from going onto the set or into the cutting room; many times it was impossible because, after the writer had finished his script, he was at another studio or unemployed. It is certainly not an accepted part of studio mores, though many of the young writers wish this were otherwise.

A good number of the successful movie writers with established literary and playwriting reputations, however, see no value, at least for themselves, in learning the technical aspects of movie production. One of them feels quite strongly on the matter and says that there is nothing for the writer to learn on the set, that the beginner has to learn only a few simple points, such as that the camera can shoot anything which is visible to the eye and that a sentence never begins with "He says" but starts with the actual dialogue. He likewise thinks it is easy to learn simple directions — such as "long shot" if an actor enters from the far end of the room, "medium shot" for a corner of a room with a few people in it, or "close-up" for the face of one actor. If the script calls for something very different such as shooting a whale in the bottom of the ocean, that is up to the cameraman and the director to worry about, not the writer. In the first script this writer worked on, he learned that it was an unnecessary expense to have a character walk through a hallway to get from one room to another, and that it was better to have people grouped by a window instead of in different parts of a room. These are small details easily grasped; if mistakes are made in the beginning, a director can quickly catch them.

This writer insists that the biggest mistakes of the writers have nothing to do with the camera or cutting, but are primarily in thinking about people and the situations in which they move. He says that the business of the writer is to know people and society, be able to dramatize conflict situations, and to know how to write dialogue. He thinks that the writer will learn more if he goes to the corner saloon, or to a political meeting, or to any other place where people are gathered, or if he sits home and reads a good book. Good taste, good judgment and a knowledge of people, he continues, cannot be learned on the set.

Another successful writer has a different point of view about training. He thinks it is necessary, but should consist of understanding how a novel, play or story is transformed into a movie and that the best training is to read the novel (or play or story) from which the movie is made and then the script; and finally to see the film a number of times. The point is for a movie writer to be movie-minded rather than camera-minded — that is, to see the whole continuity of the movie, not just shots. He does not think that this can be learned on the set by watching director or cameraman, but by the study of the movie itself.

One of the most important differences between the novel and the movie is that a character is never explained in terms of description, dialogue or background, but rather in terms of action. If, for instance, it is necessary to show that a middle-aged man is abnormal, the point can be made very well by having him slide down the bannisters without saying a word. This is the kind of thing learned from seeing movies, just as a novelist learns from reading good novels, or a playwright from reading and seeing plays. But this man says most writers look at movies not for the purposes of analysis and study, but merely to mechanically reproduce what they see in them.

The answer to what is the best training for movie writing is not in the either–or class. A knowledge of life and people and the intuitive, sensitive awareness which are the stock in trade of any distinguished writer, whatever his medium, cannot be taught, nor are there any substitutes for them. But the movie writer, like any other writer, is also a craftsman. Just as playwrights learn a great deal by seeing their play in the process of being produced, the movie writer would be benefited by understanding the techniques used in transforming the novel, play or story into a script and that into film. It is more important and more difficult to understand the essence of the movie medium than to know the jargon of long and medium shots, and the elementary points of how to break a script into scenes and sequences. Hollywood is, however, not the only place with a tendency to mistake a knowledge of terminology for understanding. This is true also in many a classroom.

The second problem, how a writer can gain more control over his material and thereby increase his self-respect and satisfaction, is important only for the able ones, a few of whom have a strong and passionate interest in what they communicate through this medium. For the majority of Hollywood writers the problem does not exist — they neither have anything to say nor any convictions, passionate or otherwise. But the gifted writers are important far out of proportion to their numbers, just as are the small number of talented directors, actors, producers and others, because it is these people who set the standards for the best pictures and through whom the further development of the medium may be expected. The problem is likewise serious for the individual able writer, who is apt to degenerate creatively, and perhaps personally, if he consistently works below his potentialities. It concerns the front office too because a system which does not utilize the talents of its most gifted employees is wasteful financially. A number of answers are given to the problem. Among them are writing originals, becoming a writer-producer or writer-director, entering into a more or less permanent relationship with a sympathetic and able producer or director, making temporary alliances with a producer or director and manipulating the relationship so as to dominate it, and finally, being so much in demand that considerable control is written into the contract or secured informally.

The solution most frequently advanced is through the writing of originals. Of the 463 screen plays which were in production or awaiting release on June 4, 1947, *Variety* indicated that 235, or more than 50 per cent, were based on originals. Of the remaining 278 properties, 187 were adapted from novels, magazines, stories or biographies, and 36 were from plays. These figures are misleading, however, because the 187 adaptations form the base for most of the A pictures, while the majority of the originals were for B pictures, Westerns and other small-budget films. Two years later,

Variety indicated that 70 per cent of the stories were new. While more of these were made into A pictures than two years previous, the majority are still used for the smaller-budget movies. However, the new trend not to depend so completely on successes in other mediums for A pictures is important.

The word "original" may be deceiving. The writers of many of these originals for B pictures pick a formula, of which there are a number. One deals with two brothers engaged in a dangerous occupation. The younger one is reckless and always getting into trouble, from which he is rescued by his more mature older brother. Another is the father-son situation in which the son rebels against his father's authority, but eventually redeems himself.

However, some scripts written for A pictures are, in the more usual connotation of the word, original. One writer, a former Broadway playwright of considerable prestige, writes in much the same way as he wrote for the stage. His originals stem out of his own experiences or from his interpretation of what he has keenly observed. Sometimes he is employed to do the script from his original story. At other times, it may be given to five writers in the usual assembly-line manner. But even if he is employed on his script, he has no control over changes which may eventually be made in it. It is significant that he has recently become a producer, because, he says he wants to recognize the film which is made from his original.

Some writers do not consider it good business to write originals. They say it is better to write first for publication and then have the studio buy it. In this way they make more money and have greater satisfaction since in writing they do not have to follow the restrictions of the Production Code and the other conventionalities of Hollywood. Others say they cannot afford to take time to write an original. One man figures that he would need eight or ten weeks to write one and that if he sold it he might get about $30,000. He says that the chances of selling it are only one in six. If he works at the studio for the same eight weeks, he is sure of $20,000 against a possible $30,000 for an original. He does not think that the $10,000 difference is a good risk against a sure

$20,000 when the chances are one in six. There is also no guarantee that if he is successful the final film will resemble his original, any more than the film will be like his script based on someone else's story. A writer may, of course, utilize considerable originality in doing an adaptation. One man practically writes an original when he adapts a story. It gives him an idea, from which he develops a script completely different from the story, and the studio may like his story line better than the one it purchased.

The problem of greater control for the writer over his material was discussed in the magazine of the Screen Writers' Guild [1] when Producer Sam Goldwyn recommended the abolition of the salary system for writers and urged them to work on a profit-sharing system. He thought the movie writers should take the same chances as the novelist or playwright and not "sacrifice their artistic aspirations for the security of a weekly pay-check." The following month the same magazine carried an answer by writer Paul Gangelin. He respected the intentions behind Mr. Goldwyn's remarks, but differed in conclusions. His contention was that in the theater, producers, directors and actors, as well as playwrights, take a capital risk every time a play opens and that the gamble is a co-operative one. To achieve this in movies the author suggests that if the writers are to put their salaries into the "kitty," let the producers do the same and let the writers have "a proportional drawing account, based on the amount of money the picture can be anticipated to gross . . . and THEN, after the picture has run its course, as is the case of plays, let the property revert to us."

A comparison of the systems in the publishing and theatrical worlds with that of the movies points up some of the major differences. The Broadway producer and the New York publisher see what they are buying and, if they do not like it, they do not buy. But if they do buy there can be no changes without the writer's consent. He is guaranteed a percentage of the sales. Except in the purchase of originals the studios do not see in advance what they are buying. Even then the producers are free to make as many changes as they please. When they hire a writer by the week, he writes according to a producer's dictation. The story belongs to the producer, since he is responsible for the inclusion or exclusion of every idea and line in the script, and its legal ownership rests with the studio.

Many more writers favor the solution of becoming a producer or director in order to gain more control. One works as a free-lance writer-producer without being tied to any one studio. He recently sold an original movie script, which was ready to be shot. The studio paid him $95,000 plus 10 per cent of the net profits, and met his conditions that he be the producer and select the star. He had already picked and received the consent of the star before the picture was written. As the producer he controls also the entire casting and can see that the script is produced as he intends. The actual business end of the production does not worry him or take up much of his time. This man believes very strongly that the writer, or anyone else in the creative end of production, can make good pictures only if he gets into an executive position which gives him control.

A former writer, who has become an important producer at a large studio, says, however, that his power is limited to doing one picture he likes out of every three or four he makes, and the only way he gets that one is by having a record of success at the box office. With a number of box-office hits to his credit and with the reputation of being a "good boy" doing the assignments handed to him, the studio wants him sufficiently to humor him now and then and allow him to produce a picture of his own choice. He accepts this situation in a matter-of-course manner.

Another writer-producer had been a successful movie writer, but then ceased functioning as a writer. He produced from stories handed to him by the front office and scripts written by others. Eventually he was disgusted with the quality of the movies he was turning out and, weary of the succession of films for which he had no respect, he asked and received permission to take a long vacation.

He tried to think through the whole matter. He had enough

money in the bank to live on for several years. He hated the idea of going back to the studio and reading all the terrible scripts which would be presented, and of producing some of them. He decided to quit. Then the executive head of the studio wired asking him if he would return as a producer to work only on his own scripts, and he accepted this offer. Recently he branched out as an "independent," which increased his power. He is an able craftsman getting satisfaction in telling his stories through movies, as well as making a lot of money. As an "independent" these satisfactions have increased, even though he does not have complete control, since the studio, which owns the other 50 per cent stock in his company, has to give its O.K. to his pictures.

Some gifted writers become directors so that they can be sure their script is translated into film in the way they intended.

One successful writer-director in a large studio is an intuitive literary person whose particular outlook on life is projected onto those pictures which he has been able to control. These are among the distinguished movies which have come out of Hollywood and have also been successful at the box office. He started as a playwright and when rather young had a Broadway hit. Hollywood studios then made offers to him which he turned down because he preferred New York and writing for the stage. Later, after a series of flops, he was broke and glad to take a Hollywood offer.

He was fired after three months. He then wrote an original and sold it with the provision that he could direct the dialogue. He did not know that this was an unheard-of request for a beginner. But he was very insistent, and won his point. He says that most Hollywood people do not know what they want and that if they do, they have not the courage to fight for it. The picture turned out to be a major success.

Then he wrote another original which, however, no one would buy. In the meantime he worked as a writer under contract and reached the $3000-a-week bracket. He still hankered to be a director as well as a writer but was not given the opportunity. Eventually, seven years after he had written it, he sold his second original with the condition that he would direct it. This was not easily secured. The studio did its best to discourage him, saying that he would be an inexperienced and poor director, and this would damage his reputation as a writer, now very high. He was willing to take the chance and kept on nagging and worrying the executives — so much, that they grew weary of hearing him and finally decided to let him direct, thinking that the picture would be unsuccessful and that he would then recognize his mistake. The picture was acclaimed as a most distinguished movie and was an enormous box-office success as well. After this he could more or less write his own terms.

He is an original person with more ideas than he can use. But he attained his present position and success in spite of the Hollywood structure rather than because of it. If he had not had the drive and courage to insist on his way against the wishes of the executives, he would be like any other high-salaried, able, frustrated writer who cannot bear to see the films produced from his scripts.

Another exceptional writer became a writer-director-producer. He now chooses the story, writes the script, selects the cast, directs them, cuts and edits the film. He gets no salary but instead a percentage of net profits, with the studio through which he releases getting the remainder. He was not always in this position of power. He first came to Hollywood in 1929 and took any writing job that came his way. At the end of three years, when he had saved $5000 by living simply, he began to select a bit what he would do. Soon his income and status were such that he could be more choosy. He worked with directors and chose those from whom he could learn a great deal. He constantly went on sets and into the cutting room, although this was never encouraged by the producers. His first opportunity to direct came on his own script when he managed to convince the front office, not without difficulty, that he could do it on a modest budget and utilize a star who was under contract at the studio and doing nothing. The movie turned out excellently, made a large profit, and the former writer was now acknowledged as an accomplished director. Later he took on the role of producer to increase his control over choice of story and cast. He, like the others in this group, says there is nothing to being a producer, and that it takes up very little of his time.

Not all writers favor this solution. One, with a prestige literary background, thinks the writer should "stick to his last," which is writing, and not be tied up with other duties and business affairs. He says that it would have been too bad if literary geniuses of the past had had to spend half their time as publishers in order to get their books written. He thinks that when a writer becomes a producer he ceases to be a writer, or at least writes much less than he formerly did. This is true many times, but not always, and all writers who become producers are not distinguished.

Still another possibility of control lies in the independent units in which a producer, director and writer team up on a more or less permanent basis for the production of pictures. Or there may be a team of director and writer working for a studio, both so gifted and with such a record of success that no producer can "buck" them. The work of one such team is so well integrated that it is difficult to tell where one begins and the other ends. Relatively few writers can become members of such teams. Instead, they may use a temporary alignment with some sympathetic person on a picture. One able writer in the higher-salary brackets, still with high ideals for his work after ten years in Hollywood, says that on every picture he has worked there has been a constant struggle to insure a minimum of its integrity and that he has never been able to win this by working alone. He is diplomatic, with keen insight not only into the characters he writes about but into the people with whom he works. His strategy is a temporary alignment with someone on the picture against whoever is opposing him. At times he is aligned with a producer; sometimes with a director or actor — depending on the particular situation.

One struggle was with a director who was afraid to do something a bit different from the usual film, although the script called for it. The writer's strategy was to influence the actors and then let the director think it was his work. In this way the director took over many of the writer's points, thinking they were his own. Another time he and the producer teamed up and won a partial victory over the director. Of course, many times he loses in spite of his diplomatic manipulations.

Another writer with considerable literary gifts had a good relationship with a prestige-name producer for a couple of years. The writer was allowed to choose the story from which he would do the script. He stayed with the film after he finished the writing, made suggestions about casting and was on and off the set during the shooting, doing any rewriting that was necessary. If another writer was to be called in, it was someone of his choice. In this relationship the writer's personality was considerably stronger than that of the producer. In the end the executive head of the studio fired the writer with the excuse that there was nothing for him to work on at the studio. No one believed this, but thought the executive feared this writer was getting too much power over the producer and in the studio. The producer was upset at the writer's departure but was not strong enough to oppose the executive.

One possible solution to the problem of control is for a writer to attempt to make it part of his contract that no changes can be made in his script without his consent. But this is extremely difficult and almost impossible to attain. Still another answer, not often suggested, would be for the Screen Writers' Guild to fight for the writers' control of their material — that is, to make it part of every writer's contract that he should have the final word on the script. The Guild is, however, not strong enough to fight for such a concession, which would be bitterly opposed by the studios, and the membership of the Guild as a whole probably would not think such control desirable. A large number of the writers would not be sufficiently capable of using this control. Many times the scripts turned in are so poorly done that changes have to be made, either by other writers, or by directors, producers, or actors.

An answer by a small number of the talented group of writers is not to give all their time to writing movies but to continue writing novels or plays. Their agents are annoyed with them because they could earn so much more money if they devoted all their time to movie writing. One agent figured out exactly how much his client, and incidentally he, lost every time the former wrote a novel. But the client continued to write his novels. Their solution is to accept the Hollywood organization more or less, but to use it only enough to secure sufficient economic security to work in other mediums, which give them more control and make better use of their talents.

The larger proportion of talented writers are sucked into the Hollywood system and eventually give up trying to be creative. A writer is asked to work on a script because he is known to have a fresh, new approach, and then the producer is afraid to use the script because the approach is different. Or he may never get suitable material to work with. One man with a reputation on Broadway as a serious playwright was assigned to writing musical comedies. During the four years he has worked at a studio he has only once been given the opportunity to write a script which was within his abilities and which he enjoyed doing. And before this script was finished, the producer for whom he was working left the studio and the successor did not want to take anything his predecessor had worked on. So the script was shoved into the discard and never used, much to the chagrin of the writer. He has received several screen credits but is ashamed of the pictures; he never mentions them except when talking to a producer and when they are necessary to get a job. This man could and does get considerable satisfaction out of functioning as a good movie craftsman. But his forte is melodrama; he cannot get any pleasure out of the second-rate musical comedies he is employed to do. However, he accepts the situation because of the large financial returns, and he has become habituated to it.

Many take out their personal dissatisfaction in cynical wit. One quite able writer, who seems to have accepted the situation, says that the writers have devised "an exquisite torture of dollar bills dropping on their heads." He adds that eventually they get buried under the dollar bills. One story is about a writer complaining to someone about all the restrictions which he has to observe, such as punching a time clock, being at the beck and call of the producer, not being able to write as he pleases because of the Production Code, or because a star interferes with him, and so on. At the end of his long tale of woe he asks rhetorically, "And what do I get out of it? . . . A fortune!"

Hollywood abounds with clever stories, with witty remarks, with groans about frustrations, and with tirades against the Production Code, or the front office, or a particular producer. But there is almost no thoughtful analysis, by writer, producer or front office, of this situation in which the large majority of writers write about life not as they know it, but as the producer or front office understands it, in dull imitation of the last box-office success, and to suit the personality or whims of a star. Nor is this question asked: Is there anything inherent in the production of movies, admittedly a big business and popular art, which makes the present system inevitable? There are a sufficient number of successful aberrations from the system to indicate that the answer might be "no."

There are obviously too many writers, at least several times more than are needed in times of greatest prosperity. Of course, any employer likes a large pool of workers from which to pick and choose. The typical insecure producer, without knowledge of storytelling, seems to find some comfort in large quantities, whether it is all the unused story properties owned by the studio or a large number of unemployed writers. He does not stop to think that this process attracts a large number of untrained and mediocre men. It may be that producers do not encourage writers to learn about the various parts of movie making, because of fear that increased knowledge and competence would reduce their own power and status. At the same time, those in power who maintain the system are dissatisfied with the writers it attracts and continue to search for talented novelists and playwrights, to whom they are willing to pay enormous salaries. Then they insist that the gifted men work in a structure that has the effect of voiding their special abilities.

Perhaps it would be advantageous to the writer, to the industry, and to the audience if scripts were written by writers rather than assembled by producers. Then able men might be attracted for other reasons besides the fabulous salaries. Then they would not have to spend time and energy in manipulating the Hollywood system in order to use at least some of their skills and talents to the advantage of the movies as well as to themselves.

But that is not one of the answers offered by Hollywood.

CHAPTER X
Directors

WHETHER the script is assembled or written, it is the director's job to translate it into a film. This is a key operation, for it is concerned with fusing techniques from the silent films with the latest technological developments and combining the unique characteristics of the movie medium with elements from theater and literature. These are not easy problems.

In any society, changes in technology and the introduction of new ideas are often accompanied by conflict and tension, since they require modifications not only of knowledge, but also of social organization, of attitudes and behavior. A familiar example is the Industrial Revolution, when machines replaced hand work. Back in prehistoric times, iron tools, when first introduced into a primitive society which had not gone beyond digging sticks and stone axes, were not always easily or quickly accepted. Many people did not know how to use the new tools efficiently, others did not like them, and makers of the old implements feared a loss of prestige. Gradually, the natives learned how to use the new tools and attitudes changed to one of acceptance.[1] Only sentimentalists, in anthropology or in the movies, long to return to the earlier forms of primitive life or of films. Even if it wanted to, Hollywood could not go back to the more "pure" movie form which existed before the invention of the talkies. The real problem is not of a return to the past, but of integration of old and new. The question then is, which elements in the Hollywood social system help this integration and which retard it?

Movies introduced a new art, the essence of which is the manipulation of movement in time and space with a camera. Cutting, that

[1] Ralph Linton, *The Study of Man*, p. 342. New York: D. Appleton-Century.

is, the assembling of the film in balanced sequences, is one of its important skills. It was the director who first learned this. He was all-important; the producer or writer was either absent or insignificant, and actors were far less important than today. The director did everything: planned the story, directed the actors, manipulated the camera and cut the film, as well as taking care of such details as designing the costumes and sets. "Film Author" was not an inappropriate title for him in those days. He constantly experimented with the camera, shooting from different angles; then, later, he used a number of cameras, placed in various positions — on the floor, near the ceiling, and midway. The camera can seem to become the actor; the audience then sees only what the actor — and the camera — is looking at. In the cutting room the director selects the most effective "takes." If he likes none of them, he can combine bits from three or four into one. It is also in the cutting room that the tempo for telling the story and the rhythm of the movie are set. Just as the same musical notes played in two-quarter, three-quarter or four-quarter time express different moods, so, by cutting a sequence into many segments, a tense mood of expectancy can be obtained, while fewer and longer segments will produce the opposite one of tranquillity. An actor walking across a room can be taken in one long shot which is not particularly histrionic. But if the same shot is broken into many segments and each step the man takes is seen separately, it becomes highly dramatic.

In the development of the silent films, inanimate objects, or "props," were useful in helping to tell the story; this trend reached its apex at the end of the silent era. The symbolism of rain beating on a windowpane, the close-up of a hand crushing a letter, two chairs placed cozily by a fire, a large pile of unwashed dishes in the kitchen sink, could be used as effectively as actors, and sometimes even more so.

While the saying that the camera does not lie is true, behind the camera are the men who manage it and who can create, if they are skilled, an emotional effect, without the actor necessarily portraying that emotion. If, for instance, an untalented actress in the past or today is unable to express frightened surprise, the director can take different shots of her face — full face, profile, and finally a close-up of her eyes; and then, by cutting from one to the other, he can produce the emotional effect which the actress was unable to register. Or, a director may turn the camera on an actor's back and show it sagging or stiffening and produce the impression he was unable to get from his face. If the actors do not carry a romantic scene well, the director can shoot from them to a landscape bathed in a full moon and thus increase the romantic atmosphere. The hand of an actor tearing up a girl's photograph may express more poignantly the breaking of a love relationship, than the expression on his face.

During the first quarter of the century, directors continued to experiment with camera, props, and cutting. Then, in the mid-twenties, came the invention of talkies. The old art of directing did not disappear and camera and cutting were as important as ever. But new elements were introduced. Playwrights and novelists came to Hollywood and brought their concepts of drama, dialogue and character to a medium which had previously concentrated on action. Actors were imported from Broadway who had been trained in drama schools, or were experienced on the stage, and some of Broadway's directors likewise trekked out to Hollywood. Even the tempo of the films changed, and the brash, quick movements of the actors in the silent movies became slower and more subtle in the talkies.

The invention of talkies and the resulting influences from stage and literature on the new medium might be compared to the giving of crutches to a healthy young child who was just learning to walk with his own feet. He naturally would have some difficulty in learning to use both his feet and his crutches at the same time.

A folk tale of the days when Greta Garbo was becoming a star illustrates some of the difficulties of this early period. Her director was accustomed to working with untalented actors and depending on tricks and contrivances of the camera for his effects. Garbo, however, showed him how she could create a certain feeling by merely lifting an eyebrow. The director was not pleased. A talented actress was getting a better effect than he could through the camera, and he felt that he was losing one of his essential functions.

Actually, talkies called for an expansion of the art of directing, but the system of movie production changed in the opposite direction and reduced the director's power. The assignment of the writer to the producer, under his authority, was probably conceived in terms of the power situation rather than in what was the best way for integrating old and new techniques of movie making. The producer's power was enhanced and, through him, the front office was better able to control both story and writer. But the director lost out, and perhaps the movie, too. In the past he "shot from the cuff" or from a briefly outlined story, depending rather much on his own ideas and inspiration of the moment. Today, he is handed a finished script which gives the structure for portraying a story of human relations. It is then the director's job to designate the manner in which the actors project them into the minds of the audience, and to so manipulate the camera and cut the film that the meaning of the script is brought out. Obviously, the director should understand and be sympathetic to the script. But this is only rarely the case. The cynical definition of a good director given by many Hollywood actors — "one who reads the script before he begins shooting" — is indicative, in an exaggerated manner, of the situation. However, custom is not uniform. A director may mechanically carry out the script's directions for each sequence; or he may direct the picture according to his own ideas and with little relationship to those of the script; or he may bring it to life and create a film through his understanding of the script and his knowledge of acting, camera and cutting.

Realistically, it would seem more sound for the writer and director to be in constant story conferences than in the present huddles of writer and producer, and for the director to have some control over the choice of story. Everyone in Hollywood, from front-office executive to script girl, joins in a refrain about how movie making is a collaborative industry. In any collaborative system of production, whether it be for primitive dances in the Pacific or for steel in Indiana, the degree of closeness of co-operation is not the same for all members engaged in it. The questions of who collaborates with whom, and how this is related to making a movie, are rarely raised in Hollywood. A system of production which keeps the director and writer out of contact with each other for the majority of movies is taken for granted. The norm is for the writer to work continuously under the direction of the producer; the director makes his appearance on the assembly line after the writer has left and the script is finished.

For only the exceptional director with high status is the situation any different. One of these was able to pick the story he wanted to film. A gifted playwright was then called in to do the script and he and the director worked closely together all the time. The dramatist would write a scene which the director would then read. This was followed by discussion. When they differed, they would argue until one convinced the other. Sometimes the writer convinced the director and at other times it was the other way around. When the script was finished, it represented both men's ideas and only a few minor changes were made during filming. The movie was excellent, winning critical acclaim and an Oscar, and it was a top-grossing and exceedingly profitable picture.

But the situation in which this movie was produced is rare. Even a director with considerable prestige, because of his well-known ability and because he is a producer-director at a major studio, still has to struggle with the front office. He can say, "No" to making certain pictures, but he cannot choose what he wants to make. He says, "I'm one of the boys here" — he has a seven-year contract, four years having been used — "and I have to go along and be agreeable. Sometimes I make a picture from a script which is handed to me and which I know is bad. In such a case the front office usually promises me that, if I do it, I will later be able to do one I'm really interested in." The pictures he has truly liked have been a minority of those he has made.

Unlike writing, cutting was not a new element in the production of talkies. But here, too, authority was taken from director and given to producer and front-office executive. Again the power situation shaped the structure. In the interests of the movie, it would seem that the closest relationship should be between the director and the cutter, with the director in authority. The usual

routine is for the director to see the rushes every day and indicate to the cutter which he wants and which can be discarded,
which are his pet ones, and how he wants certain sequences. A
rough cut is thus made day by day, but without fade-outs or dis-
solves, which are marked in red. Then after the camera has ceased
turning, the director does the first assembling of the entire film.
This right was won by the Directors' Guild. Before that, producers
were interfering even in the first assembling. Many times the cutter has had to be a diplomat in handling his various bosses. A producer and director looking at the various "takes" would differ
on which was best, the producer saying, "Use Take 2," and the
director, "Take 4." The cutter might agree with the director's
choice and when the producer left the cutting room, decide to use
Take 4 and gamble on the producer's not knowing the difference. Today, although the director does the first cutting, the producer can make changes after him and the front-office executive
always has the final say. If he orders the omission of certain
sequences, the meaning of the movie may be considerably
altered.

The director is, of course, not necessarily always right. Some
have developed a special angle and insist on it constantly, whether
or not its repetition is advisable. There are producers and executives
who can and do make helpful suggestions about cutting. But
whether their ideas are helpful or destructive, the Hollywood system gives them the final authority over cutting, in which lies so
much of the art of movie making, and relegates the director, whose
special skill it is, to a subsidiary position.

Unless a director has great prestige, it is difficult for him to defy
a producer and front-office executive, for he runs the risk not
only of being fired, but of gaining a reputation of being "difficult" or hard to work with, which is not desirable. While the
director is not continuously under the thumb of the producer, as
is the writer, a continuous struggle for power and control is waged,
openly or concealed, between them. The status relationship is,
however, not a fixed one. Nominally the producer has the higher
status, but an important director often outranks him. In the film
I Remember Mama the director became executive producer and

the credits read: Executive Producer and Director . . . George Stevens, Produced by Harriet Parsons.

Casting is also part of the power struggle with front-office executives. The director who works most closely with actors has usually little to say about choosing them, and the final authority is never his. Again the question of who collaborates with whom seems to have been decided for reasons other than the interests of movie production. These would indicate that the director chooses actors he considers suitable for the roles. But it is the producers and the front-office executives who have this power. Directors may argue with the front office, but they rarely win. There are many cases in which a director was suspended because he questioned the suitability of the studio's casting for the leading roles.

Directors work on the same kind of option contract as does everyone else and have the same anxieties about whether the studio will take up the option, and difficulties in breaking the contract when they have a better offer. One such conflict was resolved by the director's buying up his contract and paying a large sum each month (reported as totaling $100,000) out of his earnings from another studio. They also have the same problem as do actors in being loaned out to other studios at a profit to their home studio but none to themselves, and in the same impersonal kind of package deal. One director with an excellent reputation was loaned out to another studio without his knowledge, in exchange for a story which the latter studio had purchased. Although being loaned out means that he is in demand and increases his prestige, yet he feels that it is insulting to be swapped about as a piece of property. He and others naturally object, also, to not sharing in the profit which the studio makes on the deal.

The able director suffers from the same aspects of the system which irk the talented writer, namely the lack of freedom to utilize his talents to the best advantage. Directors also think that most of the executives and producers, with a few notable exceptions, have neither the intelligence nor ability to choose a good story or produce a good movie. Over and over again they say that the activity of these men is primarily in playing studio politics, dominating other people for the sake of domination, and, of course, accumulating their own fortunes. It is only the exceptional producer or executive, they add, who gets really excited about movies as a medium, who knows what constitutes a good picture, and who is interested in making one, as well as in making money.

But while the director's power is challenged in choice of story, script and cast, and in the final cutting, he is at least the boss on the set.

Directors vary not only in their ability but also in their techniques. Some, called cinematic directors, carry on the traditions of the past, depending more on the potentialities of the camera than on the actors. They might be compared to French Impressionist painters, and get their effect primarily by a juxtaposition of human beings and studio props, manipulated by the camera. This kind of director envisages the movie in terms of certain pictorial and emotional effects and he tells the actors exactly *what* they are to do down to the smallest detail. He is unconcerned with the *why* of the acting and does not explain the meaning of roles to the actors. He merely says *Do this* and *Do that*. If he is good he knows every camera trick and all the devices of cutting. In his films the story is of secondary importance and the audience tends to remember certain scenes pictorially, and their emotional impact.

For the cinematic director who also has the writer's ear the script is important too, and he visualizes the finished film in terms of story and dialogue as well as pictorial effects. A director of this kind is able to integrate the story with the manipulation of actors and props. The story holds together and the audience remembers it as a whole. Writers who become directors are apt to fall into this category, which represents a blend of old and new elements.

The actors' directors are those who depend more on the actors and who spend considerable time in explaining to them the meaning of the script as a whole and their particular role. If the actors are well trained, the director leaves the interpretation to them. Those without training he will coach. This kind of director has a thorough understanding of acting, although he may be better in the directing of one sex than the other. The actors' director frequently has a background of stage directing, or of being an actor, and he prefers to work with trained people, while the cinematic one may prefer untrained ones who are docile and do exactly as they are told. The "situational" director, who may fall into any of the classifications, is particularly gifted in creating situations so powerful and telling that they become the determining factors more than either actors or props.

No director today who is considered tops is limited to any one of these categories. It is more a matter of which he emphasizes. The classification, of course, applies only to directors with real ability, and, as in the other talent groups, their number is small. Of the 280-odd Hollywood directors, not more than 5 or 6 per cent were rated by the directors themselves as being gifted. Actors, the group who work closest with them, give them the same or slightly lower rating. By "gifted" is not meant the occasional genius, but the men with known ability who can be depended on to turn out better than average pictures. The large majority were described by their fellow directors and by actors as "traffic cops," men with some technical knowledge of their craft but with limited, if any, knowledge of drama, of acting and of people. They work mechanically, giving the green signal to go ahead and the red one to stop. They are primarily unconcerned with the meaning of the script and concentrate only on movement. Naturally, they get the best neither from the script nor from the actors. Below the traffic cops is a smaller group who are regarded as completely inept. One of these will begin a picture without any planning and let the actors wander through their parts with practically no help of any kind. This director is a nonentity and his pictures turn out poorly — unless the cameraman happens to be very good and takes over the direction.

Many directors have little understanding of storytelling, of the movie medium, or of human beings. These emphasize lavish sets, and, with enough help from cameramen, actors, editor-cutter, and others, their pictures come off in some way or other, in spite of them, rather than because of them. They work mechanically and shoot from every possible angle in the hope that one will be usable. They take an almost infinite number of retakes without any idea of what they are striving for.

There is a story about one of these directors who took forty takes of one sequence. An executive took the first, last, and the one the director had chosen as best, and asked the director to choose from these three. He was unable to differentiate between them.

Some of these mediocre men hold their positions because they are relatives of an important executive; others through playing the Hollywood game; a considerable number, particularly of those who started in the past, were actors in vaudeville or in silent movies; still others came up accidentally. One of these began as a barber, became a make-up man, then a property man; then he was assistant director, and finally director, which he still is.

It is the backgrounds and personalities of the able directors which are of particular interest and help in understanding what makes a good one. Some, with a long history in the industry, have held many jobs from the lowly one of prop boy to the skilled one of cutter, and it is this last position which they consider the most important in their training. Others have come from directing in the theater. Still others have been successful movie actors or writers, and added directing to their other functions.

Many of these able directors seem to belong to the industry in an organic sense. Mr. Proficient, in his early forties, who has been working in movies for twenty-odd years, is one. Among his many jobs have been prop boy, assistant cutter, cutter, and cameraman. His first directorial assignment was for B pictures, which meant working with a poor story, second-rate actors, and doing it all very quickly. He did the best he could, but thought the job hopeless. He was earning between twelve and fifteen thousand a year, but eventually he could stand it no longer and quit. He had saved sufficient money to live until he found another job, still not on A pictures but with better resources for B ones. His big opportunity came when he did exceptionally well with a cheaply made picture on a timely subject, which brought in big financial returns and received excellent reviews. Then he was given an A picture to direct, and this, too, turned out very successfully both at box office and in terms of critical acclaim. He was made as a director of A pictures and he has consistently turned out better than ordinary pictures, which have also made money for his studio. His aim is to do pictures in which the story springs from the characters, rather than those which consist of a string of incidents strung about a peg called a character. To do this more often, he wants to become a producer-director.

Mr. Proficient plans everything in advance down to the most minute detail, usually gets his effects in five or six shots, works well with different types of actors, from those whom he has to coach to the talented ones for whom only a word is necessary. In his work he gives the impression of potency and power, springing out of ability and real knowledge. He says he learned the "hard way"; that he did not know the right people, or play the usual Hollywood game, but that in twenty-odd years he has learned the ingredients which go into making a film. He has confidence in himself and in his work, without being conceited.

He is an ambitious man but his major drive or goal does not seem to be to gain power over men or to accumulate a huge fortune, but rather to do what he considers important pictures, which he can respect. He is engrossed with his job, works hard and enthusiastically within a well-thought-out plan, which reduces crises. He feels that he belongs to the medium and thoroughly enjoys what he is doing. He has never grown "soft" either from the climate or from success. His theory is that people who have grown up with the climate as he has are better able to resist it than those to whom it is a new experience. He rejected the usual Hollywood values from the beginning and never seems to have been much tempted by them. Mr. Proficient's values are as important in the making of his pictures as are his knowledge, technical skill and ability.

Mr. Well Adjusted, a writer and director, holds about the same position as does Mr. Proficient in the upper group of directors, and he, too, came up through the industry during the last twenty years. His calm, well-ordered manner of working stands out as exceptional in the midst of the usual Hollywood frenzy.

He became interested in the theater in college and took part in amateur plays. About twenty years ago, he came to Los Angeles and his first studio job was as property boy. At that time this job was not as subdivided as it is now and he learned not only about moving furniture and putting things together but also about painting sets, and was allowed to go into cutting rooms. One day the proper actor could not be found for a minor role and he was given the part. Then, a bit later, when the studio was doing a picture about college life, he was given a chance to work on the script since he knew about this from experience.

For a while Mr. Well Adjusted alternated between writing and directing and for a fairly long period free-lanced, going from one studio to another and making a number of successful pictures, both from the box-office point of view and that of critical reviewers. About four or five years ago he went to a large studio on contract as a director and writer. He likes best to direct what he writes, but he can also enjoy directing films written by others whose work he respects.

Well Adjusted is very proud of his relationship with everyone on the set from the stars to the carpenters. While shooting a picture he begins at eight in the morning with the crew of workingmen, all of whom call him by his nickname. He enjoys being "one of the boys" and feels that he understands their problems because he has been "through the mill" himself. He is noted for never "bawling out" anyone in public, not even a minor actor. He handles all his extras with consideration and understanding and he is also known for getting the best out of different kinds of actors. He says that one needs his confidence built up, while another, an old hand at acting, needs something quite different, and so he treats them all individually.

Mr. Well Adjusted enjoys his work, but also has a large number of outside interests which include painting and gardening. He seems to have more than the usual security, financially and personally, and so the threat of suspension does not scare him, and the studio knows it. If they want to suspend him he says "Fine!" — and he means it, because it gives him a chance to work on some of his other interests. For many people the threat of suspension is sufficient to bring them to heel, not only because they do not want to lose their salaries but also because the studio is their whole life and apart from it they do not know what to do with themselves. Mr. Well Adjusted is one of the few people in Hollywood who gives the impression of being comfortable within themselves and who might have been equally successful outside of the movie industry.

Mr. Prestige is at the top of the talented group and is a relative who made good. He entered the movie industry about twenty-five years ago when he was in his early twenties through a relative who was then head of the studio. But he did not start with a big position. He too came up from the bottom and had many different jobs, among which were stock boy, publicity writer, assistant director and cutter. His first directing job was on two-reel Westerns and later he did five-reelers and other B pictures. Although without previous experience in directing, his Westerns immediately became better than the others. He was distinguished from the beginning by his careful study of the script, by thinking and pondering on the set before he decided what to do, and then reshooting many times. He created a sensation on the set by coming in, sitting down, and, when the cameraman said something to him, answering "Yes" in a noncommittal tone which meant nothing except that he had heard. But he would continue to sit and ponder the particular problem, and eventually come up with an answer to it. This was most unusual, and maddening to some of the people who worked with him, who were more accustomed to directors who continuously shouted directions without ever stopping to think. He was considered unique because he demanded good actors for his Western pictures and took longer to do them than was customary. The budget director would "tear his hair" at the mounting expense incurred by the time in shooting and by the cost of the cast. It is unlikely that Mr. Prestige could have got away with this if he had not been related to the executive head of the studio, who was known not only for his loyalty to relatives, but also for giving them considerable leeway in learning how to make pictures. Although there was a great deal of talk about the expensiveness of Mr. Prestige's directing, this was later forgotten when his pictures received excellent reviews and made a lot of money. He was given A pictures and soon other studios were bidding for his services. Today he is at the top of the skilled directors' hierarchy.

It is, of course, not possible to get at all the factors contributing to his success. But among them are that he is a man of infinite patience, who thinks through problems before beginning to work and has a capacity for waiting around and holding out for what he wants, whether from people or the camera. His patience is evident in the infinite pains he takes in shooting.

A strange part of Mr. Prestige's directing is that he is unable to communicate to the actor what is the matter and what he wants him to do differently. He is definitely not an "actors' director." But, although actors may curse while they work with him, they are glad to be in his pictures because the final results are always excellent and their reputation is enhanced.

Another of Mr. Prestige's characteristics is his capacity to learn from other people. Very early he began to work with writers, and while he is still not a writer, through constant contact with them he has acquired what might be called the "writer's ear." He does no writing, but he is with the writer from the beginning. But the relationship is quite different from that of the usual producer-writer, since Mr. Prestige is not concerned with domination and really understands the meaning of collaboration. He is particularly good in suggesting situations in which average people can identify themselves and in giving them, on the set, realistic touches, so that members of an audience murmur to themselves, "How true!"

Just as he is with the picture in the beginning so also is he there at the end. He supervises every detail of the editing and cutting, and does not leave the film until it is ready to be released. He started this habit when he directed two-reel Westerns, which, he says, he took as seriously as he does his big A pictures today. The same patience and habit of keeping his goal well in mind comes out not only in working with actors and writers, but also with front-office executives. With them, too, he discusses and argues, and usually but not always manages to get his way because of his capacity of holding out. Tales circulate around Hollywood that he is not on speaking terms with the executive head of the studio at the end of one picture, which later wins an Oscar and is top box-office.

Mr. Prestige's interest is not limited to doing pictures on any one theme, but he will not work on any picture whose subject matter does not appeal to him. While he wants to make successful movies, ones which will be seen by a large number of people, the money motive is not the only one and seems not to be primary. He likes best, he says, to make serious pictures which people will remember and think about after they leave the theater. He leaves his stamp on the picture not just out of an egocentric drive to dominate, but out of the need which an artist feels to create. Like any artist he is completely serious about his work, and the end goal is not primarily the financial one. He truly cares about his pictures in the way that many others care only about themselves and their bank accounts.

What distinguishes this man from so many others is again not just his talent, but his knowledge, his capacity for thoughtful planning and his goals.

Mr. Newcomer, unlike the other directors described, has no long history in the movies but a few years ago came from the Broadway theater where he had directed a number of successful plays. He says that he had difficulty in adjusting when he first arrived for two reasons, one in getting used to working with the camera and thinking in camera terms, and the other because of a feeling that the environment was hostile to him, or more specifically, to his interest in the theater as an art. His Broadway plays were not only box-office successes but had been acclaimed as good theater and it was for these reasons he was brought to Hollywood. But, he says, his employers at the studio are interested only in "how to make a buck, or rather millions of bucks." He knows that commercial goals dominate over art ones in the Broadway theater too, but, he adds, not to the same degree as in Hollywood, and he thinks that Broadway producers on the whole are not so ignorant of, or so hostile to, dramatic standards as are Hollywood producers.

When he first came to Hollywood, he agreed to do a certain picture and he was told that he would be given the opportunity of reading the script and suggesting any necessary changes before the shooting. While the script was being written, or rather re-written, by the second writer under the second producer assigned to it (the original one having been "let out" because of a reorganization at the top of the studio), Mr. Newcomer was at the studio, under contract, but not working. The script was sent to him piecemeal, but he was asked to hold his criticisms until the writer had finished, the producer saying that criticisms would disturb the writer's creativeness. (The producer, however, did not take this counsel for himself.) Mr. Newcomer piled up pages of criticism in the desk drawer. Then, when the script was finished and before he had any opportunity to talk to the writer, he was told that shooting would begin in a week's time.

Mr. Newcomer was very angry and said that this was impossible and that the script must have many changes which could not be made in one week's time. He wrote a fifteen-page letter to the front office explaining in great detail the faults of the script and later discovered that this letter had not even been read by the people for whom it was intended. He then blew up and won certain concessions, the postponement of shooting for three weeks and a new producer and new writer. He had been completely unable to communicate with the former producer who talked some kind of cryptic language which Mr. Newcomer could not understand. For three weeks he, the new producer and the writer worked together incessantly and ended with a much-improved script. Newcomer was dissatisfied with the actress who was to play the lead, but had been unable to get any concession on the casting. The part called for a rather sophisticated love relationship which was completely beyond the powers of the star, who was chosen primarily for her photogenic quality and whose concept of marriage and love was limited to "fun."

However, Mr. Newcomer did the best he could and the front office was impressed when he finished it four days before it was due, thus saving a considerable amount of money. The picture was decidedly better than the average, received good reviews from critics, and was successful at the box office. Although the film did not really please him, he had some satisfaction from feeling that he had done the best he could with what was initially a very poor script and with an untalented star.

Mr. Newcomer's prestige rose. On the next picture he gained more control over both script and casting, and his power continues to increase. He is definitely an actors' director, but becomes increasingly excited about the potentialities of the camera. He has other satisfactions, too. He *saves* twice as much in a half year in Hollywood as he earned on Broadway in a year. He has bought a house; and while he does not live in luxury, he has more comfort than he has ever known. He plans to remain in Hollywood, but hopes also to direct plays occasionally in New York.

Most of the men in this prestige group have special gifts, but they all also have certain other qualities in common which set them off from the "traffic cops." Whether they fall into the cinematic or actors' type, they all have the capacity to plan in advance, to select good people and to work with them. All of them are skilled in cutting, directly supervise it, and struggle to have as much control over it as possible. All refuse to work within the normal Hollywood system which would completely divorce them from the writing. Instead, they work with the writer or, when possible, refuse a story in which they have no faith and which they cannot change. By the time one of these top directors is ready to begin shooting, he has an intimate and sympathetic understanding of the script.

This pattern of planning in advance is not common in an industry which so prides itself on crises and believes so strongly in luck and the breaks. Although the able director has planned in great detail how to interpret the script through actors, props, and camera angles, this does not mean that he never changes the plan, or that he does not experiment on the set and make use of an inspiration of the moment. The best directors combine careful planning with brilliant improvisation. The mediocre directors improvise all the time. Exactly the same way of planning plus taking the inspiration of the idea which comes at the moment of execution, as compared to complete improvisation, is true probably for all good creative work, and certainly so for writing a book or giving a lecture. In one case improvisation consists of altering a plan to improve it; in the other, the changes spring out of uncertainty as to what to do next, without relationship to any goal.

Another characteristic which all these top directors appear to have in common is that they are primarily motivated by the desire to produce an excellent film, and more concerned about their craft and art than with profits. These men are not disinterested in what they earn or in their bank accounts. It is the place that the latter occupies in their values and total satisfaction, which sets them off from the majority of their fellow directors and other Hollywood workers. And with the usual irony, the profits from their pictures are generally very big.

Today there is a tendency among the younger and able directors to imbue others with ideas and to learn from the people they enrich. These are the men who understand that collaboration is a two-way process, which very few executives or producers have yet learned. In the past, able directors, some of whom are still directing, tended to be very domineering. They "raised hell" at the slightest provocation and people obeyed out of fear.

The old argument of who is the most important in making a movie is futile. But the director has a pivotal position in fusing the many crafts and arts of storytelling, old and new, into a finished movie. Technology has forced him to change and broaden his techniques and learn new skills. Yet the Hollywood system of production has lagged behind him and suits best the mediocre directors, the "traffic cops." The power hierarchy is fearful of the gifted man's originality.

Mr. William Wyler, regarded as one of the very top directors, said in a newspaper interview:

"Mediocrity in films is the direct result of playing it safe. And audiences are not interested in mediocre films. A picture without an idea is a picture without vitality. There is still fear in some quarters of Hollywood. Until that is gone, we can never have the greatness of which we are capable." . . . He has bunked up against a situation where the top men were forced to decide between two stories and asked the question —

which is the safest? "The man who makes the selection should ask which is the best. Because the best is always the safest." To fear quality, Wyler believes, is to exhibit a fundamental distrust in the public. "A lot of people in Hollywood distrust the public. They think an artistic film is too good for them. Their idea is that you've got to feed them junk." [2]

These men who fear quality and ideas stem from the past days. They find it difficult to accept changes which they do not understand and therefore fear; and they tend to see the audience in their own image, which is not a flattering one.

The directors' problems are those of the whole industry and involve the acceptance of new ideas, new standards, new concepts of audiences, as well as new technology. Today, Hollywood is not unlike a primitive society when it first comes in contact with the ideas and technology of a modern one. For a time, the opposing patterns exist side by side, sometimes running along in parallel lines and not touching, at other times in conflict with resulting maladjustment. This may go on indefinitely, or one may win out over the other and become predominant, or a new form may emerge combining elements from both the old and new, but different from either. Changes are brought about by a few individuals more daring and courageous than others. Gradually, the exception may become the norm. The first women who went to college were nonconformists and not regarded favorably by their community. Today, college education for women is an accepted social pattern.

In Hollywood, it is the gifted directors, and others with ability, who dare to take chances with new ideas and standards. They stand out conspicuously among the many mediocre men. But the system of production is against the gifted, because at its top are too many scared gamblers, who can take chances on horses and cards, but not with ideas. This is to be expected, because only those at home with ideas, and accustomed to implementing them, can psychologically afford to take chances with them. A few talented directors attempt to combine the unique movie techniques of camera and cutting with a meaningful script and trained actors. The result is new, differing from both the silent films and theater. The men who do this are the exceptions and their courage and goals are as important as their ability. They, too, are successful in spite of the system, rather than because of it.

CHAPTER XI
Acting, in Hollywood

ACTING and directing are closely interwoven and neither can exist without the other. This is a natural union and, unlike the producer-writer relationship, not imposed by the power situation. Many of the actors' and directors' problems spring from the same causes. The actors came into a medium which concentrated on movement and cared relatively little for meaning, and one which was becoming increasingly skilled in using props for emotional effects. The new medium which had started as a small entertainment business was becoming a big industry with mass production, and, at the same time developing as an art, taking over many elements from theater and literature. The directors, who formerly had considerable power and control, were losing much of it to producers and executives, many of whom had very little understanding of acting. The technical aspects of camera and cutting provided limits and assets to the structure in which actors performed.

It is obvious that acting in Hollywood cannot be quite the same as acting on the Broadway stage. The essence of all acting, whether on stage or in films, is to give reality to make-believe. This does not make acting into a unique art, and the need to make believe is not confined to artists: children, insane people and normal ones all have the same need in varying degrees of intensity, but they lack the artist's talent and training, which give an illusion of reality to an audience. While creativity in all the arts has something in common, the actor's talent differs from others because it is so intimately tied to his body. A writer and composer project their fantasies onto a piece of paper; a painter uses a canvas; a musician has his instrument; the actor has his body. His art is projected through his voice;

through his movements and gestures, as well as through his intelligence and imagination.

This gives to acting an openly exhibitionistic quality which takes different forms. Pure exhibitionism has behind it the wish, "Look at me!" "Look at my body!" But the gifted actor thinks also, "Look what I can do!" "Look at me playing the hero, and now, look at me playing the villain!" He does not actually reveal himself in the way of the ordinary exhibitionist, because he plays a role, a character created by a writer. In one sense he conceals himself, although not entirely so. All of us have the capacity for experiencing many emotions and therefore actor, playwright and audience can identify with many different kinds of roles.[1] Shakespeare's greatness is due, in part, to his capacity to identify with such widely different parts as tragedian or jester.

The popular idea that an actor is "living his part" when he is exceptionally realistic in portraying a role is false. Only insane people "live" their roles. Actors only *seem* to live their roles. Actually, they are in intellectual control of their performance. Through imagination, past experiences and objective planning, the actor creates an emotion. He first tries to get a clear idea of the kind of person a playwright is presenting, and then to know how he would behave in the situation. If he has experienced the emotions of the character he portrays, this increases his understanding. But his final portrayal will depend on a learned technique and thought-out plan, in which the intellect is in firm control of intuition and imagination.[2] Of course, within this general pattern, there is considerable variation, some actors working more on an intuitive level and others on a more intellectual one. Again, it is a matter of emphasis rather than one-or-the-other.

An actor whose only motivation is sheer exhibitionism will always be asking himself, "How am *I* doing?" — while the actor for whom there is the strong desire to make believe will also think to

[1] Otto Fenichel, "On Acting," *Psychoanalytic Quarterly*, 1946, Vol. XV, No. 2, p. 150.
[2] This point of view was expressed by many actors in interviews, and also in *Motion Picture Acting* by Lillian Albertson. New York: Funk & Wagnalls Co.

himself, "*What* am I doing?" Of course, the two categories are not exclusive ones. Even the most pronounced "Look at *me*" type has a desire to exhibit what he can do. It is not uncommon for a young actress, who has become a star on the basis of her photogenic qualities and whose ability is limited to a song and dance act, to have an illusion that she could be a great tragedian. Neither is the gifted actor in the "Look what I can do" class completely lacking in the narcissistic characteristic.

Hollywood stresses and gives importance to the "Look at me," "Look at my body" type. All the camera tricks, the close-ups, give intimate details of the actor's physical being. This exhibitionism is carried still further by emphasizing certain parts of the actor's body. An actress becomes known for her comely legs, and these are accented in every picture. Another one is known for her bust; still another for her husky, sensuous voice. So obvious is the use of actors as sexual symbols that in a major studio a handsome star is colloquially referred to as "the penis." Advertising strengthens the exhibitionism. Billboards are plastered with sexually enticing pictures and slogans. Publicity, whether it is through the gossip columns in trade and daily papers, or in interviews and articles in fan and other magazines, concentrates on the person of the actor. Their life at home, their parties, with whom they go to a night club or preview, their favorite hobbies, and even the details of their sleeping habits, pajamas or no pajamas, accent "Look at me." Type casting, in which the actors repeatedly play similar roles, strengthens this tendency. The audience tends to identify the actor with the role and thinks it is seeing the man and not the actor. When the average movie-goer describes a picture he has seen, he gives the plot in terms of what happened to John Garfield, Bing Crosby or Ingrid Bergman. The emphasis on type casting and accent on certain parts of an actor's body fits well into the Hollywood system which had stressed so much the use of props and formulas in the making of movies.

Whether acting is of the "Look at me" or the "Look at what I can do" type, or a combination of the two, it meets a deep personality need for the actor. It is a way of living, and not just a means of earning a living. An actor is only half alive when he is not performing, and, unlike the painter or writer, he cannot work alone but must have a job in order to function. He will suffer privations for years in order to have this opportunity. The great strength of the actor's compulsion to act seems to breed an intense faith in his ability. Almost every actor, regardless of the realities of the situation, firmly believes that he could be a Barrymore or Dusè, if only given an opportunity. The stronger his personality need, the more important it is for him to believe in his ability, because if the latter is denied then his personality outlet is cut off. On the reality level, ability depends on many factors in addition to personality needs.

It is this intimate relationship between acting and personality needs which makes all actors take their acting so seriously. Even if the role is a small one, or the picture in the B class, he must do his best, not just for the sake of the studio, for the movie, or even for his reputation, but for himself. He cannot toss off poor acting as unimportant because he would be tossing off part of himself. Acting is and has to be, because of its nature, deeply egocentric. Since the movie script is rarely the work of any one person and is dominated by the producer, it is difficult for any writer to think of it as his. But, regardless of how small the part, or how much help is given by a director, it is the actor who performs. Three people may have written the dialogue, but the actor alone is talking it. One actor, now a star, says that in a long period of acting in B pictures, at $75 a week, he knew he must never sink to the level of the picture, but constantly maintain his integrity as an actor. Another star makes the same point in another context. She says that it would be very easy, after having reached the top, to grow "soft" and self-satisfied, but that instead there is a constant drive to become better, to improve one's self. To be happy most actors need to perform all the time, on and off the job. The "Look at me" type calls attention to himself through his clothes, behavior, and publicity stunts. The "Look what I can do" type is always seeking for an audience for his make-believe. The latter may be through a game of charades at a party, or acting in one of the "little theaters" when unemployed. (There are, of course, many college professors whose lecturing is not confined to a classroom and who hold forth at the slightest encouragement.)

*   *   *

There are wide variations in ability, status and income among the 4000 actors in Hollywood.[3] At the top, in status and income, are the stars. Beneath them are the second leads, usually character actors, who have star or featured billing. They are followed by smaller and bit players, among whom are also some character actors. The Screen Actors' Guild in 1948 divided their membership in the following categories according to annual income: [4]

No.	Per Cent	Earning
202	4.9	over $50,000
265	6.4	$15,000 — $50,000
1130	27.5	$ 7,500 — $15,000
2516	61.2	less than $ 7,500

It was not possible to get from the Guild how many of their approximate upper 5 per cent were in the top bracket of between $100,000 and $400,000 a year. The Treasury Department, however, gives statements for individuals in this group. It shows that in 1946, Humphrey Bogart received $432,000; Bette Davis $328,000; Bing Crosby $325,000; Deanna Durbin $325,477; Betty Grable $299,333; Ann Sheridan $269,345; Robert Montgomery $250,000; Errol Flynn $199,999; Rosalind Russell $190,104; Ronald Reagan $169,750; Rita Hayworth $94,916.[5] Other top stars were on the same income levels.

Talent is not necessarily correlated with either income or status. Stars may or may not be gifted. Some are truly distinguished; others are good; and still others may owe their success primarily to photogenic and personality qualities. It is generally agreed by most actors and directors that character actors are the most talented of all the players. These supporting players are chosen primarily for their ability and there is keen competition for the jobs. Moreover, they must make good on their own, for everything on the set is not geared to their success. Cameramen, electrician and director use most of their energy and time to getting the best results for the

[3] This is the approximate membership of the Screen Actors' Guild. There are also between 4000 and 4500 extras in the Screen Extras' Guild.

[4] Guild dues are based on percentage of income.

[5] *Variety*, February 9, 1949.

stars and have little left for the others. Often the character actor playing a second lead is, literally, a supporting player. If the star is not gifted, he carries the real burden of the acting and, through the skillful manipulation of the camera, the star's lack of ability is at least partly concealed. The character actor could be described as a brassière for the star, literally holding him or her up. Of course all stars do not have to depend on supporting players in this way, but a considerable number do.

In Hollywood, among the characteristics of the system in which all actors work and live, are: a well-defined hierarchy in which the individuals position is determined primarily by income; the power of the front office to assign roles; a legal contract which binds actor to studio for seven years; the star system, a disproportionate ratio of workers to jobs; the very high salaries for the successful; the tendency to emphasize the "Look at me" type of actor; the attitudes of Hollywood people toward actors as contrasted with attitudes of the public. The medium itself also sets certain conditions, such as the absence of an audience, the acting of sequences out of their natural order, and rehearsal of only isolated sequences rather than of the whole. Some of these conditions, even those formerly considered an inherent part of the movie medium, are undergoing change, and, as usual, this is first brought about by the actions of a few individuals who struggle against the conventional order.

The most formalized part of the structure is the contractual legal arrangement between studio and actor. The term or option contracts already described are more important for understanding the system in which actors work than the free-lance arrangement in which they contract to make just one picture for a studio.[6] The usual contract runs for seven years, with the studio having the right to take up an option on the actor's services at the end of six months or a year, with a mandatory increase in pay. If the studio does not

[6] (In 1948 there were 342 actors under the long-term contracts to studios. This is considered subnormal. During the years from 1937 to 1946, the number varied between 600 and 800. Those under contract include most of the top bracket people, as well as starlets.) (Information from the Screen Actors' Guild.)

take up the option, or wishes to fire with or without cause, the contract is terminated. But as noted before, the actor cannot, under any conditions, break the contract for its duration.

The studio's control is strengthened by a clause in the contract which specifies that the actor must accept the role offered him. If he refuses a role, he is suspended without pay. In the past the suspension time was added to his contract but this practice has not been legally permissible since 1944 when Miss Olivia de Havilland won an eighteen months' battle against the right of a studio to add to her contract the twenty-five weeks in which she had been suspended at various times for refusing roles.[7] Some stars have, because of their prestige, won the right to refuse two roles in succession but must accept the third, and an occasional star has no limitations on the refusal of roles. But these are the exceptions. The large majority must take the role the studio offers.

For all actors with any ability, getting a suitable role is one of their most important problems. A good actor can be made by a strong role which offers potentialities for him to develop, or he can be embarrassed by a meaningless one. This role problem is exaggerated by the Hollywood emphasis on type casting. An actor may get typed as the hero or villain, the "good" girl, the "bad" one, the "wholesome" or the "neurotic" type, through being successful the first time he plays any one of them. It is then assumed that he can do nothing else. This is, of course, particularly frustrating for the talented actor who wants to demonstrate the wide variety of roles he can play.

Gifted actors strongly object to doing the same role over and over again, to weak or phony parts and to those for which they are not fitted. But the Hollywood system is not sympathetic to this point of view and the actors have constantly to struggle against the studio's absolute power. The manner in which objections are handled depends on the studio, the status of the actor, and the particular producer. One studio has a reputation for immediate suspension for refusal to play a role. Another uses persuasion and coaxing, saying that the role is really not as bad as the actor thinks it is, that he, a great star, can make it into a wonderful part, or they

[7] *New York Times,* March 20, 1947.

may tell the actor to be a "good boy" or "girl" now, and next time they will get what they want. At one studio with a number of executives, the actor may be tossed from one to another, each trying to convince him that the studio knows what is best.

The actor's struggle against this aspect of the studio's power goes on continuously and takes different forms. Occasionally, a star goes to court. Bette Davis sued Warner Brothers for the right to select her own story and won her case. Now a few have this right as part of their contracts. Other stars accept suspensions and still others try to get their way through manipulation. For the majority of actors, it is acceptance of a role or suspension. One star, with an excellent reputation on Broadway and in Hollywood, was suspended nine or ten times during the seven years of his contract for refusing roles that were either repetitions or very weak. Miss Lauren Bacall refused to play the feminine lead in *The Girl from Jones Beach* because she thought the script was bad and the role unfitted to her. She, too, was suspended without pay.[8] Another star managed a bit better because he had a flexible contract which allowed him to make pictures for two studios. He had been playing the role of neurotic villain for a long time when he spoke to the head of the studio about changing it to an unneurotic pirate in a story he was interested in doing. The executive's answer was, "We spent all this money to build you up as a neurotic villain, and that's what the people expect from you. You cannot suddenly switch to a normal, lusty pirate." Then the star and his agent went over to another studio and gave the pirate story to its executive, who gave his O.K. to the picture. It was a success.

Character actors who play second leads have, of course, more difficulty in refusing roles than stars. They can accept suspension and take the loss of salary. But this is not the end of the story. The producer takes it very personally and as a threat to his power. He, a great producer, has gone to so much trouble to get a story, star, director, together, *et cetera* — and a character actor playing the second or third lead tells him he does not like the role, and will not play it. This, from the producer's point of view, is impertinence. A character actor has set his judgment above that of the producer.

[8] *Variety*, April 25, 1948.

Sometimes it is difficult for him or the studio to realize such a phenomenon. One serious-minded character actor playing second leads, who has very definite ideas about the kind of roles best for him, wrote to the producer and casting director refusing a role. There was no acknowledgment of his letters and, instead, they proceeded on the assumption that he would do the part, announcing it in the trade paper. The wardrobe person phoned him to come in to be measured for his clothes. He refused and then the fuss began. However, the studio, which happens to be a large one with the policy of keeping its actors "happy," was very polite. Also the actor is exceptionally gifted and in great demand by other studios. Just before his refusal he had been loaned out for eight weeks, his studio receiving four fifths of his annual salary for that time. He is a valuable property, to be handled carefully, and his suspension lasted only a short time.

Most of the time, actors, for whom the choice of a role is important, try to manipulate the situation. If a weak part is offered, the agent may say, "Let me handle it; I'll be the villain of the piece. You must keep in good with the producer!" The agent may or may not win. At other times, the agent may have so many irons in the fire in his complex dealings with the producer that he only pretends to negotiate about the role, and actually double-crosses his client. The actor may, of course, go directly to the producer. A character actor who was asked to do the second lead told the producer directly that he did not want the part because he neither liked nor respected it. The producer rather agreed with his opinion of the role, but pointed out that he could not very well go with such a reason to the front-office executive, who would be affronted and insulted. A character actor is not supposed to think about a part in terms of good or bad, but gladly take what is offered. However, the sympathetic producer in this situation said, "Make a test for the picture. I'll have to have something to tell the front office, and I'll say that your test is no good."

Another time, when the producer was not sympathetic and an actor thought a role, that of a foreigner, was not good for him, he asked the make-up man to report that he could not possibly be made up to look the part. Sometimes an appeal is made to the casting director not to be recommended for a contemplated role. Or, the actor may resort to telling the producer how "unhappy" he will be playing this role, the theory being that an unhappy actor does not do a good job.

In spite of all this manipulation and the many suspensions, the majority of gifted actors have to do a large number of roles they consider phony. Most of them do not expect more than a few good ones during the life of their contracts. There are two alternatives. One is to try to believe that the synthetic or phony role is a true one. The other is to accept the part realistically for what it is, but play it as well as possible. The second reaction seems the healthier.

This business of role is of serious concern only to those actors who are gifted. While these are a minority, their importance far outweighs their number, as is the case for the small percentage of talented writers and directors. The majority of actors do not know enough to judge what role is good for them. For these actors with little or no ability, who photograph well, and who play themselves, type casting is a protection. An attractive-looking young actress with very little talent or experience was cast in a naïve and innocent role in which she was quite successful, because she was playing herself. It would not have been possible for her to play the role of a girl desperately and passionately in love. The role situation is one more way in which the Hollywood system is geared to mediocrity rather than talent.

The role is part of the larger problem of script and all the able actors emphasize the importance of the latter. They know that the quality of their acting depends to a large degree on what they are given to interpret, and they bemoan the fact that so few of the scripts are any good. For this, many blame the writers, condemning them as lazy people who do not earn the money they are paid. A few, who know the system under which writers work, regard them as frustrated and glorified hacks, for whom they have no respect.

Another significant part of the contract is the right it gives the studio to loan an actor to other studios. The transfer is always at a higher salary and the studio pockets the difference. Some actors are under contract to individual producers who make fortunes selling them to their own, or to other, studios. It is always to the advantage of an actor's reputation to be in demand by different studios, but it is his producer or studio, to whom he is under contract, that makes the actual profit.

The option and loan-out rights given to studio executives seem to be accepted by the actors as an inevitability which they resent but do not actively fight. The Screen Actors' Guild has, however, tried to reduce the number of years in the contract, and a few individual stars in advantageous bargaining positions win concessions such as a straight contract without options, and with restrictions on being loaned out. But for the majority of actors, including stars and featured players, these are the conditions under which they work and part of the price they pay for their enormous salaries. Among other compensations are a guaranteed forty weeks of work a year, or pay for that time whether working or not. The basic minimum rates of pay are much higher than for comparable work elsewhere, and stars are the highest paid group of people in the country.

The fact that the movie industry is completely unionized and that the artist's unions or guilds have accepted conditions of work which most American workers would find debasing is one of the many contradictions of the community. Indentured servants during the American colonial period were bound to their masters for a number of years, but even they had a security during that period which the actors lack. College professors, most of whom are in no union or in a relatively weak one, generally have been able to secure tenure on their jobs after a probationary period, but are free to leave them at any time. The situation in Hollywood is unique in trade-union history and in economic practices since the Middle Ages.

Even with the best contract, most movie actors who have been on the stage say that there is an inherently frustrating quality in film acting. The custom of acting disconnected bits of script at different times, instead of going through a whole play in its natural order is thwarting. In movie acting there can be no gradual working up to an emotional climax, sustaining it, and then tapering off. Instead, the actor may begin with a small scene in the middle or end of the script, concentrate on it and then proceed to another sequence which has the same physical setting, but is completely separated emotionally from it. Between them are tedious periods of waiting, while lighting is tested and other details are attended to. Then there are the endless repetitions of takes of the same sequence. The day is spent in constant alternation of feeling tone, the climax and then nothing, followed by another climax and again nothing, or the tiresome repetition of the same small bit time after time. The stars have portable dressing rooms to which they retire during the long waiting periods, while others idle on the set. For all, with or without a dressing room, the idling is emotionally tiring and physically fatiguing. An actress with Broadway experience says that on the stage, when she is playing both a matinee and evening performance, she has a feeling of exhilaration at the end of the evening even though she is tired. But at the end of a day on the set, although she has acted only a couple of scenes, she is completely exhausted and let down emotionally. The reason for this seeming irrational way of acting is that by concentrating all the scenes in which the same people appear and in the same background, regardless of their order in the script, an economy is effected. Actors are employed only for the time they are doing their parts rather than for the whole of the shooting.

Another difference between movie and stage acting is that in Hollywood the actor often works with strangers. He arrives on the set and is immediately supposed to do an intimate scene with someone he does not know at all. On the stage the cast has a chance to know each other during the long weeks of rehearsals and the try-outs on the road. A repertory company, accustomed to acting with each other in play after play, carries this advantage to the utmost. The extreme of strangeness occurs when a movie actor is loaned to a studio, meets the cast for the first time, and has to play a role portraying intimate relationships with some of them. The assumption seems to be that the movie actor is a robot and that this practice, therefore, has no effect on him.

For every stage actor, rehearsals are an important part of his preparation for playing a role. A number of directors, more particularly those from Broadway, would like to have rehearsals before they begin to shoot the movie. But the expense and difficulties in arranging them have been considered forbidding. The leading actors may not be free from other studio obligations until the date of the shooting, and rehearsal time would add to the budget. However, an occasional director has experimented with a week or two of rehearsals and found that he got a better picture and saved time later in the shooting. The rehearsals then caused no additional expense. It is possible for the date of beginning a picture to be the time for starting rehearsals rather than shooting, and contracts made accordingly. But the system of production has not been geared to rehearsals and only rarely has a daring director questioned the accepted belief of the front office that rehearsals would add to the budget. The exceptions are now becoming a bit more common, because it has finally been discovered they save money. According to a report in the *New York Times*, October 30, 1949:

> From its earliest days, Hollywood has followed the practice, from which it only occasionally has departed, of shooting pictures with little or no rehearsal by the players except such as they may engage in briefly, scene by scene, just before the director calls for action on the set. Lately, however, in their efforts to find ways and means of bringing down costs, some producers and directors have discovered that time and money can often be saved — and the artistic quality of their screen plays improved — if casts are well rehearsed in advance of shooting.

Because the front office usually tends to think and work according to old formulas and is afraid of new ideas, rehearsals had to wait until Hollywood fell on hard times and then in desperation tried something different. Hard times have their advantages.

Rehearsals also provide training for young actors with small parts. A player on the stage with only a line or two goes through all the rehearsals with the cast for weeks in advance of the plays. He knows what the play is about. He sees all the actors doing their parts and watches the leading actors improve themselves in rehearsals. In contrast, the small-bit player in movies is called in to do his part for one day only, when the particular scene in which he says his line is shot. He knows nothing about the script; he may not even know what the name of the movie is; certainly, he knows nothing about the relation of his small part to the whole. When he comes on the set the director tells him what to do and how to say his few lines, and then he goes home. It has therefore been impossible for any actor to receive training by doing small parts in movies.

Training is conspicuously lacking in the studios. The large ones do have something called "training" for starlets, but it is primarily in such details as posture, speech, and the elimination of an accent. There is nothing at the studio comparable to the experience gained at a good dramatic school or by having even small parts in Broadway shows. Hollywood generally depends on the stage for seasoned actors.

The absence of an audience while acting is one of the conditions inherent in the movie medium. This problem of actor and audience is not an easy one to explain. On the stage the actor cannot see the members of the audience, but he says he feels them and knows how they are reacting through their silence, laughter and slight moments. It is difficult for any exhibitionist, actor or not, to be at his best if there is no one, seen or unseen, to admire him. Of course, the movie actor has a pleasure later in looking at himself acting, and also, the foreknowledge of an eventual enormous audience. These, however, do not seem to completely compensate for the lack of audience when he is before the camera. But actors vary considerably in their reaction to this problem. Some have great difficulty in adjusting to it, others are able to use substitutes and still others seem relatively unaffected by it.

One actress with a long Broadway experience says she first felt like a "fish out of water" on the set, and that "an actress without an audience is like a fire horse without a fire." She thinks that actors who have never performed before a real audience are at a disadvantage, because then they cannot even imagine one. Another actor who had been a Broadway star before he came to Hollywood says that he uses the people on the set — the cast, the carpenters, the electricians, the extras, the various assistants — for his audience, and that he can tell from their reactions how he is doing. Other actors say that the prop men and electricians are playing gin rummy or betting on horses while they wait around on the set, and cannot be compared to an audience which pays money to see a play. Actually, many of the crew with long experience on the sets are blasé, self-taught critics, and the occasional spontaneous burst of applause from them, as a sequence is finished, is considered very rewarding. Many actors try to use the director as an audience. They play to him and wait for his reaction. But to make this method effective, the actors say they must have a director who has a knowledge of acting — and they add that there are very few of these.

All actors, no matter what their type, experienced or inexperienced, need a good director. It is paradoxical that although acting is the most deeply egocentric of all the arts, the actor is at the same time completely dependent on other people. Gifted or mediocre, he cannot perform without a director's help. No actor can see himself while he is acting, and it is imperative that a director tell him whether his characterization is too strong or too weak in relation to other roles, and to the whole. This is the minimum function of a director. Often an actor, particularly an immature one, needs to have explained the meaning of the script and his role and its relationship to the others. This is the director's job and it is he who must skillfully integrate all the parts into a well-balanced whole. The description given by many actors of a good director is one who knows not only the technicalities of camera and cutting, but who also understands people and drama. He plans everything in advance and, since he knows the place of close-ups, medium and master shots, he does not have to waste time and money making every possible shot. At the same time, he is flexible and can incorporate good ideas from actors or anyone else, without losing the main theme. On the other hand, he must not take every suggestion, but have sufficient judgment to know what to reject and what to use. The director is the key figure in drawing out the best from both actors and script.

According to the actors the majority of directors are too mediocre to even begin fulfilling this function. Most of them, they say, are traffic cops, who simply keep actors from bumping into each other as they move from one chalk line to another. The experience of stars, featured players, character actors, bit players, starlets, is remarkably uniform. All complain about the infrequency of helpful directing. One man, a star both on the stage and screen, who goes back and forth between Broadway and Hollywood, says that of his twelve Hollywood directors, three were really good. The others were mediocre or bad. As a star in A pictures he naturally has a better chance at a good director than most actors. But he says that some of his directors did not even understand what the picture was about. One was completely dictatorial and resented any suggestion an actor made. Another took every suggestion, good or bad, made by anyone. Only three were able to give him the necessary cues to indicate if he was going too far, or not far enough.

Another star, who had come to Hollywood after playing leading roles on Broadway, says that his first picture was very successful, and because of this and his Broadway reputation, he was regarded as "terrific," and most of his directors were afraid to direct him, leaving him almost completely alone. This, he says, was bad for his acting. Of his twenty-five Hollywood directors, all in A pictures, he rates five as good and three of these as excellent. Many of the others, he says, did not know the meaning of the script or have any real knowledge of acting. They concentrated almost entirely on technical details. In one picture the director gave all his attention in an important scene to getting unusual light effects from a broken glass. But in achieving this he forgot the meaning.

A leading star, in movies for a long time, says that he has had about sixty directors, only three of whom were creative and able to help him. The creative director, he says, treats each actor as an individual and stirs his imagination, and has a capacity of synthesizing all the actor's contributions. He and many other actors test out a new director on about the fourth day of production to find out if the latter knows what it is all about. The test consists of the actor purposely doing something badly to see if the director notices it. If the latter is oblivious, then the actor sadly knows that he is on his own.

*   *   *

An actress who began with small roles and has worked up to feature parts says that of her thirty directors no one was in the superior group. None were able to help her and she has been grateful when they did not, at least, interfere. Her chief complaint is that the directors do not know what they want. She tells about one scene in which she and several other actors were sitting casually around a table and supposed to convey a certain meaning by the manner in which they exchanged glances. The actors in this scene were all experienced and knew the meaning of what they were portraying. They exchanged the meaningful glances indicated in the script, but the director did not appear to understand what they were trying to convey. He told them to repeat this scene eight or nine times. They kept on looking at each other in many different ways, but it never seemed to suit the director. Finally, the weary actors "hammed" the scene, looking at each other in a most exaggerated fashion. The director did not like this either. Then they went back and played the scene as they had done it the first time. The director then said this was O.K. The same director made another actress, who happened to be a star and talented, do the same scene twenty-five times; he was completely unable to tell her what was the matter with it — just simply telling her to repeat it. When she finally flounced off the set, very angry, the director retorted that he had been in the movies for thirty years, that there was nothing he did not know, and never had he worked with such temperamental actors. He was unsympathetic and ungracious with everyone, from bit player to star, never giving the encouraging "well done" to any of them.

Sometimes a conscientious director makes a mistake simply out of his ignorance about acting. In a big A picture the leading role was played by a popular star. Before she had been chosen, the studio had tested another more gifted actress for the part, and, although the latter had done extraordinarily well, the studio decided she was not sufficiently box-office and therefore gave the role to a better-known star, who, while competent, was decidedly less gifted. Before they began the big climax scene, for which the first actress had tested, the director spent several hours looking at this test.

He then came on the set and tried to teach the star to do it exactly as the other actress had done it. The scene turned out a mess. The star was competent enough to have given a creditable performance if she had been given moderately skilled direction. But when the director tried to turn her into another actress, he ruined her chances. He was unaware that acting is not imitation, and he did not know that the different personalities of the two actresses prohibited mechanically transferring the acting of one to the other.

How much an actor can argue with a director depends on the relative status of each. One elderly star, respected by everyone for his long history in the theater as well as movies, and for his known ability, usually does discuss the script and role with the director, but with varying success. One gave him the script to read in advance and asked him what he thought of it, and after reading it carefully, he said that the major character lacked consistent motivation. The director agreed with him and together they discussed the problem with the writer, who then rewrote the script along the indicated lines. However, with another director, this actor had quite a different experience, when he tried to tell him that more meaning should be given to the script. The director refused even to discuss the matter. The actor's explanation is that this director was insecure and had a strong feeling of inferiority, which he tried to conceal by asserting his own will. At another time the actor tried to get a director to pay more attention to the meaning, but the latter was not interested because he was concentrating on getting the reflection of a fire in a fireplace, rather than the meaning of the scene. Of his thirty directors this actor, who has played only in A pictures, says that ten were good; and of these, two or three were "tops."

Another actor, younger and playing featured roles, not as well established, says that he chooses very carefully the occasions on which he argues with a director. He does not argue every time he feels like it, but only on those situations which he considers very important, and on which he thinks he has a good chance of winning his point. If he did this too often, he would gain a reputation of being "difficult." Also, arguing upsets him, and he then cannot give the best to his role. But when things get too bad he "pitches in." He adds that sometimes he comes out with increased respect from the producer and director. Of his eleven directors, two were good and one was excellent. The latter knew and understood the script and its characters, made the actors feel at ease and encouraged them to give their ideas. Although this director had everything planned in advance he was able to incorporate new ideas. Everyone in the set felt that the making of this film was truly collaborative.

Young actors without stage experience or training, playing relatively small parts, need help even more than the older and gifted ones — but rarely get it. One, who has been playing small roles for the last four years, says, "Most directors give you no help at all." She continues, "The studio employs you for your physical type and perhaps for your ability, too, and then it leaves you alone." In only one picture, her last one, did she get real help by the director. It was a unique experience for her to have the director talking over the role with her, telling her what it meant, and helping her to understand it. She says, "An actress needs psychological understanding and must get it from someone." This director not only made her understand what she was doing, but for the first time she was put at ease. She thinks that her acting improved greatly under his direction. It was also a new experience for her to be on a set where everything was well planned in advance. She was accustomed to directors who worked in a haphazard, unplanned fashion. She is grateful for this last experience and hopes she will be able to work with the same director again.

She tells about another director who tried to establish a good relationship with the actors through a constant stream of jokes. But, she says, the funny story just before she began a sequence, distracted and threw her off.

Another starlet, who has been at a studio for three years doing bit parts, and who recently secured a featured role, describes her idea of a good director as: "One who is friendly, puts you at your ease, and is interested in bringing the best out of you. He tells you the meaning of the roles. He works with you all the time, telling you when you are too strong or not relaxed enough. He doesn't order you about but his suggestions set the tone for your acting. Many of the directors are friendly and pleasant, and you might like them personally, but they tell you nothing and give you no help. And there are others who tell you the wrong thing to do. At the moment you don't know it is wrong, but you realize it later when you see the picture."

A youthful actor, who has worked up from bit parts to feature roles, says that of his eight directors two were good. These two gave him the emotional meaning of his role and he was then able to make something out of it. The others gave him no understanding at all, but would merely say, "Make it come alive," or "Play it as you feel it," which was no help. They were primarily concerned with telling the actors to walk to this or that chalk mark on the floor, or make this or that kind of gesture, but never with the meaning. These men also never seemed to prepare in advance of the shooting date and gave the effect of not knowing where they were going.

A young actress, after eight years in the movies and with previous training and experience limited to singing and dancing in night clubs, recently became a star. Her last picture was the first one in which she had a director who explained what her role meant and the feelings underlying it, and who then worked with her on how she could best express them. She describes him as a "genius." He happens to be a very good director from the Broadway stage, but not in the genius class. But he is the first director who made her *feel* like an actress. In all her other pictures, she says, the directors were concerned primarily with the camera technique and different kinds of shots. She felt like an automaton, making this or that kind of motion, which the camera caught in long, medium or close-up shot. Actually this actress appears to fall rather definitely in the "Look at me" category. In the living room of her home the only pictures are three oil paintings of herself, two of them full length. In this movie, which she considers her best, she shows little acting talent. Yet she resents being regarded as a package of goods which photographs well and a good director was able to call forth some emotional response from her; for the first time she felt human and that she was actually portraying a character, and not simply moving from one chalk mark to another.

The attitude of the director to the actors may be pleasant and friendly, or cruel and sadistic, and is not correlated with his ability. There are unkind directors who know nothing about acting or directing and others who are able. One, whose ability lay mainly in ridicule, could make an actor so self-conscious that his performance was spoiled. This director once said, "There are only supposed to be two people in this scene; we do not need an elephant." Although the actor tried not to show that the remark had got under his skin, he became acutely self-conscious and muffed his part. Another director known for his cruelty is, however, gifted, and some actors prefer to work for him because he does know what is good for them and the film. One says if he has to make a choice, he prefers a cruel director whose work he respects to a kindly one without ability.

Whatever the director's personality, the actor needs his help. The able director can give an inexperienced actor a training which he carries with him when he leaves the picture and the studio. If the actor is trained, he still needs a director to provide the perspective on his work in relationship to the whole. Any actor can be enriched through working with a gifted director. All actors emphasize that they need a director who can go beyond the mechanics of the camera, who knows how people behave in certain life situations, and who can suggest the small touches which make a character come alive — such as, for instance, the way a drunkard crossing a street would come up on the curb. They want a director who has grown up sufficiently in the use of his medium to emphasize meaning as well as movement, which, while still very important, is not the only essential as it was in the early silent films. They need a director who sees them as something more than just other "props" — as human beings with feelings, emotions, imagination and intellect.

Ironically, the studio places great emphasis on the realness of its nonhuman props. Furniture and clothes must authentically represent the period; location shooting is desired because the background is real. But people can be robots or automatons. A gifted actor is often frustrated because at the height of climax the camera concentrates on a prop such as a broken chair, rather than on him as the director endeavors to get a synthetic emotional effect through the juxtaposition of nonhuman objects.

Actors frequently are portrayed as passive creatures, spiritless zombies, rarely registering an emotion. This seems to be an inversion of the primitive man's animism, whereby he attributes human qualities to material objects such as stone or a wood carving. In Hollywood it is the human beings who are treated as if they were inanimate objects which paradoxically are given meaning by the director. The custom began in the silent films, and long after the need has ceased to exist continues and even grows stronger. Many of the young female stars today lack all individuality. They seem to both look and act alike, and it is not easy for those who are not regular movie-goers to tell them apart. Their goal appears to be the cultivation of a completely expressionless face and voice. The older women stars, now in their forties, have more individuality than the younger ones and at least can be told apart.

What began as a necessity, getting emotional and human effects from props and material objects rather than from individuals, has remained and increased, long after the need has ceased to exist.

More and more talented actors are brought to Hollywood from Broadway. But the factory system is slow to change. Gifted actors, like talented directors and writers, have to constantly struggle to use their special skills for their own good, as well as for that of the movies.

The difficulties in getting suitable roles and helpful directors could be met by a more flexible system of production, responding to new conditions, and one in which those with power understood the nature of acting. For the front office, many of the conditions under which movies were first made still tend to be binding.

Gradually, because of the need for economy, changes are occurring. Even rehearsals, long considered impossible, are, as we have noted, slowly becoming a new trend. Intelligent planning and imagination could eliminate part of the time lag. This situation is not unique. Many a primitive society in the South Seas also keeps its antiquated system of agriculture limited to yams, taro, coconuts and bananas, long after diversified farming has been introduced.

CHAPTER XII

Stars

Stars are, of course, part of all theater. But the star system appears to dominate Hollywood to a greater degree than it does the theater. Nor is its effect restricted to Hollywood, since movie stars are among our most admired folk heroes and heroines. Considerable mythology has accumulated about them, and as in any society, myths, true or false, influence behavior. They leave their impact on stars, would-be stars, those who work with them, and the audience.

While the star system has long been a significant part of movie production, it was not initiated by the studios. In the early days, the names of the leading actors were not even publicized and members of the audience wrote to the studios for information about their favorites. The studios did not at first encourage this spontaneous fan mail because they feared that actors would demand more money if they knew about their popularity. Soon, however, the studios realized that the popularity of a star could be exploited, even if salaries did go up. From this small beginning grew a Gargantuan system which has deep repercussions on the making of movies and leaves its effect on American society.

From a business point of view, there are many advantages in the star system. The star has tangible features which can be advertised and marketed — a face, a body, a pair of legs, a voice, a certain kind of personality, real or synthetic — and can be typed as the wicked villain, the honest hero, the fatal siren, the sweet young girl, the neurotic woman. The system provides a formula easy to understand and has made the production of movies seem more like just another business. The use of this formula may serve also to protect the executives from talent and from having to pay much attention to such intangibles as the quality of story or of acting. Here is a standardized product which they can understand, which can be advertised and sold, and which not only they, but also banks and exhibitors, regard as insurance for large profits. The studios can promise exhibitors a Bing Crosby picture, one with Bob Hope, one with Ingrid Bergman and, until very recently, all were confident about their profits. The use of this formula may also give a psychological security to men who know little about the art of storytelling. It is, therefore, logical, from the point of view of studio executives, to build up and exaggerate the star system.

Stars do not fall into any single category. Among them are handsome men and beautiful women and those with just pleasant, everyday faces, tough heroes and gentle ones, straight comedians and song-and-dance ones, character actors, all ages from children to those past middle age, actors with great talent and those with very little. To stay on top for a long period, the actors must appeal to both sexes and male stars do this more often than female. Clark Gable, Gary Cooper, Bob Hope and Bing Crosby are among those who have enjoyed unusually long tenure at the top. Wallace Beery probably attained his top position primarily through a male following. Both Ingrid Bergman and Shirley Temple have also enjoyed a long term of popularity. The popularity of child actors such as Margaret O'Brien, Mickey Rooney and Judy Garland before they grew up, may be due in part to the fact that their fans included both sexes and all ages. It is impossible to know exactly why any particular actor makes the top bracket in popularity. It may be his personality, his acting, his role, and the amount of exploitation by the studio, or any combination of these factors. Claudette Colbert may have achieved her position in the past because of the success of the picture *It Happened One Night*, and to being teamed with Clark Gable. Jane Wyman later became very popular because of her poignant role in *Johnny Belinda*.

There is considerable mythology concerning how stars are made, particularly the female ones. Many of the myths are concerned with Cinderella tales of how a beautiful girl is snatched from some humdrum position by a perceptive producer, wins a contract, and becomes a star overnight. In a primitive society it is difficult to determine the degree of truth in myths and folk tales. But in Hollywood it is quite possible to find out how stars are actually made, and to contrast this with the mythology. Most everyone concerned with the making of movies is aware that the quickest and surest way to become a star is to be asked to come to Hollywood after being successful on Broadway. This means being an actor of distinction, or at least, of considerable ability. But there are many movie stars who have not come from Broadway, and it is about them the myths circulate. The success tales are, of course, not the same for each star. A combined list of the success ingredients in all of them would include photogenic looks, a personality that clicks, sleeping with the right person or persons, publicity, knowing the right people and playing the social game, perseverence, ability, good roles, and breaks.

While looks are important, great or classical beauty is not essential. Much emphasis is put on being photogenic, but it is impossible to get any consensus of agreement on what this quality is. Opinions range from its being due to the bone structure of the face to sexiness. It is a fact that individuals vary considerably in how well they photograph, and those who depend primarily on their vitality or some indefinable charm may not come off as well as others who rely on the shape of their features. But make-up, lights, and skilled camera work are often as important as features. It is difficult to define the sexy quality which comes through on the screen and which is necessary for all movie actors, whether hero or villain. Figure, gait, voice are important, but the real personality may have little to do with the matter, because some actresses known for their sexiness on the screen have a reputation for being nymphomaniacs, and others for being virginal. Even more difficult to define is what makes a personality click. Why did one of the earliest stars, Mary Pickford, become "America's Sweetheart"? Why do adolescents rave about Frank Sinatra? Why has Bing Crosby become a universal favorite? Neither their looks nor talent are outstanding, but the camera has caught some quality which the audience loves.

The Cinderella story of winning a beauty contest and immediately becoming a star is practically never true. Usually stardom is not attained by the contest winner, and when this does occasionally happen, it is after a long period of ups and downs. One young woman who had won a beauty contest in her home state waited seven years for a big part which made her into a star. She was extremely beautiful but was given only very minor roles when she first came to Hollywood. She was married at different times to two movie stars, but still did not get a big role. Finally she attained a good second lead in which she was successful. From here she went on to playing the lead and now she is a star. She had beauty, good marriages from a professional point of view, some ability, and the capacity to learn under good direction. But it took her seven years.

Another contest winner has succeeded, after many disappointments, in playing the feminine lead in Westerns. She is attractive-looking, considered photogenic, and had taken singing and dancing lessons from early childhood. Her background was comfortable middle-class. When she had worked up to amateur musical comedies and radio programs, a studio talent scout saw her and she was asked to come to Hollywood for a test. She and all her friends were much excited, and at the farewell parties they took it for granted that it would be just a short time before she became a star. She arrived in Los Angeles and the studio gave her six weeks of training in diction, posture, standing, and so on. Finally, it was time for her to take the test. She did not pass. She felt she was a complete failure and the most horrible part was the memory of all the going-away parties and presents from friends who were so sure that she would be a star. She could not go home. . . .

The casting director, with whom she had become friendly, thought the test good, and on his own initiative sent it around to three other studios, one of which sent for her and offered her a contract. For a couple of years she again took the studio training in diction and singing, and did a few bit parts which led to nothing, and eventually her option was not taken up. Then came the war and she began to sell bonds on the radio for the United States Treasury Department. A major studio sponsored a bond-selling contest and the prize was a role in one of its big pictures. She won the contest —

and now, she thought, this was her real break. According to all the publicity the role would have star billing, and so she expected her own and her friends' delayed expectations would come true. But again she was humiliated because she came off with only a very small part and no billing at all. She says, "The studio has no concern for your feelings at all. They just used me and exploited the contest publicity and then did not come across with the promised big part. It was only a small part to begin with, and then it was so cut that it became still smaller. The studios don't care what they do to a person; anything for the sake of publicity. You know how awful I felt before my friends — all this publicity about a big role and then I come off with such a little one." The role might have been cut for any number of reasons including lack of ability, or for other causes completely unconnected with her. But her humiliation and resentment are still strong after five or six years have passed.

This small part, however, was her break, because she did go on to bigger roles. She is still not a star, but has recently been signed to play feminine leads in Westerns. She is the outdoor type of girl and loves to ride and swim and, because of her early training, she dances and sings well. In the Westerns she is able to play herself and to use this early training. But she says that she wants to get away from these singing-dancing parts and become a "real" actress. In all likelihood she has reached her greatest success and will disappear from movies after she becomes too old to do young girl parts in Westerns.

These two actresses are exceptions among the contest winners. Most of them never get further than making a test. Some manage to get bit parts but that is their limit. Most of them have to be content with showing off their figures in tight pants as waitresses in the Los Angeles drive-in restaurants. But whatever they do, they feel it is impossible to go back home and face family and friends with the fact that they failed and that the Cinderella myth did not work for them.

Another Hollywood myth is that a young actress can get ahead by sleeping with the right men. The use of sex, overtly or otherwise, by women to further their ambitions was not exactly invented in Hollywood, nor is the custom of men sleeping with young women over whom they have authority restricted to that community. Businessmen have been known to have sex relations with their secretaries and folk tales circulate about male college professors who make passes at their female students. Nor are extramarital relations unknown in either the folklore or behavior of our society from *Tobocco Road* to "the 400" groups. The theater world also has its particular traditions of bohemianism and defiance of conventions.

The situation in Hollywood, however, might seem to lend itself particularly to a breaking of sex taboos. In one community there is concentrated more pulchritude than probably in any other place in the world. Here are all the young girls who have won beauty contests in their home towns, and thousands of others with exceptionally good looks, with and without talent, all unswervingly intent on stardom. Only a very few out of the thousands can be successful and competition is keen. As in most industries, those in executive positions with decisive power are usually middle-aged or older men. Directors and agents, young or old men, also have power; and attractive stars might likewise further a girl's career. Since there are so few women with executive power, the situation for the large number of handsome or attractive young men, as avid as the females for success, is a bit different. These men can only use their wiles on female stars who might help them.

But strange to say, success via the bed formula frequently does not work. The reason may be that in Hollywood, more than in most modern communities, sex behavior, particularly that outside of marriage, is so often limited to the instinctual biological act, unassociated with love, tenderness or affection; and sex there is frequently just part of the manipulation of human relationships for one's own advantage. These two attitudes do not always merge to produce success for the hopeful aspirant. The young girl is often willing and eager to use the bed to advance her career. But the man whom she thinks she is using for her own purposes is frequently through with her after the episode. For him it was simply a biological release, much the same as going to a prostitute; but in this situation the kind of payment the girl wants cannot be collected, because the affection or tenderness which would prompt it is lacking. One big executive who slept with an actress, in this case a talented European, when approached on why he had not given her a part said: "Is it not enough that I, Mr. Terrific, slept with her?" He had soon tired of her and then did not want her around. Even if some feeling is there, or a desire to keep the girl as a bed partner, it is difficult for the man to give her any major role unless she has ability which will be effective at the box office. The bank casts its shadow even over the bed. The executive is accountable to the banks, and it is difficult for him to explain losses to them in terms of sexual desires. What many girls do not realize is that profits are more important to these men than any particular girl. Sexual needs can be more easily satisfied than the urge for large returns on a picture.

Even before the bank steps in there are difficulties. A small independent producer was living with a young girl and seemed to have really fallen rather hard for her. Although she had neither acting ability nor experience, she was ambitious and the producer gave her a leading role. Her lack of ability was so glaring, and the protests of the male lead and director so strong, that in less than two weeks the producer was forced to permit them to substitute another actress for his girl friend and to reshoot what had already been done.

Usually the young aspirant for stardom does not even have the opportunity of going to bed with important people. Over the years and through experience these men have become scared of paternity suits and blackmail, as an aftermath of their indulgence, and so they prefer using a high class call-house. If they have an affair it is with someone who is already successful. One man said he would not think of going out with an actress who earned less than $1000 a week. This was not due to snobbishness but was based on the theory that a girl in that salary bracket would not have the financial incentive for a lawsuit and is interested also in protecting her own reputation.

The going-to-bed opportunities for the girls on the bottom of the ladder are usually limited to "little men" such as first, second and third assistant directors. In return the girls may get work as extras or bit players, but this is as far as they go. Agents, too, may take advantage of their position to obtain sexual favors, but a job does not always follow.

While the bed may be and sometimes is the way to secure a test or a bit part, this is the end unless the girl has some objective qualities which would tend to make her success as an actress probable. However, very few girls realize this. The majority say "yes" very easily to men at the studios, some for a combination of reasons including career ambitions and sex desire, others purely for ambition, only very few just for pleasure, and still fewer because of emotional involvement. At one studio three girls under stock contract were known to be exceedingly promiscuous. One of them, who had unquestioned ability, is now on the way to becoming a star, but the general opinion is that she would have been successful whether or not she slept around. One married a wealthy businessman and left the movies, and the third disappeared when her contract expired and no one knows what happened to her. There are also an appreciable number of successful young actresses – though definitely in the minority – whose private lives are unconnected with the studio and who do not use the bed as a means to furthering their careers. But many believe in and act on the myth, jumping into bed with anyone on even a half-promise of help to stardom. It is probable that more men have to refuse girls who make advances than the other way around.

Can the handsome young men, the masculine equivalent of starlets, use their sex appeal to get ahead? Top executives, directors, and cameramen are male, and there are very few women producers. Of course, an occasional homosexual actor can exploit this situation, if he finds a producer with similar interests. In Hollywood, as elsewhere, the ratio between the sexes is disproportionate, and there never appear to be quite enough attractive young men to fill the needs of divorcees, unmarried girls, or married women who are looking for fun on the side. Some of these women have a reputation of wanting a continuous succession of different young men. If the ambitious young actor becomes the boy friend of an important star, he is invited to parties with her, meets the right people who have power over jobs, and gets an enormous amount of free publicity. His name is constantly in the columns of the trade paper as being seen with Miss Big Star at a night club or restaurant, all of which may be to his advantage. It is, however, not possible to gauge accurately how often the boy friend technique brings success. One young actor had a whirlwind social life and became intimate with a famous star, a divorcee, and later with another who had the reputation of being "on the town," but he still has not had a big part. Such a man may ride high for a while and then suddenly be left out in the cold. The star may have a rapid turnover in boy friends and she might find it embarrassing to work with him in a picture once the affair is over. So if the casting director suggests him for one of her pictures, she might say, "Oh no, he's no good," or "I don't want to work with him." It then gets noised about that she does not think he's good. His former relationship with her acts as a boomerang.

Other times it may work out better, and the actor may get his opportunity through escorting and being seen with a glamorous star. But, as in the case of the young girls, he too must have some degree of ability or box-office appeal if he is to cash in on his opportunity. Thus one often hears that some handsome young man, who is now playing second leads, has been escorting the big-time glamour girls, and, according to gossip, sleeping with some of them. For some time he has been keeping himself well in the public eye, particularly the producer's eye. Luck may come if, as in one case, he is undeniably handsome with a crude and obvious sexiness and possesses some talent.

The female stars do not have to worry about maternity suits or blackmail and so need not be cautious about bestowing their favors. But the situation in which a young man sexually uses a female as a steppingstone for success is a reversal of our customs, and some of the stars, particularly younger ones looking for a husband, resent being so used. They would like to have the feeling that a man takes them out because he likes them rather than for publicity. One young unmarried actress who has recently received star billing says: "I prefer to go out with businessmen because they are more sincere. They'll take you out because they like being with you, while one of the Hollywood men just wants to be seen in your company. Besides, I think a businessman would make a better husband."

On the whole, with whom one sleeps is *not* the crucial element in success today. It may have been more important in the early days of the silent movies, when ability was not as important and when life in Hollywood, sexual and otherwise, was on a cruder level. But the myth still persists, partly out of the past emphasis and partly because of the sexy atmosphere. There is an obsession on sex in conversation and in print, which is somewhat similar to the attitude of adolescents when they first become sexually aware. The gossip columns in trade papers give spicy items and innuendos about who was seen with whom at a night club on Sunset Strip and whose marriage is in the process of breaking up. The whole industry revolves around sex. Hollywood knows that it is a sex symbol for the world and does its best to live up to the reputation.

This extends to the set and off it. While one picture was being shot, two stars made no secret of their attachment. They would emerge from the actress's dressing room, obviously enamored with each other, play a sequence, and then return to her dressing room. Real or phony the same atmosphere continues after the day on the set is over. A publicity man insists on circulating romantic stories about two leads in a film, and having them photographed dining and dancing together as advance publicity for the movie.

Sex may also serve in Hollywood, as elsewhere, as an outlet for frustration, as a means of excitement, or as a way of making life seem less empty. At the top of the success ladder are some people with more than enough money to satisfy all material desires, with neither creative drive nor the capacity for deep human relationships, nor any meaningful goal which would give significance to their lives. When not working, and often even when working, these people are basically bored, and sex relations are one means of reducing boredom. Their lives are dull or unsatisfying and hence the constant quest for an opiate whether it be sex, drink or drug.

What is relatively rare in Hollywood is the bohemian kind of sex life, so often associated with artists, for whom the conventions do not have the customary binding force, but for whom the emotions of love and affection are important. In other words, in Hollywood sex is regarded as a means of getting ahead, a form of excitement and fun, a function of power, a biological act. Far more rarely is it associated with love or affection, or given meaning in human relations.

Besides sex, publicity, good or bad, free or paid for, false or true, is regarded as an essential ingredient to the success story. This publicity may be directed to audiences, limited to the industry, or reach both. Each studio has its own publicity department with manifold functions, one of which is to continuously publicize the stars and build up those whom the studio is planning to make into stars. The department pays relatively little attention to character actors and supporting players. In addition there are a large number of publicity agencies apart from the studios, which actors (and also producers, directors and others) use. Among the actors who employ their own publicity men are those on their way to becoming stars, who want to speed up the process; those who are anxious about maintaining their high positions; those who have started to slip and need to regain their former positions.

A major part of the outside publicity agent's work is to make the actor more desirable to the studios, and one of his techniques is the spreading of gossip and rumors. The agent may spread tales that a British studio wants his client, or that a deal with a Hollywood one is in the air. A competitive bidding situation, real or fictitious, for the services of an actor is naturally to the advantage of the actor, as it is to anyone in our society, including college professors. They, however, usually have to show evidence of a real offer for their services, while in Hollywood a rumor quoted in the gossip columns of the trade papers is sometimes enough to produce results. Another rumor about the enormous size of a client's fan mail is usually helpful. So also are the planted items, real or fictitious, in the columns about the client spending a week end on the yacht of an important executive or star, or going to a night club with one of them. One successful actor in his late twenties has been reported engaged by columnists five times during the last two years. None of the reports was true and he did not even know two of the girls to whom he was supposedly engaged. The premise underlying the use of this kind of planted item is that the reader will assume the actor is successful because he is in the company of successful people. Interestingly enough that premise is correct, even though everyone knows many of the items originate in the publicity man's imagination. Producers have even been known to believe fictitious publicity turned out by their own studios. The magic of the printed word still operates in Hollywood.

Another technique is a build-up in the press and magazines through the gag of an award by a false company. Miss Enterprise, playing in serials at a salary of $250 a week, employed a publicity agent to help her along. He invented a nonexistent fashion institute and covered himself by giving the phone number of a New York friend who was willing to say that he was a representative of the institute. It then gave an award to Miss Enterprise as the best-dressed movie actress off the screen. The news angle of the story was that while she earned only $15,000 a year, she spent almost all of it on clothes. Magazines and papers sent out photographers to take pictures of her in the clothes — which, of course, she had to borrow from girl friends. Stories and pictures appeared in a large number of national magazines, including one enormous-circulation weekly which made her its cover girl and gave her three or four pages. Shortly afterwards she was given her first star role in an A picture at a major studio and today she is one of the big stars. The executive who gave her the role might never have heard of her, if it had not been for the build-up by the publicity man. However, even he says that the build-up would not have been successful if Miss Enterprise had not been very attractive, photogenic, and possessing a sexy quality which comes across on the screen.

At first the publicity agent was so pleased with the results that he thought he could make anyone into a star. But it did not always work. Some of the little-known actresses with whom he tried similar schemes did not become stars — for lack of sufficient ability, or good looks, or the kind of personality that clicks, or for some other unknown reason. Then he became more discriminating about choosing the actress for the build-up. He did a good job for one whom he described as a "lush, sexy" person who had somehow been passed over by the studios. He planted a large number of photographs of her in bathing suits and other scanty attire in magazines, and she became a cover girl. In this way she was brought to the attention of producers.

All publicity is not based on hokum. The publicity man in the studio or in his own agency is quick to exploit anything that has a news or story angle from the actual life of the actor. Larraine Day, before her divorce and marriage to Leo Durocher, had never been able to get good publicity, because she was regarded as a "cold personality without sex appeal," "too nice," "too conventional" — in other words, a dud from the publicity angle. Then she became notorious and front-page news as a possible bigamist in 1947 when she flew down to Mexico to marry Leo (The Lip) Durocher. She had obtained a California divorce from her husband, Mr. Hendricks, with the usual legal stipulation requiring a year's wait before she was free to marry again. But the next day she flew to Mexico, obtained a second divorce, and married "Lippy" there. Now the "cold" personality became "hot." She had thrown over husband and children and risked a charge of bigamy, all for love! Newspapers and fan magazines clamored for interviews. Typical of the way the movie columnists in the newspapers handled the actress's difficulties was the following: "Larraine Day in the seventh heaven of bliss because Leo Durocher is flying all the way from Havana on Wednesday, to fly back with her on Friday to Havana for her two weeks visit with him! If ever I saw love, this is it." [1] Earlier the same columnist wrote:

> Larraine Day's telephone bill to Leo Durocher in Havana, and Leo's to her, are reaching an all-time fabulous high. "Leo's bill for 10 days," says Larraine dreamily on the set of *Tycoon*, "was $600! And I expect mine to be even higher." Love is an expensive commodity.

But was it really so expensive? Net gains were high even after the reported $600 phone bill. A trade paper had the following item in its gossip column:

[1] Sheilah Graham, in *Hollywood Citizen News*, March 17, 1947.

. . . You're off the beam if you think that Larraine Day has been the butt of bad publicity in her current legal marital difficulties. She's combing magazine interviews out of her hair — and her price for an outside picture [off the RKO lot] has gone to $150,000.[2]

At her own studio, her price per picture was said to have gone from $50,000–$60,000 to $100,000. Nor was the actress the only one to benefit. The studio immediately planned to release her latest picture, *The Locket*, ahead of its scheduled date to cash in on the publicity, and one executive is reported to have said, "It should increase the picture's box office take by $200,000."[3] A Brooklyn theater running a previous picture, *Mr. Lucky*, changed its billing to read, "Starring Mrs. Leo Durocher and Cary Grant." The studio even considered reissuing a two-year-old movie, *Bride by Mistake*, in which she had been featured. The Hollywood proverb that "The only bad publicity is no publicity" would seem to have considerable truth behind it, even if publicity alone is not generally sufficient to make a star.

Playing the social game and going to the right parties is also always helpful on the road to stardom. It is important to keep literally within the range of executives' and producers' eyes. One young man, now playing featured parts, who has his eyes set on star roles, says: "I go to big parties not because I particularly enjoy them or have nothing else to do, but because it is good to be seen by the producers and directors who are there. Someone is bound to say, 'Who is that handsome guy?' and then think of me for some part." Eating and drinking together, playing cards, going to the races and to parties, and week-ending with important people, is emphasized much more here than in other places, for a number of reasons. There are a large number of people with very little ability, but with no limits for their ambitions; for them, knowing the right people is most important. Also, the movie industry is one in which there are few standards of measurement and in which personal tastes and hunches therefore play an important role. Social ties can influence both and they likewise give a feeling of stability in a very uncertain situation, in which there are many elements beyond the actor's (or writer's, director's or producer's) control. A gifted actor may be in an unsuccessful picture or in an unsuitable role through no fault of his own, in the same way that a talented writer or director may have had to work on a poor picture. Social ties can carry the actor over the period of the bad picture. If he is still O.K. with the powers that be, he is more economically secure; and if his good social connections are publicized, his standing in the industry is also more stable.

Getting a strong role which gives an actor a chance to display his ability is naturally highly important in the climb to stardom, and the difficulties and maneuvering to secure these good roles have already been described. Even a distinguished actress with a record of Broadway success talks about getting the breaks in such roles. They do *not* come, she says, because of her reputation.

Persistence and hard work are usually necessary ingredients of all success stories, but by themselves not enough. Ability and talent are very important too; but they do not always find their way to the top in Hollywood, particularly if they have not first been recognized on Broadway.

Miss Purposeful, in her late thirties, with some but not outstanding talent, is a star after long years of hard work. She had the advantage of a comfortable middle-class background in Los Angeles; and her mother, who had given up stage ambitions for marriage, was determined that her daughter should have what she missed. Accordingly, Miss Purposeful took dancing and singing lessons almost as soon as she could walk. Then the mother pushed her into child parts. But the parts were always small and she never achieved any real recognition. By the time Miss Purposeful was seventeen, she was still unknown, working hard to get a part in Westerns, for which she earned about $100 for a week or ten days' work. Since she lived at home, she did not suffer as other actors in the same circumstances. She was lucky, too, she says, in having a small independent agent who worked hard to make her successful. Today he works for one of the biggest agencies and would not bother with people at the bottom. Through him, seven or eight years ago, she got her first big break, a leading role in an A picture, which was a box-office success. She enjoys reminiscing about how much it meant. Her first *première*, the first requests from fans for autographs, the first interviews with the press, all had an exciting quality which is considerably lessened now that they have become part of a routine.

Miss Purposeful is exceptional in that she does not regard herself as a great actress. She says simply that acting was what she had been trained for since childhood, what she had experience in, and that it is very lucrative financially. She also likes to act and cannot imagine herself doing anything else, but she does not think of her profession as a glamorous one. She knows too well its monotonous routine and the hard work involved, even after one is a star. She gets up at five or five-thirty to be at the studio in time to have her hair washed and set, to be made up, and so on. Then there comes the long day, which may end as late as seven or eight o'clock, if there is overtime. She does not consider great talent necessary to becoming a good actress but she emphasizes that one must have a personality which comes across in the film, be able to follow the directions of the director, and work very hard. She says that a good director is responsible for most good acting. With his help she thinks through her parts, plans them carefully and gives a polished performance. Miss Purposeful is far more realistic in her appraisal of herself and of her career than are most actresses.

It is not possible to determine with any accuracy the relative significance of luck, ability, hard work, publicity, sex behavior, beauty, perseverance, playing the game, in attaining stardom. Even if it could be found out, it would not be the same for each star, and the emphasis would vary widely. It has been said that at least part of Lana Turner's success was due to either the planned or accidental factor of her becoming known as the "sweater girl." The preceding styles had emphasized the flat-chested, boyish figure, and she started a new trend by showing off her rounded bosom to its best advantage. Men liked the change from the flat-chested heroines, as well as her obvious good looks, and she clicked at the box office. As we have seen, sex behavior is not today the important element it is supposed to be by most of the young female aspirants. Publicity and playing the social game are always good, but alone are not sufficient. Perseverance and a drive strong enough to survive many disappointments are essential ingredients but again do not necessarily bring success by themselves.

All actors stress the importance of breaks. These are emphasized more in Hollywood than anywhere else because of the lack of apprenticeship, or any specific path leading to success. The little girl who has won a beauty contest in Iowa and been spotted by some enterprising talent scout, sees only the final end, stardom, and is lacking in awareness that there is any process in becoming one. Most aspirants in other fields — doctors, engineers, musicians, manufacturers, and others — are aware of the years of preparations which precede success. The heads of studios share the point of view of the young starlets, believing in the breaks whether it is for their own careers, for the success of a movie at the box office, or in the making of a star. There is rarely a well-thought-out program of how a studio could make a good star. It is taken for granted that suitable roles are a matter of accident or fought for by the actors. Real training is absent, and the studio either relies on Broadway for established stars or on accidentally having someone brought to their attention through a publicity build-up.

However stars are made, their effect on the quality and nature of movies is all-pervasive: a movie and a particular role are often conceived and made only as a vehicle for a star. Sometimes the front office suddenly tells a producer that he must have a movie ready quickly for a particular star under contract: they are paying her an enormous salary and she is not working. So a movie is written in a hurry and tailored to fit her. Other roles are of little importance. Almost any movie produced in this fashion, no matter how gifted the people concerned with it, is poor. The system also works negatively in sometimes preventing a good picture from being made, either because it is not the proper vehicle for any star under contract and the studio cannot borrow an appropriate one, or because the script does not call for a conventionally starred role.

The star system is responsible also for many drastic changes during the shooting, which are not necessarily dictated by the needs of the movie. Once an A movie of the psychological murder type was being shot and the first lead was played by a well-known female star. The second lead — a male — who played the role of the murderer, was the more gifted actor, but not as well known. When the picture was about one-third shot the producer decided that the actor playing the murderer was being featured too much and detracting from the prominence of the star, on whose build-up the studio had previously spent so much money. So, the producer suggested that *she* become the murderer. Rumor has it that the star herself was the one to suggest the change, and that the producer, who has a reputation for good judgment but weak character, was dominated by the star and front office. Regardless of from whom the suggestion first came, it was put into effect, but without reshooting the third of the picture that had already been done. Reshooting, the studio decided, would be too costly and make the picture go over the estimated budget and there was only some quick rewriting of that part of the script which had not yet been shot. In the final picture the motivation for the murder is completely confused and the picture seems to fall apart in the middle. Neither one of the two major roles comes off. When the second lead suddenly had to shift his main motivation, his role became phony, as did also the star's part. The movie, as might be expected, turned out poorly, was not very successful and actually lowered the star's prestige. The mistake in aesthetic judgment was also a mistake in business judgment. The producer of this picture happened to have far better than average taste and judgment, but was apparently dominated by the star and the front office.

In another picture the two leading characters were not young. A secondary part was that of a young woman. This was known when the script was accepted by the producer and the director, and the entire picture was shot in this manner. Then, as is usual, it was run off for the head of the studio. He decided that the young woman playing the secondary role should be made into a star and so he ordered drastic cuts in the parts of the two older leading characters. It happened that the sequences dealing with their motivation and making them believable was in the footage cut out. When the picture was released, the reason for the behavior of the two leads was completely mysterious. An executive had sacrificed the meaning of the picture in order to build up a star. This, of course, could have been done by giving her a picture in which she would have been featured from the beginning. But while most executives swear by the star system, it is not part of Hollywood custom to plan coherently even for stars.

In one picture the star insisted on an ending which was not fitting psychologically or aesthetically, because it allowed her an increased footage in certain hysterical scenes. The producer, director and writer were all in disagreement with her and wanted another kind of ending. But the star won out. Sometimes when a star sees the rushes she insists on changes being made because she is not sufficiently prominent and she is afraid another actor has stolen her scene. For this reason, a less prominent actor may be left lying on the cutting-room floor.

The system of accenting so heavily the beauty of the star causes some actresses to become obsessed with their looks. The beautiful heroine who is rescued from drowning insists that at the rescue every hair must be in place and that her looks be perfect as usual. She says, with some degree of truth, that she has been exploited for her beauty, and that this must therefore be maintained regardless of what the acting situation calls for. In one movie the star, who was supposed to have spent a worried and sleepless night, objected violently when she saw a close-up which showed a few lines in her face. She angrily told the director that she looked simply awful, worse than Miss X who appeared in the same sequence, playing the role of an older woman. (Actually the two women were about the same age, but Miss X was a gifted character actress.) The director replied, "But darling, you are supposed to have been up all night, to be very worried — and this must show on your face. Miss X isn't supposed to have spent a sleepless night." The argument continued and in this case the director, who was a strong and commanding personality, eventually won at least sufficiently to have a few lines appear on the star's face.

The type casting of stars is detrimental in many cases to the development of talent and to a long career. If a girl is cast only to display her youthful beauty, she is finished as an actress when she is no longer young. It is somewhat pathetic to see women in their late thirties and early forties still trying to play the young-girl parts in which they were originally typed. Of course some of the stars cast for their looks have really nothing else to offer and would be finished in any case when their youthful beauty faded. But it can happen that a good-looking actor also has ability. In one such case the studio exploited only the looks of a handsome young actor, although everyone who knew him agreed that he had real ability and need not have depended purely on his appearance. But the studio was not interested in giving him the kind of role which would use his talent, and did not seem to understand that a strong role would not destroy his good looks.

Sometimes it is the effect of the star system on the personality of the star, rather than any definite studio policy, which prevents his development. This was so in the case of one actor who, while not great, did have certain gifts which could have been developed further. He was, however, influenced too much by success, which had come rather easily and which included the usual big publicity build-up, very large salary and enormous fan mail. He was also unduly impressed by the polls which seemed to indicate that a picture would be successful if he was in it. He thought the public had fallen in love with him, that the publicity built-up personality was really his own, and that all he had to do was to exhibit himself. He lost any desire he might have had earlier to create a role, and became difficult to direct. The gifts with which he had originally started functioned no longer. As an actor he was undone by the system which had made him. The fact that a number of stars with ability do constantly struggle to improve themselves, to avoid being typed, and to get diversity in roles, is a tribute to their artistic integrity.

The influence of stars on movies and Hollywood is only one part of the story. They are heroes and heroines of modern society and bear some resemblance to the heroes of primitive and pre-industrial societies which also had cycles of stories revolving around highly stylized characters. The hero was always the same, as was the villain, and no one ever expected any of the characters to change their role. The plots, too, tended to be standardized. In the movies this folk tradition persists in the framework of the most advanced technology and alongside of more sophisticated forms of acting and storytelling. It would be as unthinkable for a front office to consider Bing Crosby for a villainous part as it would be for a primitive society to change the heroic role of a totemic ancestor. Most stars are so typed that it would be possible to ex-change close-ups from one film to another without noting the dif-ference. Since the star usually plays the same type, this becomes his personality for the fan. Charlie Chaplin was, until recently, the little man buffeted about by fate. Spencer Tracy is the honest-to-God well-meaning man. Bette Davis is the neurotic woman. Edward G. Robinson is usually the sinister type. Jimmy Stewart is a nice, simple guy, on the naïve and idealistic side. Jeanne Crain is the sweet, innocent, small-town girl, while Eve Arden is comic and sophisticated. Humphrey Bogart, with an occasional exception, is from the underworld, and Lauren Bacall is the gunman's moll. Susan Hayward is spoiled and headstrong or bitchy, and Katharine Hepburn is always upper-class and usually brittle. The premise is that the audience comes to see the star, rather than to watch him act.

The relationship of fans to their stars is not limited to seeing them in movies, any more than primitive people's relationship to their totemic heroes is limited to hearing a myth told occasionally. In primitive society there is a deep biological tie between the people and their mythical heroes, since these are also their ancestors. They are important to all members of the clan or tribe, young and old, and the myths and folk tales about them serve as sanctions for behavior and customs. In our society the identification of fans with their movie heroes may be equally intimate, but for different reasons.

Fan magazines give details of the star's domestic and so-called private life, with pictures of his home, his garden, his swimming pool, his family, his dogs and his cats. The columnists in the daily paper expand this with what type of underwear he wears, whether he prefers noodle soup to tomato. The fan is permitted to have a peep show into night clubs and into bedrooms, and knows with whom the hero dines and dances, to what parties he goes and to whom he is engaged, a ritual term for "affair." Through the close-up on the screen the fan knows every intimate physical detail of the hero's face — the eyebrows, the lines around his eyes if the star is male, the quiver of his lips, the expression of his mouth, the whiteness and shape of his teeth, how he sets his jaw, and many more. Likewise, he knows every tone of the hero's and heroine's voice, whether it be a husky monotone or one of many inflections. The star need not be perfect. In fact, it is easier for the audience to identify itself with a hero with some blemish. In a discussion of their favorite stars, in themes by an English class, a group of Freshmen indicated that they could identify best with someone whose figure was not too perfect, or who was not too, too handsome and beautiful. They felt more at home with such a star, in whom they could see some of their own imperfections. Part of Bing Crosby's popularity is often attributed to his being so much like an everyday, average kind of person.

Certainly no folk hero or god has ever been known so intimately by his admirers as are the movie stars. But, of course, none of the ancient gods had publicity departments. The fan clubs organized throughout the country strengthen this intimacy, as the star sends their members his autographed photograph. In our society the autograph appears to be a kind of magical symbol for the person. In primitive societies, where writing is unknown, hair combings and fingernail parings have an even deeper symbolic quality.

When stars transgress some of society's rules and even come into contact with the law most of the time their popularity does not diminish and may even be increased. In the past, Errol Flynn's trial on girl charges seems only to have endeared him more to his fans, particularly the female ones, perhaps because his strength as a symbol of male virility was increased. The judge is reported to have said during the trial that he received many letters from women who were mothers, coming to the actor's defense. Triangle matrimonial situations which make the headlines do not necessarily diminish the popularity of the principals, nor does an arrest in a marijuana raid. Rita Hayworth's charm seems only to have been increased by her publicized battles with an ex-husband, Eddie Judson, her separations from Orson Welles, and her travels around Europe with a royal prince, who later became husband number three. Often, there is the attitude that a movie hero or heroine can do no wrong, when they appear to indulge their instinctual life more than is customary. Perhaps the fan would like only the chance to do the same. What young girl would not get secret satisfaction out of a fantasy of traveling through Europe with an enormously wealthy nobleman lavishing her with attentions? However, this is not always the case. The clamor raised over Ingrid Bergman's broken marriage and her relationship with the director, Rossellini, indicates that she was a very different symbol to movie fans than was Rita Hayworth. But in general the studio's worry about actors' indiscretions is not because of their effect on fans, but because of fear of organized pressure groups who are self-constituted censors of morals.

The relationship between the stars and their admirers is further strengthened through other mass communications. Many of the popular movie actors and actresses are heard regularly on radio programs. Much fiction in popular magazines deals in some manner with movies. In a syndicated Sunday magazine section there was a story of a girl who did not marry because she could not find a man who fulfilled her glamorous ideal.[4] However, at the age of thirty-five she became scared that she might forever remain single, and married a nondescript, unglamorous person whom she did not love. After a few years of this loveless marriage (on her part),

[4] Jessica Wellner, "The Blinding Moment," in *This Week Magazine. Los Angeles Times*, March 9, 1947.

she grew frightened one evening that her husband might have been drowned on a sailing trip when he did not return at the expected time. When he comes home a bit later, she is much relieved and very happy to see him. Love has finally come to the heroine because, the author writes, she suddenly noticed that, when her husband smiled, he looked like Ronald Colman.

There is an important major difference between primitive societies and our own in the relationships of folk heroes to their followers. Movie fans are mostly adolescents and young people, and statistical studies have recently revealed that a majority of the audience is under thirty years of age. This is in sharp contrast to primitive societies where the admirers of folk heroes are of all ages and represent the entire tribe. The stereotypes of our movie stars seem to meet the personality needs primarily of the young and of adolescents, and perhaps, of front office executives. The oft heard statement of a studio head, "If I don't like a picture, no one will," is true today for only a small part of the potential movie audience. What many executives do not yet realize is that large sections of the population are more grown up than they themselves are.

But the sure potency of the star formula is now being questioned even in Hollywood, and an occasional executive expresses skepticism. Mr. Selznick says: "It is much less public taste than traditional and outmoded thinking in the industry itself that keeps the illusory stellar names working." [5] *Variety* has a story with the headline **Stars Ain't What They Used to Be,** and continues:

Overturn of many long-accepted ideas on the value of stars to pictures is, in fact, one of the most significant results of Hollywood's disturbed state. Aside from the established lure of a handful of these, perhaps, twenty-five at the most, who provide producers with "insurance" — or the "illusion of insurance" as David O. Selznick put it last week — many students of the industry are coming to the conclusion that there are mighty few players who count for a dollar at the b.o. [6]

[5] *Variety*, March 10, 1948.
[6] *Ibid.*

A number of months later, the paper had an article under the headline **Hot Stars with Cold Yarns Give Hollywood Lukewarm Profits,** and gave the following account of the situation:

> Film stars proved no longer enough to "insure" pix producer profits – the role in which they have been traditionally cast. Weighing stars against stories in a survey of top grossing films of the year, balance appears definitely on the story side in terms of profit to the producer. In other words, he has a much better chance of turning a fast buck with a hot yarn and a lightweight cast than with a top marquee name and not much of a script. Top profits, of course, generally lie in the perfect combo of a solid script backed by players powerful at the b.o. But a surprising number of top-grossers of the year owe their coin almost entirely to the story and a cast that is competent but not highly marquee worthy.[7]

Until the Rossellini affair, Miss Ingrid Bergman has been at the top in almost every poll for popularity. She rated as being able to make a picture a box-office success on her name alone,[8] but the *Arch of Triumph,* in which she starred, was not successful, grossing only $1,700,000 according to reports. Other pictures with stars who had been considered as sure insurance for big profits which disappointed their studios in returns were: [9]

Mr. Blanding Builds His Dream House with Cary Grant and Myrna Loy
The Paradine Case with Gregory Peck
It Had To Be You with Ginger Rogers
So Evil My Love with Ray Milland
Winter Meeting with Bette Davis
Time of Your Life with James Cagney
Saxon Charm with Robert Montgomery

On the other hand there have been a number of large profit-making films in which the leading roles were played by actors not regarded as having box-office pull, some of them having previously played second leads only. Among these are *Naked City* with

[7] *Ibid.,* Dec. 22, 1948.
[8] *Ibid.,* May 21, 1949.
[9] *Ibid.,* Dec. 22, 1948.

Barry Fitzgerald, *Red River* with John Wayne and Montgomery Clift, *T-Men* with Dennis O'Keefe, *Sitting Pretty* with Clifton Webb, *Street with No Name* with Mark Stevens and Richard Widmark. Only recently has effort and money been put into selling pictures without star names. This is one of the new trends, running parallel with the strongly intrenched star system which is still regarded as an essential part of the formula in making movies. Only a few have dared to question its efficacy.

Stars are obviously one of the essential ingredients of all theater, including movies, but it need not be taken for granted that they have to dominate and supersede every other element in production. Nor is there any reason why movie stars should not work in a system which gives them training and emphasizes the quality of acting. The problem is tied up with the general Hollywood attitude to movie production.

Actors Are People

WHAT are actors really like in their relationships with the other members of the industry? How does Hollywood's own stereotype of actors compare with the glamorous one which the world has?

In Hollywood, actors are not regarded as ordinary people, either. But instead of being admired, they are looked down upon as a kind of subhuman species. No one respects them. The cliché that there are three kinds of people — men, women, and actors — is heard over and over again. They are often described as children who do not know what is good for them, immature, irresponsible, completely self-centered, egotistical, exhibitionistic, nitwits, and utterly stupid. Part of this description is reminiscent of white attitudes in the Deep South toward Negroes. Hollywood attitudes towards actors range from pitying condescension to contempt, hostility and hatred. It is difficult to find anyone who has a good word to say for them. Usually one hears, in belligerent tones, "I can't stand actors." The star system has decidedly boomeranged in Hollywood.

The actor is regarded by the studio as a valuable but synthetic product of make-up department, cameraman, publicity agent, director, producer, and front office. Rarely is he given credit for having any ability, and the front-office executive, who thinks of himself as the creative source of everything from stars and scripts to the final movie, sincerely believes that it is he who created the star. Did he not bring him from Broadway, or, according to the legend, snatch her from the soda-fountain stool? Provide the script, the director, the publicity and all the resources of the studio — not to mention the negotiations with the bank for the necessary capital? An executive often talks as if his was a disinterested act of creation, in which his own rewards were quite secondary. There is, how-ever, the disconcerting fact that his object of creation is human and, worse, not always grateful, and even at times impertinently critical and resentful. Over and over, almost like a refrain, is heard, "Look what I did for the s.o.b., brought him over from Europe and paid his passage" — or, "Took the bitch from a night club floor"; or: "Look what I've made them into; look at their swimming pools, at their popularity rating, and do they ever say *Thank you?* Do the bastards know what gratitude is? No! They dare tell me that the story I paid seventy-five thousand for is no good, that they are tired of playing the same role — telling me, who made the s.o.b.'s famous and spent a fortune building them up!"

To make life even harder for the executive, this ungrateful cre-ation must be pampered and kept in good humor with all kinds of blandishments. For if he is in bad humor, it may be reflected in his acting. Or, if he gets mad, he may feign illness and stay home causing great financial loss to the studio. It is reported the actor may even go to a hospital and have his appendix removed merely to spite the studios. The executive's attitude is a combination of cracking the whip to the tune of the contract and at the same time cuddling and wheedling with endearments. Terms of address are always "darling" and "sweetheart" between males as well as males and females, followed by the most exaggerated compliments. These and costly presents, parties, and week ends on a yacht or in the desert seem to be like the oil which the mechanic uses to grease his machinery and keep it running smoothly. Underneath all the blandishments, the executive regards the star as not only his creation, but as his property, legally owned for seven years, which he can use as he pleases or loan out for a profit, and on whom demands can be made continuously, away from the studio as well as on the set. And the stars, talented and untalented, in-telligent and stupid, know this and resent it. As they recline in an easy chair on the patio facing the swimming pool, or converse over the lunch table at The Players or Romanoff's restaurant, they give their reaction in no uncertain terms. They hate their bosses, whom they regard as ignorant and stupid fools.

It is the big stars who tell, with malice aforethought, the biting tales to expose, what they consider, the stupidity and naïveté of executives and producers for whom they work. One tells how the head of a major studio was entertaining at luncheon a European diplomat and had invited a number of top stars and producers to be present. The diplomat had given an informal talk, saying how impressed he had been with the way people could think as they chose in the United States and with the high degree of diversity permitted. When he finished his speech, the head of the studio arose and said that if anyone did not think the United States was the best place in the world he should be either shot or deported. The diplomat's face was red. Another kind of story which stars gleefully tell is that concerned with the past backgrounds of the big executives. Many, according to the tales, were bankrupt failures from small businesses before they came to Hollywood. One had been a notorious gambler. Another never learned to read and must have a story told to him. Another knows more about horses than movies. All have made many and costly mistakes. And these are the men, the stars continue, who are paid enormous salaries and who have the power to make the actor toe the line. The feeling is shared by the character actors, the second leads, and the bit players. One star recalls her feeling of resentment of five years ago when no one in the studio thought of phoning to tell her she had her first big part, for which she had been so anxiously waiting. She learned about it through an announcement in the trade press. The same bitterness comes out in the discussion of the way a studio loans them out. Even though it is to the actor's professional advantage, they resent not being at least told in advance, and to being given no share in the studio's profit.

Important in the buying and selling of actors is the agent, a middleman who handles negotiations between them and studios and, in return, receives 10 per cent of the actor's earnings. Although he is usually regarded by them as the manipulator of a horse trade he, too, fancies himself playing God, a lesser one than the executive and producer, but still important. Every agent has a tale to tell of how he is responsible for making a certain star. He discovered him, or he secured the role which made him click with the public, or he arranged a deal by which the star got his first big picture, and so on and on to the same tune.

The agent is supposed to be working continuously for his clients' interests, by securing better roles and creating a demand for him. Actually the agent's role is not on such a simple level, but is very complicated and becoming more so. His activities consist of a clever and skilled juggling of many factors. This is particularly true when he is connected with a large agency which owns a block of stock in one or several studios. The agency therefore has two interests, one, its clients', and the other, the clients' bosses. The actor may be a pawn in a very complicated game and can never be sure whether the agent is working for or against him. There are wheels within wheels and the "package deal" is becoming more and more common. The agent may sell to the studio a number of people — an actor or actors, a director, and sometimes a writer — assembling the various ones necessary for a picture in one package. The individual actor's gain is not, therefore, the sole goal; he is arranged with other pieces of property and sold at the largest profit to the agent.

In one situation an actor with star billing, playing second leads, was under contract to a studio, which was not using him at the time when he was in demand by several others. The actor preferred one of the studios who made a bid for him, because he liked the script and the role it offered. But he did not get what he wanted, because the agent found it more advantageous to sign him up with another studio which was also bidding for his services. The agent was trying to get into a good relationship with this studio, in order to place another client. The first actor was used as part of a trade, to help place the second one, and this took precedence over the first one's personal interests and preferences. Sometimes when various deals are in the offing, the actor may not know whether he is coming or going, and is constantly on the phone trying to learn where he stands. It is this function of juggling men's professional lives, making deals and various combinations, that makes the agent feel he, too, is God. He also considers his role a paternalistic one, guiding the steps of the immature actors and advising the older ones; and one agent even mentioned casually that he was sending a client to a psychoanalyst. But most of the actors feel that their agents would sell them down the river if that were profitable. The essence of the actor's attitude is the acceptance of the agent as a necessary evil. He usually thinks that the agent is really helpful only after success has already been attained. There are, of course, the exceptions. An occasional actor trusts his agent and there are several agents who are trusted by all who know them, including their clients.

The actors probably have less contact with the writers than with any other group in Hollywood, but each group talks with great emotion and in the most unflattering terms about the other. The writers join the chorus of how utterly stupid all actors are, how their only aim in life is to exhibit themselves, how adulation has gone to their heads spoiling any ability they might have had. One writer describes the actors' status in Hollywood as that of foul-smelling cattle. At best, they are said to be puppets, unintellectual and emotional. Columnist Frank Scully writes:

> I view the crediting of brains to such people [actors] with something like encroachment. . . . Thinking is a writer's property-right, not an actor's. The greater the thinker, the greater the writer, and the greater the imitator the greater the actor.[1]

The actor returns the compliment by saying that writers are good-for-nothing hack men, and, even if they have some ability, are too lazy to use it.

The strongest mutual hostility exists between actors and publicity men. "All actors stink" is the practically universal attitude of Hollywood publicity men, and the detailed descriptions of their clients as arrogant, vulgar, and completely stupid make the actors seems almost unhuman. When this is pointed out the answer is, "Well, they aren't human!" Publicity men grant that there is

[1] *Variety*, April 30, 1947.

an occasional exception: perhaps three or four actors out of the four thousand belong to *Homo sapiens*, but that is all.

The publicity men of course join the Hollywood chorus of "I made the star what he is." They feel they are the ones who have created the glamour, and pulled the strings. They are the ones who arrange for and accompany the stars on their personal appearances, who get them out of jams, and who, in the publicity men's own words, act as nursemaids. When the stars are making personal appearances away from Los Angeles, for the opening of their movies, they are accompanied by publicity men. If one of the stars drinks too much and there have been several occasions when he has been too drunk to make his appearance, the publicity man never lets the actor out of his sight, arguing, coaxing, and sometimes forcibly keeping him from drinking. Or, an actress comes in after a long day of public appearances on an out-of-town junket — tired, with wet feet — no curl left in her hair — and he has to persuade her to see a press representative who has been waiting for her. It is part of the publicity man's job to see that the junket gets as much space as possible in the papers and therefore that the actress is nice to the press. Or an actor to whom the publicity man is assigned has a fight in a café, which has potentialities for unfavorable publicity. The nursemaid gets him home as quickly as possible and then passes out drinks to the reporters who swarm about for news of the brawl, keeps them from taking pictures and, as far as possible, from writing about it. A publicity man may be assigned to an actress whom the studio is priming for stardom. He corrects her clothes, tells her with whom to go out, builds up interesting stories about her past, arranges some of her dates, and sits by protectively guiding the conversation when she interviews reporters and columnists. All this is just part of the daily and nightly job of publicity men, whether on a junket or in Hollywood.

What they gripe most about is when the actor goes highhat on them. Every publicity man tells of the stars who, he says, without him would still be playing bit parts, and who were nice and cooperative before becoming successful. Then the story changes. They appear to believe the publicity about their importance, and become difficult, rude and arrogant. They keep the publicity man waiting for hours, and treat him as if he were an infectious plague. Nevertheless, he has to grind out stories. A good one can usually get some kind of story from even an unsuccessful interview. The actor will have said at least one little thing which can be built up. But, the publicity man complains, once the actor is a star he refuses even this, although the studio expects the publicity to go on. So, when the star is difficult or refuses an interview, the publicity man writes a story from his imagination. Being human, after he finds out how much easier this is than trying to get interviews, he is not apt to bother about them. Most of the publicity men think that the reason the stars are difficult to interview is not because they do not like publicity, but simply because they are too lazy to grant an interview. According to the publicity man, the stars consider themselves as "personalities" rather than real people, and they cannot see why the publicity man should not dream up stories about the "personality" and not bother them. And the publicity men, who do not really regard the actors as human beings, cannot understand why these synthetic creatures should not want to have their so-called private lives publicized in magazines and newspapers.

Some actors get quite excited on the subject, calling publicity men "dishonest parasites." All resent the publicity men's claims that they have "made" them, since they say that publicity cannot make an audience like an actor or make him into a popular star, which, they contend, is due to the actor's own personality and ability. One of the top stars says that publicity men do not make fans, but simply cater to the latter's never-ending desire to hear more and more about their beloved heroes. He says that the fans come into existence because thousands of people all over the world like an actor when they see him on the screen. Publicity, he adds, cannot make this happen or make an actor good, although he does admit that even an able actor may be helped by publicity.

Although all actors resent the publicity man's claim that he has made them, their reasons vary. For the talented actor, secure in the knowledge of his own ability, training, and experience, and for whom publicity has been relatively incidental to success, there is a natural resentment at the publicity man's claim to credit. Others not conspicuous for their talent and who do owe much of their success to publicity, cannot afford, psychologically, to have the belief in their own ability threatened by the publicity man's claim. It is human for anyone to want to believe that his success is due to his own ability, beauty, charming personality, or combination of them, rather than to the stories a publicist has dreamed up. For the actor whose profession meets such deep personality needs, this is probably even more necessary than for other people. So, regardless of the truth, or lack of it, in the publicity man's claims, he is resented by all actors, talented or merely photogenic. The actors are also exasperated by the kind of publicity that is turned out about them. Stupid or intelligent, they do not like having their private lives, from the state of their marital affairs to the kind of cereal they eat for breakfast, either truly or falsely broadcast to the public. The premise on which such publicity is based is that the whole person of the actor is the property of the studio to be exploited for its benefit. The fact that it may redound also to the actor's profit does not negate his deep and bitter resentment to being so exploited.

The business managers, whom most actors and other Hollywood people making over $25,000 a year employ, do not participate in the refrain of "I created the stars," but they share in the general attitude of treating their clients as children. The institution of business manager has become increasingly popular partly because of high and complicated income taxes. However, this is not the only reason. For almost all the top successes in Hollywood, great wealth is a new experience. They are without training in the handling of big money as compared to those whose wealth goes back at least a couple of generations. Also, among these, the control of wealth is usually in the hands of the older members of the family, while in Hollywood the stars are relatively young. Again, the star has not as much assurance of continued income as has the big industrialist, and there is hardly a star who does not have at least a twinge of anxiety when he sees a former star of the old silent films now working as an extra. The business manager has therefore become an institution. He works out a budget for his client and family, with specific amounts to be spent for running the house, for clothes, for personal allowances for husband, wife and children, for payments to dependents, for contributions to causes, and for other expenses. After the agent has deducted his 10 per cent, he sends the actor's salary checks directly to the business manager who pays the bills, makes out the various allowance checks, and saves or invests the remainder. This means that there is very little about the actor's life the latter does not know. If a mistress is being supported or there are large losses at cards or on horses, the manager knows it.

Most business managers are deeply earnest about their work and see themselves in the combined role of guardians as well as businessmen who handle money. They tend to regard their clients as children, to whom they give allowances. A business agent may refuse to allow a client to spend too much money on expensive presents for a boy friend or girl friend and argue him out of what he considers other foolish extravagance or scare him with stories about what happened to a star who did not save his money. Interestingly enough many of the clients seem to forget that it is really their money which is doled out to them. One business manager who handles top-bracket people says he will not keep clients who lie in an attempt to wheedle money out of him. The $100,000-a-year star who tries to get some cash on false pretenses just does not remain his client.

Another business manager, who takes his role equally seriously, is accustomed to receiving phone calls at all hours to come to the aid of his clients. One phones at six in the morning that he is in trouble at a gambling joint and will the business manager come quickly. The trouble may be money or a fight. Or the wife of a client calls him, angry and excited, to tell him that her husband came home drunk at four A.M. and crawled into bed with the Negro maid, and she is never going to sleep with him again and is going to start divorce proceedings at once. The business manager rushes over and effects a reconciliation. The wife remains, but the maid leaves.

The star is thus regarded as the ward, property or creation of business manager, agent, publicity man, producer and executive. Besides all these, the technical crew, including carpenters and electricians, has a power of its own to bring an actor to heel. Although this group is low in the social hierarchy, on the set it can sabotage and disrupt an actor's work. If a "grip" (handy man) does not like an actor, he can drop a monkey wrench or make some other seemingly accidental noise just when the actor is at the height of a climax, and then the scene has to be shot again. A "gaffer" (electrician) may drop a sun lamp next to the actor and terrify him, and the lights can likewise be used to the actor's advantage or disadvantage. When an actor is rehearsing a sequence, a carpenter can look at him in a peculiar way, or make unflattering remarks under his breath, the purport of which the actor gets and which is disturbing. Or, the crew can carry tales to a newspaper columnist about a star who loses his temper and has a tantrum on the set, tearing off his wig and flinging things about, which is bad publicity.

What do the crew of workers have against actors, that they should want to sabotage them? Electricians and carpenters are self-respecting, middle-class skilled workers, who in traditional American fashion do not accept a class system. They do not like to be high-hatted, and so they do not like a star who emphasizes social distance between them or who is not hail-fellow-well-met. They have also the conventional morality of the middle class and do not like actors who they think are too free and easy with young girls or who make obscene jokes before the latter. One actor was hated because his idea of a good time was to indulge in the custom of "goosing," or tickling the posterior of a person and causing him to jump in a startled fashion. The technical crew often serves as a kind of moral control over the actors' behavior on the set.

The long waits which occur every day provide many opportunities for the tone of such relationships to be set. Most of the actors are friendly with the crew, either because they actually enjoy joking and kibitzing with them or because they think it is necessary. Of course, this hail-fellow-well-met relationship ends abruptly when the working day is over.

The field worker is struck with the intensity of reactions to actors by everyone from the front office down. So rarely does anyone have a good word to say for them! There are a number of reasons for what seems to be this overreaction. First, there is a deep well of envy — envy of the actors' enormous salaries, envy of the way they are glamorized, envy of their publicity. To the public Hollywood means the stars, and the names of even important producers, directors, and writers are frequently unknown. In the movie advertisements in many small-town newspapers, only the names of the actors appear along with the title of the movie and even the studio's name may be omitted. All Hollywood has concentrated on selling its product through the stars, and now seems to be resentful of its success. The constant negation of the actor's ability and the chorus of "I made him what he is" has a compensatory quality for the godlike position the stars occupy. The executive, the producer, the publicity man try to get some comfort through the refrain, "Without me he would be a nobody." With the exception of the top executives, the stars also earn more money than anyone else in Hollywood. Even though the level of earnings for everyone in the movie industry is higher than anywhere else, this does not lessen the envy of the stars' fabulous income.

Some of the envy may be on a deeper level than jealousy of salaries and adulation from the public. Resentment of the exhibitionistic quality of the actor's personality is stressed over and over again. Now, some degree of exhibitionism is part of being human. But our culture frowns upon any excessive display of it and has very strong taboos against sexual exhibitionism. Probably most members of our society have at some time or other in their lives, in infancy or later, been frustrated in not being as exhibitionistic as they desired. In Hollywood, and the whole show business world, there is a higher level of permissiveness for exhibitionism than in most other areas of living. But no one in all Hollywood can compete in exhibitionism with the actors. And, groan the envious ones, these actors are paid huge salaries for *that!*

There is probably a selective personality factor underlying the choice of acting as a profession. This is true for many professions. Philosophers and theoretical physicists tend to be rather introverted. The reformer and crusader usually have another type of personality, and the doctor still another. Some of these may be strongly exhibitionistic, too, but they do not literally cash in on it as do actors. Even in Hollywood, where almost everyone struts and where boasting is carried to superlative heights, the actors are the only ones who receive hard cash for exhibitionism. Hollywood has created a mammoth machine to exploit the exhibitionistic quality of its actors and the people who have done the most to build the machine appear deeply envious that they are not the objects exhibited.

There is a particular intensity in the venomous feelings which the publicity men have towards their clients. For this there are additional causes. The men who write publicity are more anonymous than anyone else. In one studio the publicity department has a sign, "Anonymity Department." The publicity men are also much less well paid than other Hollywood people and refer to themselves as the poor relations of the industry. Both these reasons add to their hostility. Then, too, many publicity men are highly intelligent and superior to the work they do. Some are ambitiously writing novels, plays and scripts on the side. They do not respect their publicity work, whether directed towards the industry or the public, and are generally contemptuous of the kind of hocus-pocus they spend their days turning out. But they stay on the jobs because these provide higher salaries than they can earn elsewhere. It may well be that the publicity men deflect at least part of their scorn and contempt from what they write to the objects about whom they write. This is a rather common psychological mechanism which helps make the job more bearable. Another possible reason for the extremity of the publicity men's scorn for their clients is that they are with them so continuously in the role of valet nursemaid, which traditionally does not lend itself to an attitude of respect.

The general contemptuous attitude of Hollywood to actors is based on a stereotype, that of the star without any ability, unintelligent, chosen almost entirely for some photogenic quality, and earning a fabulous salary. He is considered to be a puppet made by the various studio departments and this is strengthened by "type" casting. This stereotype does exist, but it is not representative of all actors. There seems to be as much diversity in intelligence and ability among them as there is among Hollywood writers or any

other group of people, in and out of Hollywood. The character actors are almost uniformly talented and many of them intelligent.
But the publicity men hardly ever come in contact with them.
Their work is almost entirely among the stars. Among these, too,
are intelligent and gifted men and women, as well as stupid people
whose only aim in life is sheer exhibitionism. But it is these who
have become the stereotype for the entire actor group. Only the
directors, who work closely with all kinds of actors and who really
are concerned in their success, have a more realistic concept of their
diversity and are less hostile to them. For most Hollywood people,
the thinking is confused, as thinking always is when based on a stereotype and motivated by envy. Many actors are quite aware of the
contempt in which they are held. A few have accepted the stereotyped picture as some members of a minority group accept the position accorded them by a dominant group. One actor and his wife
boasted that they did not go socially with other actors, but they
were an exception. Most of the actors react with bitterness to the
scorn which underlies the "darlings" and "sweethearts."

To answer the question, *What are actors really like?* it is necessary to know that while they share certain traits in common,
there are also wide differences among them. Many are extroverted
in nature, exhibitionistic, generous and warm. Some are gay but
quite a few, particularly the comedians, are serious. Some are gifted,
highly intelligent, and keenly alive to the world they live in, while
others have very little talent, are stupid, and might as well be living in the Middle Ages for all the understanding they have of contemporary society. For these, the disparity between earnings and
ability is particularly glaring, although the discrepancy is present
for the gifted, too, when compared to the earnings of equally gifted
people outside of Hollywood.

Some stars have remained relatively unaffected by the synthetic
glamour and idolatry so carefully nourished by the publicity department, although it is not easy for anyone to be completely
untouched by it. Others seem actually to believe the publicity circulated about them and to accept the built-up synthetic personality as their real one. The ballyhoo publicity acts as a kind of

self-poison and is reminiscent of the situation in Nathaniel Hawthorne's story, "Rappaccini's Daughter" — in which a doctor pathologically interested in experimenting with poisons feeds his daughter on them until she becomes immune and is unable to live on anything else. A normal existence would cause her death. So, too, for some stars: synthetic glamour has become essential for their continued existence.

Miss Manifest Destiny is one of the people who has become a victim of her own publicity. She is now in her mid-twenties, with limited ability, and, after many years' struggle, has recently become a star. Her background is one of poverty, with a father who died when she was an infant and a mother who had once been ambitious to be a dancer and had become a waitress. As a child Miss Manifest Destiny's formal schooling was spotty but her mother insisted on dancing lessons. Growing up meant working long and hard to become a successful dancer. When old enough she began dancing in night clubs, and eventually came to one in Hollywood. Someone from a studio saw her and she was given a contract. But nothing much happened. She made many tests but got no parts. She says that while she learned a little about acting during the two years at the studio by playing with others who were also making tests, it was a depressing period. Her roles were limited to bit parts in B pictures and she did not even have many of these. She had just about decided that it would be better to go back to night club dancing, when her agent took her over to another studio to make a test. There, a producer happened to see her sitting in the casting director's office and said he would like to consider her for a role. He had a big name and the picture he was planning was in the A class; the role, while not the star one, was featured and important. It was her first opportunity at something other than bit parts in B pictures and she felt that if only she could secure this role she was made. For two months she made all kinds of tests, eager but worried about the outcome, and finally she was given the part. She was still on a relatively low salary but at the end of the picture she was given a $5000 bonus and her salary went up fast, as she became a star for A pictures.

The effect of success on her personality is of interest. Although she had been quite successful as a night club dancer, she now looks down upon all dancing and her goal has completely changed. She fancies herself as a serious dramatic actress and as a great singer, and talks about how she would like to sing the title role in *Carmen* and be a soloist with a symphony orchestra. Her regret is that her mother sent her to dancing school instead of to dramatic and singing schools. She is absolutely sure that if she had been given this training, she would have been a great dramatic actress and singer.

Now she takes singing lessons and musical composition to enable her to read music, and she goes to one of the best dramatic schools in town, for all of which training the studio pays. Her comment on the studio paying the bills is: "I am box office for them and they make lots of money from me. So the better they make me, the better it is for them." She thinks she is doing the studio a favor when she gives her time for these lessons, particularly since some occur from six to seven in the evening after a day's work. Although she talks very seriously about the dramatic school and their use of a modification of the Stanislavsky method, she gives the impression that she is learning words rather than acting. For instance, in explaining this method, she says: "If you are tired, you must be tired during the entire scene; that is, if you are sitting in a chair and supposed to be tired you must not spring up out of the chair as though you are not tired, but must get up languidly. You must not put the tired feeling on and off."

Combined with great ambition is a belief that she is fated to be great. She says, "I believe people are destined to be great actors or commonplace mechanics, that people are meant to be small or big. Some people are just born to be important and others not to be." However, she continues, although she is destined to be a great actress, she knows she has to work hard to achieve this. She thinks that all the talk about equality is nonsense; if she is fated to be successful and also works hard to achieve it, then she deserves a big house on top of a hill with lots of servants and a swimming pool, and horses to ride. The people who are born to be mechanics are doomed to live in little houses at the foot of the hill.

She describes herself as a reactionary, and uses the term without any feeling in her voice. She adds that she rarely goes to meetings of the Actors' Guild, that she does not understand "that kind of thing, but hopes to learn about it some day." She accepts some of the things she has to do for publicity in somewhat the same spirit as she does the Guild. She describes her participation in the publicity stunts arranged in a city, which was the setting of a movie in which she starred. Although she boasts that she drew greater crowds than some of the older stars, she does not appear to have really enjoyed the junket. She was a bit scared at having to meet a lot of people and resentful of not getting enough rest. "But," she adds, "I suppose it is necessary and someday I will understand what it means to these people to see a celebrity." Actually Miss Manifest Destiny would be better described as medieval than by her own term reactionary. Her theory of predestination, of success which has been mysteriously ordained but for which she also has to work hard, is reminiscent of the Protestant Reformation. Calvinists likewise believed that they were destined for salvation and the proof that they were of the elect lay in their hard work and good deeds. But Miss Destiny stresses only the former.

She goes to many big parties and frequents night clubs and has a reputation of being "on the town." She is worried about her present lack of marital status, and says enviously that all the other stars her age have been married, and many divorced and remarried. She feels that the many reports of her engagements and the equal number of reports of the engagement being broken (one engagement was reported on and then off at least six times) by the columnists, publicizes her personal failure on this point. She complains about the difficulty of finding a husband, saying that the actors with whom she goes out are interested only in themselves and their careers and that they go out with her because it is good publicity for them, and this isn't fun for her. In the next breath she says, "And I don't want to settle down and be a little wife looking after a man. I must have my career." She thinks the difficulties with an actor would be insurmountable. Now she is looking for a cattleman or, perhaps, she hints, the anthropologist might know a likely doctor who would be a good husband.

It is unlikely that Miss Destiny's career as a star will last longer than ten years, since she has little real ability outside of dancing, and not enough intelligence to learn how to become an actress. She is amenable to direction, has a capacity for hard work, and is concentrated completely on herself and her ambition. But it is unlikely that these will be enough to maintain her status after she loses her youthful looks. She gives a sense of pathos, of an unhappy person straining for something unreachable, of being manipulated by a system of which she has no understanding.

While Miss Manifest Destiny represents a large number of actresses in her age group, there are many others who are quite different personally and professionally. Miss Serious has a Broadway background. Her father and mother were actors and she began her career by understudying on Broadway. Occasionally she was lucky enough to be given a part. She rose to being a lead in a play which, however, flopped after a week or so on Broadway. But before it closed, the head of a major studio was in the audience, and, impressed with her performance, signed her up with his studio.

Shortly after her arrival in Hollywood she was given a part she describes as "medium good." She got fine notices and people at the studio considered her good. But after this picture she did nothing for two years. She was on the studio's payroll and did not have to worry economically, but she says she nearly "went crazy," because she was not acting. Eventually she was cast in a featured role in an A production. The producer and casting director had wondered if she was old enough for this role, but everything was being done in a great hurry and the person for whom the role had originally been planned was not available. So Miss Serious was given the part and sent on location where some of the scenes were being shot. However, when the front-office executive looked at the rushes he decided that she was too young and could not be made up to look old enough for the role. She was out of the picture. This was a great disappointment although she was assured that it had nothing to do with her acting.

A short time later she was again selected for a good part in a big production. This time she thought it was sure and that this was her big break. She had been measured for her costumes and everything was in readiness. Just before the shooting was to begin, a new director was assigned to the picture and another actress was brought in to fill her role. Once more she was out. She never did understand the reason, but as far as she could learn from the grapevine, it was not the new director who insisted on bringing in another actress. The change had been made by someone in the front office. Now she thought there must be something wrong with her and that she was a failure. A bit later she was given a small part in a picture and she was so nervous over her fear of failing that it affected her acting; but the director was understanding and reassured her that she could act.

After these disappointments and three years of feeling that she was getting nowhere, she was glad when her agent mentioned an opportunity in another studio. Here she was given a good role with star billing which she played with considerable ability, receiving excellent press notices. Now she is under contract to this studio, which she likes much better than the first one. She had been surprised when she arrived in Hollywood from Broadway to find no one at that studio willing to help her. On Broadway, she says, it is customary to receive help from older and more experienced people, but at this studio everyone seemed afraid of someone higher up. She commented also that no one seemed to take acting very seriously. At the actors' lunch table, there was never any serious talk, just funny, and off-color, stories and gossip. It was all very impersonal and there were no real friendships. She felt lost. At the studio where she now is, she is impressed with the seriousness of the people and their concern about the film on which they are working. She adds that they consider the script more important than make-up.

Miss Serious has been married to an actor for the past two years and he agrees that she should continue her career. She lives quietly and does not move in any gay Hollywood circles. When she and her husband are both acting they have little time for social life. She is, of course, a member of the Screen Actors' Guild, but rarely goes to meetings. She has no interest in social problems although she has some vague rather inarticulate feeling that underpaid people should get more money and that the "poor carpenters" suffered when they were out on strike. Her whole being is centered on acting; she is seriously concerned about becoming a distinguished dramatic actress. She is intelligent enough to know that she cannot continue too long to play the young-girl romantic leads which she now has, and so she tries hard to get a strong role which will offer dramatic opportunities.

Miss Manifest Destiny and Miss Serious have both been successful. Miss Frustrated, after seven years, is still not even within sight of success. She has had no formal training and before coming to Hollywood her acting was limited to amateur theatricals and a small local stock company. But she is completely convinced that she has the makings of a great dramatic actress and all her life is centered about this intense ambition. Now in her late thirties, she knows she cannot play young-girl parts and so she concentrates on trying to get character roles. Her acting record during the last six years has been no more than twenty-five weeks of work, of which three were in one small part, fourteen in her biggest role, a character part, and the rest in odd days when she was called in for bit parts. She has managed to earn enough to live on through occasional radio work, clerical and other odd jobs. She thought the character part in the A picture, for which she was paid $400 a week, was her break, and tried to capitalize on it. Her agent, a small one, refused to help with any publicity; the studio had no interest in publicizing her since she was not under contract and they had no plans for using her further. At her own expense, she put an advertisement about herself in a trade paper and sent her photographs to local newspapers. But there were no results. She was offered nothing but a few bit parts in B pictures. Several years later she still struggles on, lives very economically, and takes odd jobs. She is not exactly unhappy because she is convinced that she is a great actress. It is not possible to know whether she has confused her intense personal need to act with ability. Since she has no training or accepted dramatic experience, no financial reserves, is no longer young and knows none of the right people, her breaks appear to lie in some never-never land. There are many others like Miss Frustrated.

Starlets are a group of young hopefuls under stock contracts at the major studios. The traditional policy has been to sign any pretty face in sight, give them training in diction and posture, and occasional bit parts. Their salaries range from $100 to $175 a week at the beginning, with increases of $25 to $50 at the end of each six months. Rarely do they go beyond the bit parts. One starlet was a pretty girl in her early twenties, from a middle-class background in a small Midwestern town. She had long wanted to be an actress and took part in amateur shows in high school and in a small local college. While still a student she began to earn her living as a model, and it was on one of these jobs that a studio talent scout saw her and arranged for her to come to Hollywood on a contract. She hung around for a number of years, doing an occasional bit part. When her contract was not renewed she went back to modeling.

Another stock contract actress is very different. She has a serious kind of beauty that is not the usual Hollywood type. She is a farmer's daughter and very early was ambitious to be a dancer. When still young she took dancing lessons in a town near her father's farm, and later gave lessons in the same town. She saved her money and went to New York. There she had the usual ups and downs with jobs as a model and dancer, and knows well the experience of being broke. Eventually she went on the road with a dancing and singing show which performed for two-week periods throughout the country. This was an extremely lonely life, spent in hotels in strange cities, but all the time she was trying to make herself into a better dancer. She never gave up her idea of dramatic dancing, even though she was not doing it at the moment. One of the Hollywood talent scouts saw her in a night club show and she was given her present contract with the studio. She came in at a higher salary than most of the other girls — $175 a week. She lives very simply in a rented room and saves as much money as she can, because there is always the fear that she will be broke again. She regrets that she cannot save as much money as she would like, because she has to spend so much on clothes, as she is expected to dress well. Her ambition has changed to becoming a dramatic actress. She is intensely earnest, working constantly on her lessons. At the studio, she is regarded as a person with ability. However, after a year there in which she has not been given any parts, she is impatient and she has decided to leave and try to get into an Eastern summer resort theater.

Interestingly enough, when any of the starlets do have success it is usually at a studio other than the one that first invested in them. A studio often seems to lack the necessary confidence in its own judgment. Recently there has been a new trend to fill small roles in A pictures with Broadway actors who are tested for the particular parts. One of Metro's Eastern talent scouts says:

> U. S. film makers are becoming increasing hep to the fact that fresh faces in minor roles add a special kind of excitement to pix. British and Continental producers regularly employ this stratagen with good results.[2]

It seems that if a number of the foreign films had not been profitable, it would have never occurred to the U. S. film makers that well-acted minor roles are important in making a good movie. Even now is it regarded as a "stratagem," or a new gimmick.

On the whole the male actors in Hollywood seem to have more ability and experience than the females. Looks, being photogenic and sexy, count for them too, and they need the same perseverance and faith in themselves as do the girls. But there appears to be no male equivalent of arriving in Hollywood through winning a contest, real or fictitious. Most of the men have come to Hollywood with some kind of theater experience. Those who were stars on Broadway are naturally stars in Hollywood, and the stories of their struggles for stardom belong to Broadway. But some did not arrive in Hollywood as stars.

Mr. Qualified, in his forties and a successful character actor with featured billing, has been in Hollywood about eleven years. He had always wanted to be an actor as far back as he can re-

[2] *Variety*, July 6, 1949.

member, and after being in high school and college theatricals and local stock companies, he went to New York. Over the years there he managed to get only minor roles and was never in any of the long-run hits. He and his family came to Hollywood because they found it increasingly difficult to live on his earnings from the Broadway stage.

During his first year in Hollywood he was pleased when he earned about $5000 and assumed this was just the beginning and that he would go up quickly to the higher brackets. So he saved nothing, although the $5000 was considerably more than he had ever averaged in New York. But he earned practically nothing the second and third years, and for no reason that he could understand. He was able to secure only bit parts and these only occasionally. However, Mr. Qualified did not lose faith in his ability and eventual success. Besides, there was no other place for him to go. He and his family managed to live during these two lean years through the help of friends. Then Mr. Qualified played a bit part so well it was expanded to a larger one. From there he went on to a number of small but important parts, and eventually into bigger, featured roles. Now, after eleven years, he has a very good income, lives in a beautiful home, and is regarded by everyone as quite successful. But he does not feel secure, and he is always talking about buying a farm — not because he is interested in rural life, but because for him a farm spells security. Mr. Qualified has never played the Hollywood social game or done the usual night-clubbing and parties. He and his wife choose their friends, many of whom are not connected with movies, on the basis of congeniality. He is regarded as liberal and his interests cover social and political issues of the day. He is an active participant in both the Actors' Guild and community life.

Mr. Apollo, a handsome young man of about twenty-six, is quite different in background and personality from Mr. Qualified. He, too, always wanted to be an actor, but he never played on Broadway. He went to a good dramatic school and later played in the theaters of his home town. When he came to Hollywood, he had little difficulty in getting a good start and was making fast progress, which was interrupted by the war. After that was over, he resumed his career. Mr. Apollo knows just what he wants. He turned down the male lead in a big A production because he considered the role weak and ineffectual. He tries to get strong roles, which permit him to show off his ability. When not working he takes lessons from a distinguished dramatic coach to keep in trim and improve his acting. He regards both his career and private life as a business. He employs a publicity man whose main function is to keep unfavorable publicity out of the papers. He goes to *premières* and other public rites because he thinks it is good to have his pictures taken at them, and to big parties in order to keep constantly within the vision of executives and producers who, he says, can see only as far as their finger tips. However, he rarely frequents night clubs, partly because he does not enjoy them and partly because he thinks it is bad business. He says that today producers do not want an actor to be a gay man about town or a heavy drinker, but rather do they want a hard worker who knows his responsibilities and whom they can count on to do the job.

A striking aspect of Mr. Apollo's personality is his complete and humorless seriousness. He compares himself to the President of the United States, saying that both must comport themselves in public with great dignity. He cannot afford to dissipate his body which is the vehicle of his talent, nor his reputation which is tied up with his career. He feels very strongly that his life should be aloof, dignified and circumspect. When he makes a public appearance and gives autographs, he never feels that he is one of the crowd or part of it in any way. He is conservative in his opinions and uninterested in politics. Although a member of the Screen Actors' Guild, he is not active in it. Mr. Apollo's colossal seriousness might be labeled in different ways. Some would call it conceit. Others might think of it as consecration to a profession, not unlike that of a religious man to a noble cause. He is typical of a whole group of very serious young actors and actresses who are a long way from the Fatty Arbuckle type of old days.

Mr. Bitter, in his middle thirties, and good-looking, has not yet been successful. He grew up on the West Coast and says he has wanted to be an actor ever since he was fourteen and took part in a school play. When he finished high school, however, he went into the real-estate business with the idea that he would quickly become rich and important. Instead he was bored. He happened to meet one of his former schoolmates, who was acting in a local playhouse and receiving dramatic training. Mr. Bitter begged his friend to help him get in, and he was given a walk-on part. From this he progressed to bit parts, and eventually to leads.

This playhouse was not far from Los Angeles and a studio talent scout saw him and offered a contract. He started at a low salary, but he was sure that his great ability would soon be recognized and that he would go up quickly. However, he was disappointed by going no further than small parts in B pictures. Then the war came along, and for three and a half years he had important roles in army training films. When the war ended and he returned to Hollywood, a studio offered him a contract. During its first year he acted in only one film, which was four or five weeks' work. The rest of the time he drew his salary, but did not act. This was most frustrating. He would go to the studios two or three times a week, have lunch with people who might be of help in getting him a part, such as a casting director, but nothing happened. He says it is terrible to have nothing to do. When asked what he did while he was not working, he replied. "Nothing." Later, he said, "Well, nothing constructive," and mentioned that he went to the races a great deal and made considerable money. He did odd things such as painting his car and looking for a new place to live.

Finally he landed a small part in a big picture. Desperately and with great emotion he begged the director to let him do his part on the sympathetic side so that he would get favorable notices. "For God's sake," he said, "give me a chance; I must get ahead; I can't stand this any more!" The director was willing. But although Mr. Bitter did get good notices, he has been unemployed. However, his belief in his own talent is unshaken as he awaits his break. But he is resentful; he says that he has been passed by because he has not been aggressive and because he has not played the part of "wolf" with young actresses who are stars. Instead, he lives rather quietly with his wife. Politically he is conservative and seems al-

most a-political, although he is vaguely for the "common man."
He goes quite regularly to Guild meetings and thinks it has done
wonderful things for the actors.

The social life of most actors is usually limited to those in the
same financial bracket. At the top are the stars with their beautiful
homes and swimming pools, symbols of Hollywood success. Some
of the stars are in the process of forming a new aristocracy. They
send their children to the best private schools and a preferred marriage is into an old, established family of wealth. Some members of
this new aristocracy make a cult of normality, as they understand
it. The women have children, differing from the stars of the past
who feared babies might reduce their popularity. Today, the actresses are merely careful to space their babies between pictures.
What is considered normal is, of course, always conditioned by the
group. In some communities it is normal for a businessman to get
drunk on Saturday nights, go to church on Sundays, and carry on a
secret affair with his secretary during the week. In Hollywood the
normal in social life is now quite different from what it was in
the early days. Wild parties and late nights are completely out
during time of production. The hours required by the studio are
so long and exhausting that no star would have the energy left for
a late night, after a day on the set. Besides, the night-before dissipation shows up in the face and voice of the actor and neither he
nor the studio desire that. Parties, gaiety and late nights are restricted to the periods between pictures. Vacations are frequently
spent in the desert resorts, on a yacht, in Hawaii, Mexico, or Europe.
Racing and gambling may be major interests, or it may be something quite different such as painting or acting in "little theater."
Or it may be sex and extramarital affairs which take up spare
time. Of course, one hobby does not preclude others. While publicized parties are lavish and ostentatious, the tendency is to make
them respectable. Publicized immorality may not lessen a star's
popularity with his fans and has been even known to increase it,
but the studios fear the clamor raised by self-constituted censors
of actor's morals. The trend is, therefore, for indecorous and loose
sexual behavior to be private. Some actors are also personally

anxious to dispel the traditional concept of unconventionality connected with their profession and long to be considered normal rather than different. Actually, the personal lives of many actors, when they are not working, are not too different from those of any other very wealthy group. These are the playboys and playgirls, who are seen at the night clubs and whose flirtations and doings are subjects for gossip columns. They may be unmarried, or between marriages, or married, but gay night life (when they are not doing a picture) is an important part of their existence.

Another group of actors with a certain coherence because of a similarity of background is quite different. They come from the Broadway stage and received their training in the old Theater Guild, the Eva Le Gallienne group, or some such theater group. These people, mostly character actors and a few stars, regard themselves as professional artists. They do not go in for lavish social life but spend much of their free time in something connected with the theater world. Among them is found more of the bohemianism usually associated with artists. There are other actors who do not belong to any group, who live fairly quiet lives, either happily or unhappily on the personal side, and have various outlets for their free time — politics, Guild activity, or a "little" theater. But for most, big and little, what to do with their spare time is a problem. When employed there are the long hours of activity, which meet personality needs. Then the picture is finished and a period of inactivity follows. Even if the actor is under contract and there is no financial worry, the situation is not an easy one. There is the well-known lost feeling when not acting; they do not really enjoy the substitutes such as rounds of parties, flirtations, sex orgies, drinking, betting, racing, painting or working for a cause. For them, the only really satisfactory way of living is acting. All other activities are poor makeshifts.

These are the actors — successful or unsuccessful, stupid or intelligent, merely photogenic or very talented, untrained or experienced, those who will ruin a film to increase their footage and those with the integrity of an artist, those for whom the publicity ballyhoo has had a malign effect and those who have survived it.

For all, acting is a way of life as well as a means of earning a living. They work in an industry which exploits to the utmost their personal need for exhibitionism, and at the same time views it as one the darkest iniquities. They earn more money than any other group of people in the country, but work under serf-like conditions and in a system geared to the mediocre rather than to the talented. They are regarded as property, to be bought and sold at a profit. They are pampered, flattered, and glamorized for the public, and at the same time scorned, and hated by those who give the flattery and do the glamorizing. They live in luxury and have considerable power, but are treated as adolescents subject to the many controls of contract, front office, agent, business manager, publicity man.

If proof were needed that the actors are people, it would be their deep resentment to this situation. For all members of our species, not to be regarded as human is a severe threat.

These then are the actors, glamorous stars and folk heroes to their admirers all over the world; inhuman pieces of property, scorned, hated and envied in Hollywood.

CHAPTER XIV
Emerging from Magic

HOLLYWOOD bustles with frenzied activity, and makes use of the most modern technology. Yet at the same time it gives the impression of being only half awake in its slow emergence from a dim prehistoric past of illusions, fears, and magical thinking. More strikingly than any other section of our society, it seems to span all the ages of mankind. In it, too, are represented all the ages of individual man, from infancy to adult.

In any human society the presence or absence of a particular body of ideas limits and affects the development of behavior as much as do technology and environment.[1] Therefore to comprehend the social organization in which movies are made and to understand the behavior of people in Hollywood, it is necessary to know how they think. All peoples, whether in the South Seas or in Hollywood, try to make the world intelligible to themselves, and to exercise some control over it. The particular ideology of any society shapes its institutions and molds the behavior of its members.

Since its beginning, the human species seems to have been aware that not all phenomena are of the same order. But the division between the animate and inanimate has not always been clear. In order to make the inanimate intelligible, primitive man often ascribed human attitudes and motives to the nonhuman world. (This is called "animism.") It was easier for him to do this than to imagine different processes or to admit his ignorance. As Ruth Benedict has pointed out: "Throughout man's history it has been the mechanistic

[1] Ralph Linton, *The Study of Man,* Chapter IV. New York: D. Appleton-Century.

theory of the universe that he has found fantastic, not the animistic one." [2] So, in many primitive societies, human qualities have been attributed to fishes, birds, trees, rocks, and ancestral spirits, and gods. Men could therefore use towards them attitudes and techniques, such as cajoling, scolding and making gifts which has been found effective in dealing with human beings, and expect similar responses. For instance, primitive peoples sometimes denounce their ancestral spirits and at other times propitiate them with gifts, to gain their help.

Animistic thinking is not restricted to primitive man. Many folk tales of historical civilizations show a confusion between the animate and the inanimate and our own society still exhibits attenuated forms of the same thing. Most everyone who has owned an old car has had the experience of talking cajolingly to it when it mysteriously stalls. A child who hurts himself by falling over a rug may hit the rug in retaliation, as if the rug could feel a spanking. In Hollywood, however, there appears to be a much greater confusion between the animate and inanimate than in the larger society, although it works in an opposite manner from that of primitive man's animism. Hollywood people seem more at home with the inanimate, with property which can be measured in dollars and which can be manipulated to increase itself, than they are with human beings. They therefore attribute the characteristics of what they know best to the unknown — which is, for them, the world of human beings and the art of storytelling. These become intelligible as they take on the characteristics of the known — property — and become functional as they contribute to the goal of wealth. The psychological process appears to be the same one by which primitive man makes his environment intelligible by projecting what he knows about human beings onto his canoe and ancestral spirits.

Much of Hollywood thinking has the characteristics of this inverted form of animism and, as we have seen, the history of movies helps make this possible: props were early used to produce emotional effects. In the legitimate theater, on the other hand, actors were important from the beginning, and elaborate stage settings

[2] F. Boas and others, *General Anthropology*, p. 636. Boston: D. C. Heath and Co.

came later. In literature, the art of storytelling preceded the invention of printing, which has never superseded it. But what the men who founded the movie industry knew best was property, the accumulation of which was their highest goal. Artists and the art of storytelling were strange to them.

Among primitive peoples, magic is one of the techniques used to control supernatural and other forces which they do not understand. The Stone Age agriculturalists in the Southwest Pacific were well aware through observation and experience that the ground had to be cleared before planting their taro, that the plants should be a certain distance apart, that weeds must be pulled out, and that a fence built around the garden would help keep out wild pigs. All these were natural elements controllable by hard work and foresight. But there remained the uncertainties of weather and other factors beyond human control, which also influenced the crop. So before starting a garden, men made magic to coerce or cajole these elements to bring them success. The Melanesians did not think the magic eliminated the need for weeding, or that weeding made the magic unnecessary.

Deep layers of magical thinking still remain in the unconscious of modern men, and sometimes on the conscious level, too. But most of us no longer view magic as an operational tool. We may unconsciously or consciously long for a magical helper and for miracles; but we know that writing a book, getting a job, or making a garden depends on hard work, knowledge, ability and planning, rather than on coercing the supernatural; we usually act on this awareness. We may vaguely feel that disease can be the work of an evil spirit or a punishment for sin, but when we become ill we consult a doctor, who utilizes the latest scientific developments in medicine. Over the centuries of man's development, magical thinking has receded more and more into the unconscious and become less and less a conscious instrument to achieve his ends. The growth of modern civilization has been due, in part, to a constant widening of that area of our thinking based on rational knowledge and experience of reality, and to a corresponding shrinking of the supernatural sphere. It is unlikely that either area will ever disappear, but the proportional significance of each in our conscious thinking and behavior changes considerably.

In Hollywood, however, there appears to be a greater use of magical thinking on a conscious level and as a tool for achieving success than elsewhere in the modern world. The concepts of breaks to secure success, so emphasized in Hollywood, belongs to the supernatural sphere. Most successful people, no matter what their occupation, believe that luck has played some role in their lives. But they usually emphasize far more the contribution of hard work, perseverance, training, or of particular gifts and aptitudes. In Hollywood the quite considerable difference in the degree of emphasis on luck is important, for according to the familiar philosophical principle, a sufficiently large quantitative difference may produce a qualitative one. Almost everyone in the movie industry from front office executives, producers, actors, directors and writers, to those who play minor roles, such as assistant directors and agents, attribute their own and other people's success to forces lying beyond their control in the world of chance. This belief indeed corresponds with reality as most Hollywood people have known it. An executive without previous training or experience in the art or business of storytelling makes a colossal fortune because he had the breaks; perhaps the breaks for him consisted of coming into the industry when it was very young and success easy. A producer becomes a millionaire and important in the industry, because he had the breaks of knowing in childhood, or later on, an executive. An actress becomes a star because a producer chanced to notice her and gave her a role in a picture which happened to be a hit. A writer has the luck to work with a sympathetic producer, or to hit on a very clever gimmick, or to get credit for the script of a movie which makes big profits for the studio. The profits themselves are believed to be the result of luck, too, since whether or not an audience will like a movie seems unpredictable. Most people who live in Hollywood are wholly committed to this philosophy and regard it as an inherent and necessary part of movie production. They do not think movies could be made differently.

This type of thinking, whether in New Guinea or Hollywood, produces appropriate attitudes and behavior. The Melanesian puts his faith in coercing the supernatural through using a magical formula, which consists of a spell and rite handed down by tradition. Hollywood people have their formulas too: stars, gimmicks, traditional plots. Just as the Melanesian thinks failure would result from changing the form of a spell, so men in Hollywood consider it dangerous to depart from their formulas. Each group can point to the times it worked and conveniently forget or rationalize the other occasions. The Melanesian placates hostile supernatural forces through a series of taboos; Hollywood attempts to appease its critics and enemies with the MPAA Code. Primitive men often make sacrifices of whatever they consider most valuable — food, animals and occasionally human beings — in order to court the favor of the supernatural. In Hollywood money is more highly valued than anything else and this is sacrificed in large amounts.

It is earnestly believed that the more money spent on a picture the more successful it will be. *How* the money is spent — on the highest paid stars, on the most lavish settings, or on a series of expensive writers, or whether there are realistic returns for it, does not make too much difference. Knowing the right people in Hollywood is also not too unlike the ritual behavior prescribed in family, clans, and other social groups among primitive peoples. In each case the ritual behavior is important: not only the maintaining of one's own status, but the very life of the people, and of society, is believed to depend on it.

In most societies in which supernatural elements are important in attaining success, some form of divination is practiced, because foreknowledge is one way of control. In parts of East Africa, the entrails of chickens are used for divining the future, while among the Karen of Burma it is the gall bladder of a pig; in Hollywood polls are used to determine the mysterious tastes of the audience. Will they like this or that title and this or that plot, with this or that star? The methods now used to determine, a year in advance, the tastes of potential audiences is not too different from trying to foretell the future by examining the spots on an animal's liver.

This comparative *tour de force* can, of course, be carried too far, but success in Hollywood appears to be more closely related to the realm of the supernatural than it does for primitive men. The average producer seems less clear in his thinking about those elements in movie production which are knowable and those where chance plays a role than the Stone Age man is in his occupations. The latter does not confuse the practical work necessary to making his canoe seaworthy with the need for magical rites and taboos. But studio executives have depended more often on formulas, breaks, and following the Code than on the quality of script, directing and acting. But enough good movies (which have also been profitable) *have* been produced with intelligent planning to indicate that the prevailing pattern need not be the only one.

Hollywood seems as wasteful of talent and brains as primitive peoples are neglectful of many of their natural resources. Valuable minerals often remained hidden in the earth which Stone Age men inhabited, because they were ignorant of their presence or use. Natural resources in Hollywood are its talent and brains as well as the technological assets. The industry makes good use of the latter. But the human properties of the artist, his sensitivity, his imagination, his ability to create, are utilized in only a very limited way. Most people have more intelligence and ability than they use, but in Hollywood the discrepancy between potentialities and actualities is more glaring than elsewhere.

The two major characteristics of Hollywood thinking, the belief in chance or breaks, and the confusion between the human and nonhuman, dominate every concept of creativity there. Creativity is not thought of as human in Hollywood. Human sensitivity to the joys and sorrows of life, human imagination, an awareness of human limitations, the decencies of human relations are relatively unimportant, nor is their portrayal regarded as the part of man's capacity to think and plan. As the original founders of the industry, the executives tend to think of themselves as its totemic ancestors, omniscient and omnipotent. They boast about how they manipulate the emotions of millions in the audience, causing them to tense with excitement or to laugh with relief. Even more important is the executive's control and manipulation of everyone connected with production, from star to script girl. The front office knows in some mysterious way — through instinct, they say — everything about script writing, about casting, about cutting, and what the audience will like. Primitive man conveniently forgets the times his magic does not work, and the executives also do not remember when their instinct has been wrong.

The emotional ferment of creativity is an inner one, and there is excitement, with stimulation and satisfaction, in the creative expression of ideas and fantasies. No matter how collaborative or how many contributors, behind every human creation is an idea in one individual's mind. Nor does it spring full blown into being as an instinctual act: preceding it are training, discipline, and work. The artist's intuition is quite different from the showman's instinct. The former rests on deeper than average sensitivity to human beings and to the complexities in the world about him. The artist's reaction is personal and individual, and it is this which he tries to express. He works primarily to please himself, experiments with new ideas and new forms, and leaps ahead into the unknown, not sure of the outcome. When he succeeds he has an inner satisfaction, and he likewise enjoys any honor and payment which society gives him.

The average movie is produced in an entirely different way. The excitement has nothing to do with genuine creation, but is all on the outside. The producer strides up and down his office at the frequent story conferences, phone calls are made at midnight, the front office or star demand changes which precipitate crises, and so on and on. Similarly, in many movies the feeling of excitement is limited to external factors, such as noise, music, props falling, thunderstorms. Rarely does the star's passive face or acting give any indication of an inner emotional ferment. Underlying the studio's bustle and excitement is the tension of the unanswered question, "Will the public like it?" Everyone is aware of the enormous costs of production. Will a large profit be made after these are covered? In this situation, it is rare for writer or actor or director or any other artist to feel the satisfaction of creating something which pleases him and which he respects. He is a cog in the machine.

Although the idea for a film originates in the mind of one person, its execution and final consummation is the result of collaboration with many others, who may be equally creative in their own ways. But collaboration takes different forms. In the production of most pictures, the relationship of one individual to another is direct, one personality impinging on the other in terms of their respective power statuses. In the production of a few pictures, however, the bonds between the individuals are those of mutual connection with a creative activity, and this objective relationship is allowed to take precedence over the power one. Suggestions from writer, executive, director, actors, are discussed in terms of their logic and appropriateness to the film, and the results of the discussion are not foreordained in terms of who has the most money or power. One idea may be recognized as better than the other, or out of the discussion may evolve a totally new idea, containing elements from the several points of view. When problems are discussed in this way and no one person always has the final word, the creative process functions collaboratively. The resulting film is the joint product of many minds, even though the initial idea was conceived by one. Any creative collaboration is of this type. A good teacher-student relationship, at any level from kindergarten to university, is oriented to the objective of knowledge and understanding, rather than to the teacher's using his authority to impose his ideas on the student, and the latter's critical remark or contribution is as much part of the teaching as are those of the learned lecturer. Actually, all human relationships, including the intimate family ones, are apt to be easier if the ties of the individuals to each other are based on a mutual objective interest, rather than exclusively on age, sex or power difference.

In any factory or business, management does not want too much interference from its employees. Although men on the factory assembly line want some say over conditions of work, such as hours and salaries, most of them take for granted that they work rather mechanically under the foreman's directions, and this does not impair their efficiency. But writers and other artists do their best work only when they have some freedom to try and please themselves. Working on the assembly line and following orders do not bring good results and are basically inefficient from the point of view of profits. Hollywood is an industry, but daydreams are its product and these cannot be successfully produced as if they were cans of beans.

Although Hollywood production has factory characteristics, the general atmosphere pervading the studios is no more that of a factory than it is of a creative human enterprise. Rather it is that of the gamblers' den. The psychology of the gambler has been well described.[3] Outstanding characteristics of all gambling are the importance of chance in determining success or failure, and the lack of emphasis on skill. The neurotic gambler, as Dr. Greenson points out, is driven by unconscious needs and cannot stop. "It [gambling] has an irresistible quality: the tension has to be satisfied by action, not thinking, and immediately, not by postponement."[4] Winning, for the neurotic gambler, means not only the jack pot, but proof that he is favored by Fate, and a token of power.[5] He mistakes his yearnings for omnipotence, for feeling that he is omnipotent. Yet he cannot quite repress his doubts, and so he is always looking for signs to confirm his shaky belief. This longing and belief in omnipotence, is thought to be a regression to early infancy since infants, too, are thought to have a feeling of unlimited omnipotence.[6] "It is this feeling which the neurotic gambler unconsciously is attempting to recapture."[7]

Winning in the Hollywood gamble means being connected with a movie which is a box-office hit. This is then regarded both as a sign of having been favored by Fate and as a token of omniscience and omnipotence. The award of an Oscar is another such sign. It is easy to understand that when an actor, writer, or director dares to question an executive's decision, he is by implication attacking the executive's belief in his own omnipotence, and the reaction is accordingly violent. For to permit omniscience to be questioned

[3] Ralph R. Greenson, M.D., "On Gambling," *The American Imago*. Vol. 4, No. 2, April 1947, pp. 61–77.

[4] *Ibid.*

[5] *Ibid.*

[6] Cf. Sandor Ferenczi, *Contributions to Psychoanalysis*. Boston: Richard Badger. Otto Fenichel, *The Psychoanalytical Theory of Neurosis*. New York: W. W. Norton.

[7] Greenson, *op. cit.*

would destroy it, and any such attempt therefore arouses great anxiety.

Just as the neurotic gambler cannot stay away from his game, so also there are many people in Hollywood who cannot leave, who cannot imagine any existence apart from it. Successful or unsuccessful, lucky or unlucky, they must remain. Nor is their gambling limited to the making of movies. The same people spend much of their free time gambling with cards and betting on horses. Gambling is for them a way of life, just as acting is for the actor.

This is the atmosphere in which movies are made and which is thought to be inherent and essential to their production. Most people do not imagine that movies could be made differently, any more than Stone Age man can imagine that irrigation might replace rain magic. Since crops do grow and many movies do make money, magic appears to work a sufficient number of times to make giving it up seem risky and dangerous.

Men usually think that their particular way of life is inevitable and such beliefs are strengthened when the way also answers their neurotic needs. It appears easier for primitive men to replace rain magic with irrigation, once they have learned about it, than it is for many Hollywood people to give up their claims to omniscience and omnipotence, and to substitute thinking. Perhaps they mistake their deep emotional needs for the inherent conditions of movie making. Perhaps they oppose change not just for economic reasons, but because the *status quo* suits them on a deep and personal level.

Movie production does give many men the opportunity to live out their deep personality needs for gambling and power, and in so doing to make great fortunes. Yet they can never be satisfied because their needs are insatiable. No matter how large the profits, how many Oscars, they must go on constantly striving to prove to themselves that they are supermen. A pause in the activity — and questioning voices might be heard; the only way to silence these voices is through further activity.

All gamblers and others with pretensions to omnipotence and

omniscience are scared men. For Fate can, and sometimes does, stop smiling; the pretense can never be complete. The only way out is to continue gambling — when not on pictures, then on horses and cards.

While Hollywood provides a situation which meets the needs of gamblers, the conditions for creativity which would satisfy artists are lacking. The artist, as well as the gambler, has deep personality needs. An artist wants to use his talent and training in expressing as well as he can his ideas, his fantasies, his interpretations of life. It is believed that the daydreams which he expresses in his work signify repressed wishes, and that the public acceptance and approval of them reduce his anxieties.[8] In Hollywood, however, the writer does not express his own fantasies, but those of a producer or front-office executive. Even when permitted to use some of his own imaginative thinking, he knows in advance that the script will be changed by other writers, producers, stars, directors, and anyone else with power. He knows that at the end his contribution will probably be distorted beyond recognition. To work as an artist, a gifted director must have a script in which he believes, but he usually has to direct whatever is handed him, whether or not he even respects it. For the actor, it is important that he respects both his role and the script, but he rarely has any choice over either, nor is it possible for him to have a variety of roles and not to become stereotyped. He needs likewise a director who can help him make his role an integrated part of the whole, but rarely does he get this help. The artist can rarely even work toward this goal. Other men, front-office executives and producers, have in their omniscience and omnipotence taken over the artist's functions while the artists have replaced their own values with those of the businessmen.

There is nothing inherently bad or wrong about artists making millions of dollars. Money is not necessarily the root of all evil, as the old proverb says. It can be the source of much pleasure and human good. But the making of money has a nature of its own and

[8] Hanns Sachs, *The Creative Unconscious*, p. 38. Cambridge, Mass.: Scie-Art Publisher.

follows certain laws. Creativity has another nature and follows other laws. They are not interchangeable. The nature of creativity is such that it is defeated if anything is substituted for its goal. If an artist in expressing himself succeeds also in giving form to the inarticulate dreams or needs of many people, and is later rewarded with a million dollars, that need not affect him, if his creative drive is strong. But if he works on something he does not believe in or respect, *in order* to make a million, then he and his work deteriorate. It is the change of goals which is important. Very few gifted people are always at their best. Everyone has his off periods when he is not up to his own standards — whether giving a lecture, writing a book, composing a score, or performing an experiment in the laboratory. But it is a very different matter for either artist or scientist deliberately to lower his standard in order to make a lot of money. Corruption of both work and man is inevitable, and if it extends over any length of time there is no going back. The artist who thinks he can beat the game, stay in Hollywood and clean up his million, and then return to his own creative works, is usually fooled. There are well-known examples of writers who finally shook the dust of many years of Hollywood from their typewriters, only to turn out mediocre plays and novels which resemble far more the movie scripts on which they had made their million, than their pre-Hollywood work.

This happens much more often to writers than to directors and actors. Of all the creative workers in Hollywood, the writers are the most frustrated because they are allowed to function least as artists. They write to dictation, expressing someone else's fantasies, and even this is later changed and mangled by others. The gifted actor or director, no matter how weak or corny the role or script, can still give it his best. They have at least a partial satisfaction of using initially weak material as well as possible. However, gifted directors also experience some of the writers' frustrations. A director may work hard and creatively on a movie, and at the last minute the front office cuts out certain scenes and so changes others that the effect he has striven for is lost. When the picture is released under his name, he is ashamed of it. An actor doing his best still may not be able to take away the corniness of his role. But the actor and director at least do play their professional roles regardless of the outcome, while the writer rarely even does that.

Of course the truly gifted people for whom the problem of creation is important are few everywhere. Only a small percentage of novelists, painters, musicians, scientists, anywhere in the world, are talented. But there are many more in Hollywood than one would expect from looking at movies. The industry entices them, with big salaries, from New York, London, Paris and Milan. Once Hollywood gets them, it makes them part of that system which prevents their gifts from being utilized to the best advantage. This is costly and wasteful to the studio and to the banks which finance production. It is corrupting to the artists, to the movies they help produce, and a decided disadvantage to the movie-going public.

Many people beside Hollywood artists are frustrated. College professors frequently feel frustrated because of lack of money and the difficulties of bringing up a family and maintaining their social status on the professorial salary. Many artists outside of Hollywood know economic frustrations. While these frustrations are wearing and burdensome, they do not usually cause an individual to lose respect for what he does, or for himself. This is a heavy load for any personality to carry.

The really important people in the development and growth of the movies, as a popular art form and as a profitable industry, are the small group of artists who continuously struggle to function as such, and the occasional executive who appreciates their goals because they are partly or wholly his own. We have therefore stressed their significance which is far greater than their numbers would seem to warrant. It is these men and women, who are not primarily gamblers, who do not confuse the animate with the inanimate — the human with the supernatural — who are responsible for any human creativity that there is in Hollywood. They have a point of view, the expression of which is important to them; they have a capacity for sustained hard work, and they prefer thoughtful planning to constant crises. They regard people as human beings. Although comparatively few, they can be found in all parts of movie production. They struggle constantly for power within the Hollywood system, power not to dominate other human beings, but to bend the system so that creation becomes human. Many times they lose, but sometimes they win; and the fighting, whatever the outcome, relieves some of their frustration.

One strategy for the artist who understands the system and wants to improve it is, first, to meet the front office's standards by making money for the studio, following the conventional formulas. Then by persistent nagging he may gain the opportunity to create something to please himself. This opportunity is granted to keep him in good humor and prevent his going to another studio. If, to the studio's surprise, the humoring of the artist turns out to be good box office, he is given more control over his work. But first the artist must show that he can work within the executive's scheme of values. The executive does not have to prove that he can work within the artist's scale. It is a one-way road.

When occasionally an executive does demonstrate that he understands and appreciates the artist's standards, and is objectively more interested in the movie than in power, he can usually have his pick of talent.

The mediocre would be so in any situation. In Hollywood, they enjoy the illusion of being creative and some of them even emulate the frustrations of artists. They work in a system geared to mediocrity, which enables them, if successful, to earn more money than in any other place in the world. They have the same gambling psychology that the front-office executives have; their faith in breaks is so strong that often they hang on for years and years even when Fate has not yet smiled. As the front office manipulates them, so they manipulate everyone else that they can. Their economic insecurities, however, are greater than those of the front office. But if moderately successful they enjoy material comforts and luxuries far greater than anything they could have outside of Hollywood. For people without marked ability, whether they sit in the front office, in the producer's office or in that of the writer's, whether they direct or act, a system in which success depends upon breaks is far more reassuring than one in which talent or special gifts count. For people without imagination or with understanding of writing, acting, and storytelling, a system which mechanizes the whole process is fitting. For people whose whole lives are concerned with the accumulation of property, a system which emphasizes property above everything else is understandable. For people whose drive is toward power over others, a system which encourages manipulation is desirable. For those whose inner need is the excitement of gambling rather than the stimulation of creation, the system is congenial. It is these people — the majority in Hollywood — who shape and perpetuate that system, in harmony with their own needs rather than with those of movie making.

Yet these people suffer and sometimes have mental breakdowns. Hollywood gives only a neurotic answer to their needs, which are therefore not really satisfied. A man with almost no writing ability becomes an important movie writer because an executive producer is his friend, or for some other reason unconnected with writing. Although he is regarded as a success and enjoys a very big salary, he knows, consciously or unconsciously, that the success has no foundation in ability, and suffers anxiety over whether it can last. He plays the social game in a frenzied fashion to prove to himself and to others that his position is secure. Since in our culture success is supposed to be the result of hard work and ability, he may suffer undue guilt. The anxiety may become too much for him to handle, leading to neurotic symptoms, to breakdown or failure.

The creative person, particularly if he has functioned as such in the past, likewise suffers. He, too, may break down or become maladjusted when his deep aspirations are repeatedly aroused and then left unsatisfied, when his imagination is stirred and then not permitted to function. He, too, knows guilt and anxiety — over his corruption as an artist.

In this collaborative industry, there is also, with a few exceptions, a striking and complete lack of mutual respect as well as trust. The *esprit de corps* of the industry is exceedingly low. People who do not respect each other cannot work co-operatively. Just as morale is necessary to the successful functioning of an army, so is a high level of *esprit de corps* important as a motivating force in any industry. Its absence in Hollywood endangers the industry, injures both the people who work in it and the movies they produce.

In the usual Hollywood production of movies, the quality of the movie is much less important than the assertion of the ego of any individual. When the executive insists on cutting a picture so that the motivation of the leading characters is lost, when he refuses to pay any attention to a director's idea about casting, when the star demands that her footage be increased and that of a minor character cut, when the producer dominates a writer or writers, insisting on carrying out his own ideas, good or bad, when the director refuses to listen to suggestions of a gifted actor about his role, when talented people are fired because they threaten the power of some one higher up — then, of course, it is the movie which goes to pot.

As noted, the kind of thinking which dominates Hollywood stems out of its past. Hollywood is, however, not a sealed chamber. New people, new ideas from literature and the theater, new values, have entered and continue to do so. Also, an increasing number of Hollywood people are now involved in shooting movies in every part of the world. The industry has been quick to accept new technological improvements whether in sound, in color or in some other process, but slow to incorporate those new ideas, which may seriously threaten the power situation. If actors and directors and men of literature are successful in turning out profitable pictures, then the omniscience and omnipotence of studio executives is endangered. If men with talent, ability and intelligent planning can produce better pictures, then the people who have depended on breaks and frenzied activity have no place. Naturally they are not apt to favor such changes.

Whether or not the industry likes new ideas, it is forced to meet unsettled world conditions. Foreign markets and ratios of imported pictures are constantly changing. There is increased foreign competition at home and shifts in audience standards and tastes. Federal court decrees separate production from distribution and exhibition, and costs of production climb upward. The country goes through inflation and recession. All these and many more contemporary changes directly impinge on Hollywood.

One very important consequence is that the margin for error in movie production has very much decreased. In the early days vast profits could be made regardless of mistakes, extravagances, and quality. Movies were at first something of a novelty and for a long time there was little competition. The early audiences were mostly working people who went to see any movie. Much later, during the war years, most people enjoyed larger incomes than ever before and the tensions of war and long hours of work increased their need of entertainment. Today, the situation is very different. While the costs of making movies has spiraled upward, people have less money to spend on entertainment and their standards are changing. They therefore exercise more thought in their choice of what to see.

The upward educational level of the whole country continues. The vast movements in the popularization of knowledge through adult education, museums, books, radio and other media has also done much to broaden the base of the educated public.

But more important than any other change is the loss of homogeneity in the movie audience. Today, this represents as much variety in tastes and backgrounds as does the population of the country. There are still the teen-age girls infatuated with movie heroes who go to see any picture in which their favorite stars perform, and who squirm in their seats when the hero passionately kisses the heroine. But in a preliminary study of audience reactions of high school juniors and seniors a large number, in discussing a movie or one part of it, used the phrases and adjectives "weak," "corny," "no motivation," "couldn't happen." Moreover, the audience is not limited to adolescents, critical or otherwise. People over thirty who count movies as one of their pastimes, naturally have different tastes from those of adolescents.

Hollywood has been slow to catch on to this new audience, which asks for something more than movement and excitement. The success all over the country of the so-called "art theater" has startled some of the Hollywood people. In the postwar period there was an influx of foreign pictures and the art theaters were an outlet for the better ones. Today, many regular theaters play foreign movies part of their time. According to *Variety*, there are 57 theaters which are out-and-out art-houses, and 226 which play the foreign-made product part of the time. Ten more are now under construction. It is of interest that the art-houses are called "sure-seaters" in this trade paper, which says:

> Despite the dwindling grosses which have hit regular thea-ters, distribs serving the art-house operation claim that the field is generally a lush one. Out of every 10 sureseaters now doing business several are highly lucrative, two are in a wobbly stage, and one is in the red, it is said." [9]

The same article attributes the success of the art-houses to their low cost of operation without all the "expensive plush" and to their having a steady and stable group of customers. Nor are these art theaters clustered in large cities in the East. Every city of 200,000 or over, except Newark (which suffers because of its proximity to New York) has at least one art theater. Texas is particularly strong in them. In Detroit, four neighborhood movie houses changed into art-houses in 1949. From places as scattered as Syracuse, New York; Salt Lake City, Utah; Tacoma, Washington; Dayton, Ohio, come reports of the openings of new art theaters.[10] These are one indica-tion of changing audience tastes.

Hollywood is not unaware of many of the changes and new trends and has attempted to meet the new situation in various ways. Metro-Goldwyn-Mayer has tried to attract an older audience by casting older people in its movies.

> "More than ten Metro pictures are soon to be made with top players over sixty years of age. Eight others are nearing re-lease. It's all part of a drive on Metro's part to lure patrons over 35 back to the theater.[11]

If this plan is carried through to its logical conclusion, Holly-wood would merely develop a new formula of teaming the age of the star to the age of the expected audience, which is even more fantastic than some of its past formulas. It is rather doubtful that

[9] *Variety*, July 27, 1949.
[10] *Ibid*.
[11] *Ibid.*, July 13, 1949.

adults now frequenting the art-houses will rush to see MGM pictures because they star actors over sixty years of age.

Studio executives, trying to analyze the success of *Pinky* and *All the King's Men*, classify them as "gimmick" pictures and are now hunting for other "gimmick pix" to beat the "b.o. Nix." [12] The executives appear unable to break loose from the bonds of their past thinking in terms of gimmicks and formulas.

They might learn from some high school students, who when asked for their favorite type of movie, indicated their preferences — musical, serious, drama, Western — and then added: "But it has to be *good*." As an example of what they meant by good, some students mentioned *All the King's Men*.

Another suggested solution is improved public relations for the whole industry. Hollywood takes great pride in its showmanship and spends more than any other industry on advertising and publicity. Yet, as is well known, its public relations are very bad. It is a popular pastime to take a crack at Hollywood at every opportunity. This symbol for sex and lavish wealth to the whole world is a target for continuous criticism and hostility. Anti-Hollywood diatribes are familiar to anyone who reads the American press, and George Seaton, President of the Screen Writers' Guild, returning from a trip to Europe, said there is "too much anti-Hollywood prejudice in the world." [13] Different causes underlie all the hostility towards Hollywood. One is probably the envy of fortunes so easily earned; and there may be resentment or envy, or both, of the supposedly freer sex life of Hollywood people. But perhaps there is a wider awareness, more than Hollywood executives' realize, of the enormous gap between the potentialities and the actual product that is turned out.

The industry knows well that its public relations are bad and suggests many different remedies. An advertising-publicity chief suggested a campaign to combat what he considered the public's misconceptions of the industry: that it is "red," immoral, extravagant, and screwball in its thinking. The office represented by Mr.

[12] *Variety*, March 8, 1950.
[13] *Ibid.*, March 16, 1949.

Eric Johnston emphasizes more the need to effect good will within the various sections of the industry (production, distribution, and exhibition) and the cessation of publicized intra-industry quarreling. He called meetings for this purpose. The Motion Picture Association of America tries to sell what they call "The constructive angle" on Hollywood, and sends out articles — such as "Music in Films," "Literature in Films," "How Films Teach History," to critics and exhibitors and to schools.[14] But what historians, musicians and those concerned with literature would say on these themes, is another story. Plans are made for an American Film Festival similar to those held in Europe, to draw the attention of Americans to their own film industry.[15]

Other plans are for increasing profits through economies in production. "Big name" stars under contract now do more pictures per year. In 1948, Van Johnson made two pictures, *Command Decision* and *The Bride Goes Wild*, while in 1949 he had a schedule of five pictures. Since he received $5000 a week whether he worked or not, the savings to the studio were considerable.[16] But against this new trend, the old one still persists. Deanna Durbin's salary from September 1948 to September 1949 was $300,000 and she did not make a single picture.[17]

As late as 1948 it was news in the trade press that planning in advance produced economies. Mr. Mamoulian emphasized that he was able to make the technicolor musical "Holiday" (*Holiday in Mexico*) for the relatively low budget of $1,800,000 because it was shot in 56 days instead of the average 100–125 for musicals, and that this was possible because of "thorough advance preparation."[18] Rehearsals which had long been desired by the talented directors and actors, but discouraged or forbidden by the front office, gradually have become part of the economy wave. It has been finally discovered that rehearsals actually save money because they prevent the needless extravagance of the cast and highly paid technicians

[14] *Ibid.*, August 3, 1949.
[15] *Ibid.*, July 20, 1949.
[16] *Ibid.*
[17] *Ibid.*, August 10, 1949.
[18] *Ibid.*, April 21, 1948.

standing around while last minute changes are made. In addition, rehearsals bring some of the advantages of the stage to both actors and directors on the set, cause better pictures to be made, and so probably improve the box-office intake.

Stars are as important as ever and even the economy wave has not reduced their earnings, but there is a move away from picking up pretty-faced newcomers toward one of selecting experienced young Broadway players with talent.[19] It is no longer so easy, but still not impossible, to achieve stardom only through beautiful legs, sensuous appearance, or being brought to the attention of an executive through faked or real publicity.

Many executives and producers repeat the timeworn adage, "There's nothing wrong with the picture business that good pictures can't cure." Yet there is considerable difference of opinion on what is a good picture or how to make one. For some, the best method is still to spend more money. Henry Ginsberg, president of Paramount Pictures, warns against "becoming cost-conscious to the point of forgetting the entertainment needs of a picture," adding that "any picture costing less than $1,000,000 is a B."[20] But other executives have gradually learned that money may not be the whole story. The same paper quoted Adolph Zukor, regarded by many as dean of the motion picture industry, as saying, "Pictures require brains, not money. The talk that high-cost films attract the public is not correct. Give me brains and I'll make good pictures. The others can have the U. S. Treasury behind them but if they don't have the talent, their money will not produce good pictures."[21] Mr. Nicholas M. Schenck, president of Loew's, Incorporated, also thinks that money is not the most essential factor and is particularly concerned about whether the writers are earning their salaries. He says:

> The motion picture industry cannot throw its weight around and its money around without sincerity of purpose. That purpose must be to give the public the best possible entertainment. This cannot be done merely by cutting costs. It

[19] *Ibid.*, August 10, 1949.
[20] *Ibid.*, July 6, 1949.
[21] *Ibid.*, July 13, 1949.

has to be done by making the costs worth while. . . . It means that writers have to try to fully express themselves in their work and not write pictures as a device to get easy money.[22]

Mr. Zukor does not consider the problem of whether the industry knows how to utilize talent, and Mr. Schenck does not raise the questions of *how* the costs can be made worth while and whether writers are permitted, as he says, "to fully express themselves in their work." A talented writer would like nothing better, but this is difficult with the present methods of production.

Both these presidents have gropingly hit only the surface of the problem. They seem not to know that gifted and intelligent people *cannot* function well without a certain amount of freedom to express themselves, and, even, to take some chances and make mistakes. Talented people with more freedom to follow their own goals might find easy money less important to them, because they would have other compensations; and the studios might get more for less money.

Even men of acknowledged talent and the highest prestige, winners of Oscars and responsible for many box-office hits, do not now possess this freedom. Mr. William Wyler is widely regarded by everyone as one of the top directors in Hollywood, and he has additional power as a producer-director. His many successes are a matter of record; he is in the unusual position of sharing with the studio the right to pass on story material. Yet Mr. Wyler, in a newspaper interview, talked about the difficulties he experienced because of the "hyper-caution" of the studios. He . . .

. . . ruefully added that he had lost considerable time seeking "mutually satisfactory" properties. Half dozen of his suggestions, some of which are now being produced by other companies, have been turned down, he said. . . . "The safest yardstick for any company is to trust someone to make the right choice or else kick him out. If you don't trust him, the best thing to do is to get rid of him and hire people you can trust." [23]

[22] *Ibid.*, January 5, 1949.
[23] *Ibid.*, April 27, 1949.

It is just this quality of trust which is lacking in Hollywood. Almost no one trusts anyone else, and the executives, particularly, trust no one, not even themselves. Trust is impossible to men whose major drive is to exploit and manipulate other human beings. Gamblers who base their play for huge profits on instinct rather than knowledge, are for all their pretensions deeply unsure of themselves. The structure of Hollywood engenders distrust, which in turn breeds the excessive caution of which Mr. Wyler complains, and the enormous cost of a picture reinforces the caution. Even gamblers pause before risking $1,500,000. They are naturally more scared about taking a real chance than a gifted director whose security lies in his actual knowledge of the art of storytelling. This is a better guarantee for financial success than magical claims to omniscience.

To liberate the unused resources of talent in Hollywood entails changes in the way of thinking, in the system of production which reflects the way of thinking and, finally, in the allocation of power. When men give up an exaggerated emphasis on breaks as inherent in movie production and a magical form of thinking, and face the world of realities, which encompass logical thinking, hard work, knowledge and talent; when they cease being primarily gamblers reveling in crises and become good businessmen with a capacity to plan in advance; when they have the courage to try out new ideas as well as new processes in color tinting; when power for the sake of dominating other human beings as if they were property ceases to be the major goal and is supplanted by a human form of collaboration in which the interests of the movies and the movie public are important — then only will the real gold in Hollywood replace the glamorized tinsel.

Change does not take place quickly or by sudden decree. It is slow and happens as the result of many causes rather than of one. The exceptions to the rules are sometimes the beginning of change. A new invention, a new idea, a new form of behavior are usually first introduced as alternatives to already existing ones.[24] To replace

[24] Ralph Linton, *The Study of Man*, Chapter XVI. New York: D. Appleton-Century.

them, the new forms must be shown to be better. When automobiles were first introduced, the horse and buggy continued to exist, and for some time both were used. In the beginning many people were afraid of the new cars. By now the automobile has almost completely replaced the horse and buggy, because of its obviously greater efficiency.

For the exceptional patterns in Hollywood to replace the universal or prevailing ones, they must make more profit. Writers who write to please themselves rather than a producer have turned out some successful scripts, from which box-office hits have been produced. Gifted directors and actors who have gained more control over their work by becoming producers have likewise turned out successful pictures. Of course, neither they nor their pictures are always successful. Sometimes, without even knowing it, they have taken over the standards of their bosses and then their movies do not improve. But they have a high batting average. Pictures which carry a ring of honesty in human relationships rather than phoniness have been box-office hits. Some studios have learned that while beautiful legs for an actress are important, a girl with talent may have them as well as a nitwit, and that there is no reason why legs should preclude other types of actresses. Many different kinds are needed and are not necessarily in competition.

Whether or not these alternatives become universal is more complicated than the matter of automobiles replacing the horse and buggy. It is relatively easy to learn how to drive a car. It is exceedingly difficult for many of the people in Hollywood, who follow the universal patterns, to learn how to use the new alternatives. Their magical thinking, and belief in breaks rather than ability, their lack of real knowledge and training, their claims to omniscience, make it almost impossible for them to change. The alternatives threaten their major goal, the desire for power; and new ideas which threaten existing authority are always resisted.

When a primitive society comes into contact with Western civilization, frequently the old men, who are the powerful ones in the tribe, fight the innovations which the young ones accept. Rarely in the history of mankind has any group with power given it up voluntarily. But bankers and presidents of the industry, who are the powerful ones behind the studio executives, are interested in profits; and if an artist can bring in profits, he is their man. It is they who asked a former writer to become vice president in charge of production at a major studio. An independent studio headed by an executive who has emphasized quality in his films for a long time has been making money. There are other independent men and studios with similar values and the number is increasing. The picture of Hollywood can be painted in many ways, all true to a degree. It is a place of innumerable contradictions, some of which represent the norm and others, the exceptions.

No salary can compensate for being dehumanized. The star and the third assistant director alike realize this, however dimly. They can strive for more and more money yet they cannot accept the denial of their own humanity. The front-office thinking, which attributes nonhuman qualities to human beings, has more far-reaching consequences than primitive man's projection of human qualities on to the inanimate, because mere objects can have no reactions. Human beings *do* react.

The denial of one's human characteristics is the most degrading insult that can be offered any man or woman. All members of minority groups in our culture have suffered it to some degree. In Hollywood, members of minorities can rise to the highest prestige, wealth, and power positions — but the supreme insult is offered to them, and to everyone else.

In one sense the psychological situation is worse than that of slavery. In that situation, owners regarded their slaves as property, but the slaves themselves did not necessarily share this attitude. They were in bondage but they did not sell themselves to the highest bidder. In Hollywood, no master forces men to sell themselves for the duration of a contract. No one even forces people to come to Hollywood. They come of their own will and voluntarily sell their freedom to the highest buyer. Yet men who have known freedom cannot give it up without resentment and bitterness. The fact that they give it up of their own will adds ambivalence and guilt to an already difficult situation.

One of the most hopeful characteristics about the human species is that its members know that man is unique and they do not want to give up their human heritage. The basic problem of Hollywood lies in man. Technological improvements, distribution methods, and foreign markets are all important, and each brings its own problems. But of even deeper significance are the problems concerned with human values, with ways of thinking, with human relationships there and in the movies.

Some element of chance will always exist, just as some tensions and crises are inevitable among people working together. But enough successful pictures have been produced with intelligent planning and the wise use of talent to show that tensions, crises and superficial excitement are not the essential ingredients of good movie making. Enough people with humanistic goals have attained power to prove that successful movie production can be human, and that people working in Hollywood do not have to lose all freedom and dignity. The magical thinking and system of production which flows from it are probably no more necessary to making movies than the corn dance of the Pueblo Indians is needed to making corn grow.

Man in his long history has moved more slowly in some areas than in others. It has always been easier for him to use his intelligence, reason and inventiveness to control his physical environment than to apply them to his human relationships. In the less than fifty years of Hollywood's existence, it has recapitulated much of man's thinking. As it gradually emerges from the age of magic into the present, its future is tied with the future of mankind.

CHAPTER XV

Hollywood and the U.S.A.

THE ANTHROPOLOGIST sees any segment of society as part of a whole; he views Hollywood as a section of the United States of America, and both in the larger frame of Western civilization. The problems of the movie industry are not unique to it. But some characteristics of the modern world have been greatly exaggerated in Hollywood while others are underplayed. Hollywood is therefore not a re-flection, but a caricature of selected contemporary tendencies, which, in turn, leave their imprint on the movies. It is a three-way circular interaction between Hollywood, U.S.A. and movies.

Many people would agree with the characterization of our society by the poet W. H. Auden as "The Age of Anxiety." The present generation has known two world wars and is worried about the pos-sibility of a third, even more devastating. We won the last war and are probably the strongest nation, and yet we are insecure in our relations with former enemies and allies. Our country is prosperous and we have demonstrated an enormous capacity for production, but we are worried about a possible recession and unemployment. We live in a fast changing world but have lost faith in our belief that change is always for the better, and that progress is inevitable. We are not so sure of the happy ending.

Man has become increasingly lonely. Although people live in close physical contact, their relationships have become more and more depersonalized. We have a sense of being with people, and yet do not feel in any way related to them. In cities we are accustomed to having strange people beside us in street car, bus, or uncomfortably close in the subway. The technique of business and many other organizations, in trying to personalize their selling relationships, such as by announcing the name of employees to customers, really fools no one. The fact that the name of the post office clerk, the bank teller or the person who handles complaints in the department store, is posted, does not really influence their relationship with customers. The market place is still basically impersonal. Over the radio, we listen to the voices of strangers relating intimate domestic stories or giving us their opinions about the latest national or world event. All these factors give an illusion of companionship which, however, only increases the feeling of being alone. This loneliness is particularly striking when we compare modern to primitive man with his web of personal relationships within his clan. From birth to death he was tied through reciprocal duties and responsibilities to his clan kindred. Clan membership could not be lost and was as fixed for the individual as was his sex. He belonged to his group through basic biological ties and isolation was rare.

Many other factors contribute to modern man's anxiety. The traditional American belief that anyone, by working hard and industriously, may rise in the social hierarchy and become rich and successful is being questioned. There is considerable evidence that the American worker realizes that social mobility is decreasing. Workers increasingly believe that hard work no longer counts for as much as it did and that opportunities for advancement are restricted.[1] Many employees do not even understand the immediate aspects of their work situation. A study made at an electric company, which had an unusually good relationship with its employees, showed that there was much that the worker did not understand about his job, even including the method of payment. The author thought that this lack of understanding caused a feeling of exasperation and sense of personal futility on the part of the workers.[2] Modern man lives in a world which is difficult to comprehend. He is prosperous or unemployed in recurring economic cycles about which economists talk in learned words of cause and effect. But the average man sees only the effect, and is confused as to the causes.

In Hollywood there is far more confusion and anxiety than in the

[1] William Lloyd Warner and J. O. Low, *The Social System of the Modern Factory*, p. 182. New Haven: Yale Univ. Press.

[2] Elton Mayo, *The Human Problems of an Industrial Civilization*, 2nd ed., pp. 119-120. New York: The Macmillan Co.

society which surrounds it. Even in its most prosperous periods when net profits were enormous, far surpassing those of other businesses, everyone was scared. Now, when diminishing foreign markets, increasing costs of production, competition with European pictures, and changing box-office tastes threaten the swollen profits of past prosperity, fear rises to panic. Anxiety grips everyone from executive to third assistant director. The happy endings of at least 100 per cent net profit for the studio and a relatively long period of employment at high salaries for employees, are becoming less common. Yet, although this is well known, many individuals still cherish the fantasy for themselves. In the movies the happy ending is still almost universal. Perhaps the people who make the movies cannot afford to admit that there can be another kind of ending, and many of those who sit in the audience prefer this fantasy, too. But an increasing number are becoming dissatisfied with the so obviously contrived nature of these endings. The neat and unrealistic movie solution to all problems is neither satisfying nor entertaining.

Attitudes stem from the past and change slowly. In a rapidly changing society such as ours, some attitudes born out of a past situation continue under new conditions, even when inappropriate. Today there are people who will still believe in the *laissez-faire* economy of the frontier days and are hostile to planning designed for a country which no longer has a frontier. But many who stubbornly cling to the old *laissez-faire* thinking are uneasy lest they fight a losing battle, while many of those who plan are afraid that the planning may go too far. Neither side is really very sure of itself. In Hollywood the lack of planning and extemporizing has been carried to extremes probably not known even on the frontier, and greater certainly than in any contemporary industry. Even more important, extemporizing without a plan has long been regarded by many as a necessary and inherent part of movie making. However, the proper accompaniment, the frontier self-confidence and courage in taking chances, is very rare in Hollywood. The distinguished director-producer William Wyler appeals for . . .

" '. . . men of courage' in Hollywood to reach out for a wealth of picture material which the industry has shunned so far." He continues, "We need men of courage in high places who will not be intimidated or coerced into making only 'safe' pictures — pictures devoid of any ideas whatsoever." Too often he has bunked up against a situation where the top men were forced to decide between two stories and asked the question, "Which is the safest?" Mediocrity in films is the direct result of playing it safe.[3]

The men who make these decisions do not trust the public to like a picture which has ideas in it, Mr. Wyler says, in the same interview. It might be added that the men who do not trust the public usually do not trust themselves.

From the frontier past comes also the tradition of individual aggressive behavior. This persists although industry has become increasingly regimented and co-operation more essential. In the movie industry which depends on the collaborative effort of many people, the aggression is more ruthless than any described on the frontier, although, due to the insecurities of most people, it is masked under "Darlings" and "Sweethearts" and costly presents and parties. In the movies, however, the hatred and aggression comes through with a bang. Here is undiluted violence. This may meet the needs of the makers of our daydreams, as well as of those who consume them. Many people in our society experience a high level of frustration but are unable, either because of social pressures or inner fear, to express their resentment. In the movies they may find comfort and encouragement for their fantasies.

We have also inherited a Puritan tradition, stressing the sinfulness of human nature and giving us taboos to curb it. Today the doctrine of the innate evilness of man has lost much of its force and is far less a part of the conscious beliefs of many people. There is a growing awareness that babies are born neither sinful nor virtuous, but with potentialities for many different kinds of behavior, and even the definitions of sin and virtue continue to change. Hollywood, however, even more than the rest of society, feels the weight of Puritan traditions. The industry has imposed on itself a set of taboos derived in part from seventeenth-century New Eng-

[3] *Variety*, October 12, 1949.

land Protestantism, in order to appease the Catholic Legion of Decency and other would-be censors. No one in Hollywood, and very few outside of it, believe in the Code, nor are the censors appeased or pleased. For while the taboos are applied in the production of each movie, they fail completely to achieve the Puritan concepts on which they are based. They serve merely to make movies more dishonest, which is the natural result of any hypocrisy.

The activities of the various censoring groups spring not only from our past Puritanism, but also out of our social system in which pressure groups are accustomed to playing an important role. Labor, big business, farmers, and others try to influence legislation and get what they want through their organizations. Pressure groups are not restricted to modern society. In primitive ones, the whole tribe may bring pressure on recalcitrant individuals to follow the mores. But the pressure groups which try to influence Hollywood represent only a small part of the population and of movie audiences and are always negative in their intentions. They try to enforce a list of "Thou shalt nots." Most people interested in good entertainment usually know enough to realize that good movies cannot be created by such actions and so do not belong to these groups. This raises the whole question of the function of pressure groups in different areas of society. It is possible that legislators can pass adequate laws through balancing the claims of different pressure groups, and the pluralistic theory of government has long been an accepted democratic practice. But legislation is one thing, and making a movie is another.

An important focus for much of the anxiety in our modern world is in our changing values and goals. The anthropologist knows that the important differences between groups of men are not biological, but lie in their goals. Among the same people the goals may change from one historical period to another, such as from Elizabethan to Victorian England, and they obviously vary from one society to another. In the early Middle Ages religion provided the sanctions for most behavior. Since then the church, while still a functioning institution, has continued to lose much of its vitality. As Kluckhohn writes:

The anthropologist must characterize our culture as profoundly irreligious. More than half of our people still occasionally go through the forms, and there are rural and ethnic islands in our population where religion is still a vital force. But very few of our leaders are still religious in the sense that they are convinced that prayer or the observance of church codes will affect the course of human events. . . . Belief in God's judgments and punishments as a motive for behavior is limited to a decreasing minority.[4]

Even more important relatively few people today, as compared to a couple hundred years ago, have the kind of relationship with God to bring them security or comfort. Our society stresses the search for a good time rather than the quest for salvation.

Traditions, however, have a habit of living on in the deeper levels of our consciousness, even when they are overtly denied. Comparatively few people give the impression of really enjoying their wealth or their good times. Many of them appear to be consumed with an obsession to merely fill up time with more and more activity, and space with more and more costly objects. The frenzied and compulsive activity in the studios and outside of them is one of Hollywood's most striking characteristics. Another is the evaluation of not only objects, but people too, in terms of how much they cost. In making movies, this is reflected in the idea that the more a picture costs the better it must be. The tendency towards lavish sets, costumes, and other extravagances is now being curtailed because of the need for economy and the trend to shooting on location. But, with a few exceptions, the correlation of the value of pictures with their budgets is still the prevalent type of thinking in Hollywood. The greater the cost the more sure the studio feels of success, and hence high costs become one way of reducing anxiety. Actually, money can no more guarantee dramatic values than it can insure accuracy or significance in research.

The U.S.A. has been labeled by many students as a business civilization as contrasted to a religious one. This is obviously true, but not the whole truth. Roger Butterfield has described the

[4] Clyde Kluckhohn, *Mirror for Man*, pp. 247–248. New York: McGraw-Hill.

dominant themes of American life as "the desire to see all men free and equal, and the desire to be richer and stronger than anyone else." [5] This conflict between human and property rights has, as this author points out, generated much of the drama of American life. The political idealism and humanitarianism of the eighteenth and nineteenth centuries, as well as the earlier Puritanism, still influence our business civilization. In our Declaration of Independence is the quintessence of idealism, expressing for the first time the idea that all men have a right to happiness. If the anthropologist interested in our contemporary society digs under the top layers of people's beliefs, he will find still surviving the archaic concepts that money is not the road to happiness, or, at least, not the main one. If he is historically minded, he will note that when private capitalism was developing, the man who accumulated wealth through his own hard work was respected and admired; but that later when private capitalism changed to a corporate form, the corporation was regarded as an enemy of the people. Theodore Roosevelt became famous as a "trust-buster." No man in the U.S.A. becomes a national hero just through making a lot of money. He must have made some contribution to the welfare of his fellow men; most of the nation's heroes have been humanitarians.

In Hollywood the concept of a business civilization has been carried to an extreme. Property is far more important than man and human values have to struggle hard to exist at all. But, while the heroes in Hollywood are those with the most money, in the movies we find the opposite extreme. The wealthy tycoon is almost always the villain and the hero is the man of good will. The hero or heroine may be rich, but wealth does not give them their status. Often we are asked to admire the poor little rich girl who breaks away from her luxurious environment to marry the poor hero whom she loves. Hollywood leans over backward to sentimentalize love, which in the movies is always more important than wealth. Earning a living is never shown with any sense of reality and making a fortune is rarely portrayed sympathetically. True, most of the characters in the movies are better dressed and

[5] *The American Past: A History of the United States from Concord to Hiroshima*, p. 5. New York: Simon & Schuster.

live more luxuriously than do their counterparts in real life. The secretary dresses like a wealthy debutante and the female psychoanalyst like the popular concept of a Hollywood star. But neither they nor any other heroine or hero are shown as fundamentally interested in or concerned about the problem of making a living or becoming rich. It is only possible to speculate on the reasons for this almost complete negation of economic motives which are so prevalent in our society. The very extremes to which most movies go in the negation may mean that the executives who control the contents of the movies have themselves some hidden ambivalence about their goals. After all, the executives, as well as the actors, do belong to the human species and are not completely unaffected by the conflicting values of our society. Or, they may think that this underplaying of economic motives in the movies is desired by the audience. Neither reason precludes the other, and both could be true, as well as other unknown ones. Whatever the reasons, Hollywood represents a caricature and overelaboration of the business motives and goals of our society, while the movies consistently underplay the same characteristics.

Art and aesthetic goals have always been less important in our society than either business or humanitarian ones. The artist in all societies has traditionally been a kind of barometer, more sensitive to nuances and changes than others, because he is more deeply immersed in his culture and more interested in its meanings. Since he rarely completely accepts all the conventions, he has a certain degree of objectivity and freedom, which of course also makes him seem different from other men. While the artist's status declined in all Western societies after the Industrial Revolution, many of the European countries with their older traditions of painting, music and literature, accorded him a higher position than he enjoys in the United States. Here, he is still considered peculiar, abnormal, sometimes feminine, and unimportant unless he achieves a commercial success comparable to that of a businessman. A Hollywood caricature of this concept is portrayed in the movie, *A Kiss in the Dark*. The hero, a successful concert pianist, played by David Niven, is scared, nervous, withdrawn, and obviously infantile. He is saved by noticing, with appreciation, a model's legs (those of Jane Wyman). She has no interest in his music and leads him to her world of jazz and trombones. He finally frees himself from being an artist and wins his girl by using his musician's hands to knock down the heroine's fiancé, a former athlete. The hero is now a he-man, throws his practice keyboard away, and embraces the heroine as the train carries them away on a honeymoon.

So in the actual production of movies in Hollywood, the American concept of the unimportance of the artist is magnified. Those who know most about storytelling, who are gifted with imagination, and who have a knowledge of human beings, all raw materials which the camera transforms into a movie, do not have sufficient status to use their abilities. As one director expressed it, "the environment is hostile to them." The environment favors the latest developments in sound and color, but discourages new ideas from its artists. These men, who traditionally have known considerable freedom in expressing themselves, work under the direction of businessmen.

The movies have to earn their living. Unlike some of the fine arts, they are not privately endowed nor are they an esoteric medium for the enjoyment of the few. The goals of business and art are each justifiable and not necessarily irreconcilable. When art meets the needs of a large number of people in our society, it inevitably makes a profit. Some of our most creative popular artists, such as Chaplin, Gershwin, Walt Disney and Irving Berlin, have made fortunes. The problem is not the simple one of art versus business. The artist can contribute to business. But his stock-in-trade is not only his technical know-how: it includes the ability to interpret man to himself. This is true in folk art, popular art and fine art. But it makes little difference to the businessman whether he assuages man's anxieties by interpretation, or whether he exploits them; but the latter is easier. Or, if phoniness brings in money easily, why bother about the details of honesty? The front-office executives are not completely blind to humanitarian issues, but they seem far more interested in profits than in man. Most of them are not conditioned to be otherwise. Artists have a different kind of conditioning. While they are concerned about money, they must also, in order to be reasonably contented, use their gifts to give their interpretations. It has already been indicated that while only relatively few of the Hollywood writers, directors and actors are artists in this sense, they are far more important than the host of mediocre people.

The social organization of Hollywood has, however, permitted the businessman to take over the functions of the artists and to substitute his values for theirs. The movies are the first art form of any kind, popular, folk or fine, to become a trust. Quite early the major companies combined in their efforts to restrain competition and to blacklist those who would not do their bidding. The struggle between the Independents and the organization of the major studios still continues. At the same time movies increasingly make use of a developing technology and of the heritage from theater and literature. Under any circumstances such a combination would create complex problems. In this particular situation, the men with power have known how to exploit the advantages of a trust better than they could utilize the assets of literature and drama. They have not seemed to realize that the efficiency of the factory is possible because it turns out identical products, whether automobiles or coffeepots, and that this principle cannot be applied to the making of movies. Since these businessmen have neither understanding nor respect for the artists' ability, they attempt to negate or destroy it, partly out of ignorance and partly from a desire to satisfy their urge to dominate men. It is only an exceptional executive who does not give the impression that he would have been equally satisfied as a tycoon in any other industry.

Outside of Hollywood there is a certain freedom in choice of goals. A man can decide to be an artist, a scientist or a college professor, which means that most likely he will never be rich. Or he can plan to be a big business executive and have the possibility of acquiring great wealth. In Hollywood the same freedom of choice does not exist, because whatever role the individual plays, the goals of business are paramount. In the country as a whole there is the combination of humanism and materialism. But in Hollywood, money is always more important than man. It is this difference in goals which accounts for much of the deep hostility between the front-office and the artists' group. People with the same goals may argue and differ on how to achieve them, but they speak the same language. People with conflicting goals speak a different language. The real artist in Hollywood cannot be completely satisfied, even though he earns a fortune, if he is not functioning as an artist, and this the head of a trust cannot understand.

Another trait of our civilization is its high level of ingenuity and inventiveness in the mechanical skills. Our heroes include men like Thomas Edison, Alexander Graham Bell, Eli Whitney and Henry Ford as well as the humanitarian, political figures. We are justly famous for the enormous number of additions to material culture which make life more comfortable. Movies are themselves a remarkable invention in their integration of electricity, photography, color, sound and acting. The history of inventions from the first stone ax is a fascinating story and one peculiar to our species. For only man is a tool-making and tool-using animal. Each succeeding example of his ingenuity and cleverness has brought, however, its own problems. This has always been true, but only recently has atomic energy forced a public recognition of the serious social consequences of technological developments.

The control of machines and of all our inventions for the benefit of man is one of the most pressing problems of our time. Machines can enslave people or free them. The Industrial Revolution brought young children into sweatshops and kept them and their parents for long hours at machines. Gradually changes in the social and economic organization reduced the hours of work, set age limits for workers, and enabled them, as well as other people, to enjoy the higher standard of living which machines made possible. But even the most casual observer of our society today recognizes its machinelike character. Not only do machines increasingly replace human labor, but what is left of it grows more mechanical. The role of the individual worker on the assembly line tends to be more and more automatic and he has less and less understanding of its relationship or his own to the whole. The ironic climax is his attempt to escape into fantasies and daydreams, themselves manufactured on an assembly line, far more concerned with technology than with meaning.

The way in which Hollywood has mechanized creativity and taken away most of its human characteristics again exaggerates the prevailing culture pattern, which gives little prestige to creativity not technological. This, of course, does not apply to the genius: an Einstein, Picasso, or a Rachmaninoff is given due honor. But we do little to bring out the creativity which lies in all human beings. Most people — just the everyday garden variety, not the geniuses — have far more potentialities for being creative than they use. But very few of them have the courage or desire to carry through their own ideas, big or little, because they have been conditioned to think routinely and follow the crowd. Our society tends, particularly today, to prize uniformity in thinking more than originality. The concern with the "know-how" rather than the "why," with technology rather than meaning, permeates much of the thinking even in the social sciences when method becomes more important than problems. The use of the most exact scientific methods on a sterile and meaningless problem is not too different from the employment of the most technically advanced camera work to produce a banal movie. It is the same when our educational system stresses the accumulation of facts rather than the meaningful relationship between them, and the taking of so many courses that there is little time for thoughtful reflection. The radio with its "Information, Please" and other quiz programs continues the emphasis. It is not that factual knowledge or scientific methods are unimportant, but rather that they are of use only in the larger context of problems and meanings. Hollywood expands these two features of our society to such an extent that it discourages and sometimes even forbids creativity in the very people whom it presumably pays to be creative.

The problem of power has been important since the beginning of mankind's existence. Its history follows no straight line, but lunges forward and backward, always correlated with the concept of what is human nature and with the meaning of freedom. In the very beginning of his history, man was more at one with the natural world than he is today. He might think he was descended from a totemic animal and there was a close tie with other animals and to the world of nature. Primitive man was also more closely linked with his kindred than is modern man. Much of life in Stone Age societies consisted of a series of reciprocal duties and responsibilities between members of an extended family, clan or other social group, which continued even after death. In this system of close relationships there was little room for emphasis on individuality. Differences between people might be noted, but were not considered particularly important. Rebels from traditional customs were few. If head-hunting was a way of proving manhood and becoming eligible for marriage, it would be unusual to find one of the young men of the tribe staying behind, murmuring "I'm not the type," as the others went off on a head-hunting expedition. Some primitive societies do have institutionalized modes of behavior for people who do not fit into the norm, such as homosexuals; but on the whole little attention is paid to the less striking individual differences. Traditions are followed, and power to implement them lies with the elders.

The process of the emergence of the individual from these primary ties Erich Fromm calls "individuation." He points out that the same process occurs in the life history of an individual.[6] Birth involves a biological separation from the mother and the beginning of an individual existence, even though the child is functionally dependent on his mother for a considerable time. Mankind as well as the individual struggles through the ages to free himself from primary ties. Familiar landmarks in this history are Christianity, with its emphasis on the importance and value of each individual's soul to God, the end of Feudalism, the Reformation, the Industrial Revolution, political revolutions with their overthrow of monarchies, and the development of political and economic democracy. During this process power has gone through many re-allocations, from the tribal elders to feudal lords, popes, kings and emperors. Gradually it was diffused from the hands of a few to the many, who include elected political representatives, owners of industry,

[6] Erich Fromm, *Escape from Freedom*. New York: Rinehart. Fromm discusses this whole problem and its relation to freedom in detail.

leaders of labor and others. This century has seen revolutions which reversed the process and concentrated power again in the hands of a few dictators. Man, as Fromm says, both wants and fears freedom; he struggles to gain it and he gives it up.

The meaning of the word "freedom," of course, is not the same to all men, or at all times. There are many freedoms and none is absolute. Most of them connote freedom from some form of constraint, either in society or within man's personality. But, underlying all freedoms, as Ralph Barton Perry writes, is the freedom of thought. This implies choice and an awareness of alternatives, based on both imagination and knowledge.[7] The *exercise* of the freedom of choice may be restricted, by institutions and customs, or by psychological forces within man, due to ignorance and fear. The degree to which freedom of choice is permitted is always linked with society's particular concept of the nature of man. Today, at one end of the power scale is the idea of man as a passive creature without ability to choose for himself, manipulated by a powerful few who claim omniscience. Men are puppets pulled by strings, seen and hidden. They are told what to think politically, scientifically, morally, and aesthetically. Spontaneity in thinking is discouraged and conformity is the goal. Choice of an alternative which involves different values is not presented in this concept. When all the manipulation is done by the state and when the strings are pulled by a dictator, it is called totalitarianism.

The form of thinking underlying totalitarianism and some of its accompanying behavior is not confined to the countries labeled as such. It is present everywhere and not absent from our own society. However, here, it is in conflict with a different concept, the democratic one, which emphasizes the uniqueness of man in his greater capacity for thinking as compared to other species. Both the desire and ability to choose between alternatives is regarded as an innate part of being human, which increases as men grow up and break their dependency on primary ties. This theory of human nature is imbedded in our formal charters, the Constitution and the Declaration of Independence, and is part of our tradi-

[7] Ralph Barton Perry, *Characteristically American*, pp. 148–149. New York: Knopf.

tional behavior as represented by a multiple-party system; freedom of choice at a secret ballot box; freedom of religion; diversity of ideas in sciences and arts, and choice of different goals.

The democratic concept of the nature of man is in continuous conflict with the totalitarian one, but the struggle is not confined to the political level, or to international relationships. It is part of the texture of our daily lives, in the family, in school and college, in courts, in Congressional and State legislative committees, and in every other area which has responsibility in human relations. There appears to be an increasing tendency in some of these areas to stifle, overtly and subtly, the expression of opinions which are not those of the majority, to overstress conformity, and to so prevent freedom of thought and of choice.

The conflict comes out particularly clearly in education. On one side there is the emphasis on discovering individual aptitudes and developing the unique capacities of each student. The goal of small classes so that more attention can be paid to individual students is everywhere recognized, even if not always attained. But even in graduate work, there is also the tendency in the opposite direction: one graduate seminar at a well-known university had eighty members. Still, the idea of the educational process as one which trains the student's capacity for critical and independent judgment is sincerely believed in by some, and given lip service by most educators. The ninetieth birthday of John Dewey, more responsible than any other one person for shaping our concept of democratic education, was celebrated nationally. At the same time there are opposing tendencies, political and pedagogical, which negate the whole concept of developing the students' capacity to think for themselves and to choose between alternatives. The censorship of ideas in books and magazines of which school boards or influential pressure groups do not approve generates an atmosphere of fear for teachers and students, which is hardly conducive to independent thinking. Nor is training in critical judgment necessarily provided by the emphasis on accumulation of facts for ritual examinations.

In family living and bringing up of children, there are also opposing trends, with the democratic one gaining. Implicit obedience to parents and the idea that "children should be seen and not heard" belong to the past mores. In this country, there is the trend, sometimes carried to extremes, of self-expression for children and for parents to be friends or pals with their children, rather than authoritarian figures. The emphasis is on the development of the child's capacity to make decisions for himself, as his knowledge and experiences broaden. This type of thinking, accenting spontaneity rather than conformity, appears to be gradually becoming part of our mores. The family, one of the most significant conditioning forces in the life history of the individual, is decidedly non-totalitarian in our society.

Family life, education, and political organizations have always been conditioning forces molding the lives of people; but mass communications are new. Certainly they have enriched our culture. Without the invention of printing, literacy for masses of people would be impossible. Radio gives a speed and ease of communication undreamed of by our ancestors. Movies can bring drama to millions of people who otherwise would never enter a theater. But the mass communications, like every other advance, bring problems as well as advantages. Among the most serious is the capacity of these communications to manipulate the ideas, opinions and emotions of vast audiences. More and more do people depend on what they read in their daily newspaper or what their radio commentator says, for their opinions. This means that man functions passively, taking over opinions, ideas, and prejudices ready-made from others, rather than actively examining a number of choices and making up his own mind. In a totalitarian society all the mass communications are controlled by a ruling clique, and no choice is permitted the citizen. In the United States there is a choice, but relatively few people avail themselves of it. They do not all seem to realize that almost every newspaper has its own line, whether it be the [New York] *Daily News* or the *Daily Worker*, as has each radio commentator; and many do not bother to examine different lines. Albert Schweitzer thinks that our whole society is geared to what he calls "the renunciation of thinking," and he labels our age one of spiritual bankruptcy. He writes:

The organized political, social and religious associations of our time are at work to induce individual man not to arrive at his convictions by his own thinking but to take as his own, such convictions as they keep ready-made for him. Any man who thinks for himself and at the same time is spiritually free is to the associations something inconvenient and even uncanny. He does not offer sufficient guarantee that he will merge himself in their organizations in the way they wish. All corporate bodies look today for their strength not so much to the spiritual worth of the ideas they represent and to that of the people who belong to them, as to the attainment of the highest possible degree of unity and exclusiveness. It is here that they expect to find their strongest power for offense and defense.[8]

The tendency of our age is not only to take over our thoughts ready-made and to lazily conform, but to continue the same pattern with our emotions. This is to be expected, since the dichotomy between thought and feeling is, of course, artificial. In manipulating and defining our emotions and ideas about human relations, mass communications are among the most powerful agents. For instance, the pulp literature, advertising and movies all hammer home a similar concept of love. Advertising both uses and abuses man's basic need for love to sell its ware. The young woman who rides the subway or bus to work, daily reads that holding a husband is dependent on using certain soap flakes which will keep the color of her underwear fresh; and in the past, there was the negative campaign of "Always a bridesmaid and never a bride" unless a certain mouthwash was used. Not only does advertising sell its products, but it also sells a concept of love and human relations. The pulps and movies sell their concept of love, too, with the movies being probably far the more powerful, since in them, love objects are dramatically portrayed by glamorous or highly attractive men and women. Love, in most movies, is limited to instant biological attraction without any other elements. The hero sees a girl waiting for a bus; one look at her well-shaped legs, strutting bosom, and

<hr>

[8] Albert Schweitzer, *Out of My Life and Thought*, p. 255. New York: Henry Holt.

golden hair is sufficient to tell him that this is his mate for life, and the pursuit begins. In actual life in Hollywood, and elsewhere, the end of such a pursuit would usually be only the bed, quickly reached. Censorship, of course, forbids this portrayal, and so the ending is transformed into the romantic one of happiness ever after. This confusion between love and infatuation or an adolescent "crush" is repeated over and over again. Another recurring theme in movies is the loss, or threatened loss, of a love object; the solution is usually suicide, murder, or insanity. Finding another love object rarely occurs, although our divorce and remarriage rate indicate this is a fairly frequent modern solution. Love is also supposed to be the mainspring for all creative work, whether in science or the arts. In the lives of great artists and scientists which have been filmed, the hero is usually dependent for his accomplishment not on his own genius, intelligence, or hard work, but on the loving devotion of his mate, or more colloquially, "the little woman."

The other emotional behavior most frequently emphasized in the movies, besides love, is violence. Radio, comics and headlines are vibrant with it. Like love, violence has long been a part of all drama. But, as John Houseman writes:

> What is significant about our contemporary "tough" films (critics and ladies' organizations to the contrary) is *not* their surface violence but the neurotic reaction that accompanies it. It is not the act of brutality that is repellent, but the indifference with which it is regarded by those who commit it and those whom it affects.[9]

As Houseman points out in his discussion of the characters in *The Big Sleep*, "It is these people — spiritless zombies, utterly lacking in moral or tragic sense — that are really frightening, not their forays with blackjack and pistol."

There are a number of points of view about violence in movies. It may serve as a catharsis for the conscious and unconscious desires of the audience, as all drama does to some degree. But whether or not the function of catharsis is served depends on whether the

[9] John Houseman, "What Makes American Movies Tough?" in *Vogue*, January 15, 1947.

violence is treated in its tragic and human aspects. As noted earlier, it is possible that a succession of movies in which violence is portrayed by glamorous stars and in which there is no sense of inner morality, even though the "sinners" are punished at the end, may not be cathartic at all but, instead, give this behavior a kind of permissiveness. At least, these movies do not act as a deterrent and movie solutions, other than violent and easy ones for difficult situations, are often ignored.

The problem of aggression in our society is not an easy one. The ordinary frictions of life generate an aggressive attitude and it is a necessary ingredient underlying much success. Yet aggressive behavior in general is not approved. Rarely is an outlet permitted in the family. If an adolescent or person in his late teens is angry with his father or mother, instead of letting his anger out on them, he is more apt to rush out of the house and go to a movie. Here, he can find an outlet for his feelings. But his relationship with parents and the situation which caused his aggression remains unchanged. Many other older people are afraid of showing their aggressive feelings, because they fear loss of love or affection. Movies provide a vicarious outlet, but the basic insecurities of the individual are left untouched.

The heightening of suspense is part of most pictures in which violence is a part. These movies aim to increase tensions and their advertisements feature the breathless suspense, excitement and horror. An element of suspense is part of all drama. But never has it been so intense and so exaggerated as in most current thrilling movies. A possible hypothesis is that people cannot permit themselves to be fully aware of all the suspense and fear involved in the atomic bomb, a possible third war, and the future in general for themselves and the world. Although they try to evade the problem, the anxiety remains. The suspense of finding out "who done it" in the movie or detective story may be one way of relieving the greater suspense of what is going to happen to them and their children in the future. The suspense gags of a man dangling on a clothesline between two high buildings and wild hysterical automobile chases, in all of which no one gets hurt, may offer some relief. In a typical Abbott and Costello comedy, *The Buck Private*

Comes Home, Costello drives a midget car in a race and through all kinds of fantastic obstacles. He does not know how to drive, is unable to control the car, and throughout the whole race is scared stiff. Through a series of miraculous escapes he comes out safely and wins the race. An audience who feels helpless to control an equally fantastic social situation, would like nothing better than a Costello victory through a miracle.

The manipulation of behavior as well as emotions is common to our society. Salesmen are important in our business civilization and success in selling is attained primarily through the manipulation of people. *How to Win Friends and Influence People*, and all the books similar to this best seller, attempt to give the techniques. Knowing the right people is regarded as more important to success in many jobs than knowledge, experience, or integrity. Many young men go to prestige universities in the East in order to make "contacts," which will help them in Wall Street or business careers after commencement. There is hardly a profession, even those in which skill and knowledge count, that does not number among its successes a goodly number who have come to the top primarily through the slap-on-the-back and similar techniques. Of course, knowing influential people and getting their help is part of human relations in every society. But our society exaggerates the pattern.

While these are some of the totalitarian elements which exist in democratic societies, there are basic differences between them and totalitarian ones. In the latter, the manipulation of people is carried to the greatest extremes and, even more important, is always done by a few powerful men at the head of the state. In democracies, the manipulation is done by many different forces with diverse goals and often in conflict. The differences between the totalitarian philosophy of man as an obedient robot and the traditional democratic concept of man's freedom and independence are very significant. These differences in social organization and in philosophy should not be underestimated. Totalitarian elements in our society, whether in school, home, politics, are only one of a number of alternatives. For, while democratic ideas and behavior are not always implemented or used, there are opportunities for freedom of thought and behavior. It is true that sometimes the citizen merely repeats opinions he hears over the radio or reads in the newspaper. But there are other times when he bursts through all these synthetic ideas and thinks for himself, as he has demonstrated in several presidential elections. The election of President Roosevelt in 1944 and of President Truman in 1948 ran counter to the majority of editorial opinions and radio propaganda. As far as is known, the citizens of the totalitarian state is not given this opportunity to choose or the family and educational conditioning to utilize it. In American society, as in many of the Western European ones, there are present conflicting trends of totalitarianism and democracy.

Hollywood represents totalitarianism. Its basis is economic rather than political but its philosophy is similar to that of the totalitarian state. In Hollywood, the concept of man as a passive creature to be manipulated extends to those who work for the studios, to personal and social relationships, to the audiences in the theaters and to the characters in the movies. The basic freedom of being able to choose between alternatives is absent. The gifted people who have the capacity for choice cannot exercise it; the executives who technically have the freedom of choice do not actually have it, because they usually lack the knowledge and imagination necessary for making such a choice. Much behavior is compulsive, springing from fears, hidden and open. The careful planning and good judgment of the exceptional people have been already described and are in dramatic contrast to the hysterical behavior of the others.

The Hollywood atmosphere of crises and continuous anxiety is a kind of hysteria which prevents people from thinking, and is not too different from the way dictators use wars and continuous threats of war as an emotional basis for maintaining their power. As the late Dr. Harry Stack Sullivan pointed out, there is considerable difference between fear and anxiety. Fear, he said, is often provoked by a new or novel situation and wears off as one becomes accustomed to it. Anxiety, however, arises out of relationships with other people which are disturbed, and "from its mildest to its most extreme manifestations interferes with effective alertness to the factors in the current situation that are immediately relevant to its occurrence, and thus with the refinement and precision of action related to its relief or reduction." [10] Put more colloquially and applied to Hollywood, this means that a stage director who directs a movie for the first time might have some fear which would disappear as he became more accustomed to the new situation. In the meantime, the fear would not inhibit his learning as much as possible about the new situation and applying his knowledge and talent to it. But the anxiety of the average producer who has been in movies all his adult life springs out of his character and interpersonal relations, and the Hollywood situation calls forth and increases what is already there. Nor is it possible to become accustomed to anxiety-provoking situations. The very anxiety prevents an awareness of the factors which call it forth and of realistically doing something about them. These anxiety-ridden producers and executives of Hollywood try to reduce anxiety by spending more money, buying a best seller whether or not it is appropriate for a movie, using ten writers instead of one, having three "big name" stars in a movie, and so on. But none of these formulas rids him of his anxiety. Even where a picture is a big success, he knows the same anxiety on the next one.

In *Mein Kampf*, Hitler wrote about Fate as sometimes cruel and other times loving. Whether it is called Fate, destiny, or breaks, the underlying concept is the same: man gives up the attempt to exercise some control over his life through his own intelligence, because he thinks forces beyond his domain completely direct it.

The totalitarian concept of man is not limited to human relationships in Hollywood, but is reflected in many movies. Life, success or misfortune is usually portrayed as caused by luck or an accident. Only rarely does a movie show the process of becoming successful or the process of disintegration. Either one is treated as a *fait accompli* in the beginning of the picture or as caused by accidents during the course of the movie. Most movie characters, whether hero or villain, heroine or jade, are passive beings to whom

[10] Harry Stack Sullivan, "Multidisciplined Co-ordination of Interpersonal Data," in *Culture and Personality*, p. 179. Proceeding of an Interdisciplinary Conference held under the auspices of the Viking Fund. Published by the Viking Fund, New York.

things happen accidentally. Rarely do they even try to think through the situation in which they find themselves. They are buffeted about and defeated; or Fate smiles on them and almost magically they are successful. A few pictures have freed themselves from this formula. In *Home of the Brave* the Negro hero is shown as suffering realistically from prejudice. His escape is not on a magic carpet into a never-never world but through a painful psychological process, which the movie plainly says is kaleidoscoped. The Negro problem is seen as part of a larger human one. Nor is the problem over at the end of the picture. The hero merely understands it better and has a way of handling it.

The totalitarian concept likewise extends toward the audiences, often regarded as suckers whose emotional needs and anxieties can be exploited for profit. Hollywood producers are, of course, not the only people with undue anxieties and many of the movies cater to the same kind of anxieties in their audiences, strengthening rather than reducing them, and contributing nothing to understanding. Only men who are not completely ridden with anxieties and who have some understanding of their own, as well as mankind's problems, can make other kinds of pictures. "The people," however, are always used as a rationalization — by dictators who say they rule for the good of the people, and by Hollywood producers who say they give the people what they want.

Until recently Hollywood offered very little more choice to audiences than it did to its artist employees. Today, because of competition from both exceptional Hollywood movies and foreign films, there is more choice.

The ultimate in totalitarian power is power for its own sake, although dictators offer various rationalizations for propaganda purposes. Some of the men with power in Hollywood present the same picture. These men have made millions, and more money means very little to them; but they cannot get enough of power: power over human beings in the studio and power over the daydreams of men and women who sit in the darkened theater.

For men of this type there is often enjoyment also in the power to humiliate, which they exercise in their relationships with their employees. There is a story about a well-known director, Mr. John Mighty, who was sleeping with the star of the picture he was directing. One morning she came on the set about a half hour late, and he bawled her out in loud, scolding language before the other actors, a crowd of extras, and the workmen. She tried to tell him that the hairdresser and make-up had taken longer than usual, but he refused to listen. Instead, he made her repeat after him an abject apology to the crowd on the set: "I apologize because I am late, and because I have caused loss of money to the studio and loss of time to all of you, and more particularly, because I know I am an actress without ability." At this point, she broke down and, crying, said, "But please, John!" She got no further. The director bellowed, " 'John' in bed, you bitch; 'Mr. Mighty' on the set!" Humiliation as a technique for maintaining authority and for enjoyment is not confined to big people: assistant directors often show the same pattern in their treatment of extras. Those who take pleasure in degrading other people, whether in Hollywood or in a totalitarian state, are themselves degraded and may be even subconsciously aware of it.

Of course Hollywood is no more completely totalitarian than it is completely primitive. The genesis of Hollywood is different from that of any totalitarian state. In the latter the dictators either seize power through revolution, or attain it by making promises to relieve the misery and anxieties from which people suffer, or they do both. In Hollywood most of the men who enjoy power have it simply because they got there first and were able to form the social structure of movie making as they desired, rather than in the interests of movie making. The Hollywood dictators have not been able to make converts, in the way of any successful political dictator. He gets his subjects when young, and conversion begins in the kindergarten. The subjects in Hollywood arrive there as adults with fairly well-formulated ideas about how they can best work and live. They accept the dictatorship only nominally, because of the high salaries. They rarely accept it emotionally and, instead, are filled with resentment and bitterness toward it.

The rebels, in this case the artists, do not struggle in underground movements to outmaneuver the studio executives. They fight openly to gain power, that is, to get into positions in which they can make important decisions and influence the movies. A sufficient number of gifted writers, directors and actors are succeeding to indicate at least a trend which offers a variation and may, eventually, modify or change the system.

These exceptional individuals receive little help in their struggles. The Federal Government tries to reduce the monopolistic power of the industry and to regulate its buying and selling practices. Censorship groups attempt to regulate the morality of the pictures and succeed only in making them dishonest. Guilds fight for more money for their members, but do nothing about a contract, which allows the employer almost literally to own his employees for its duration. The exceptional individuals, with great strength of character and drive, with high talent, and with a true morality, work on their own as they try to dent the power situation in Hollywood, alter the human relationships, and give meaning to their movies.

Totalitarianism, whether in a foreign nation or in Hollywood, represents one of the backward swings in history. But primitive societies seldom knew the degradation that modern man can suffer under a dictator. Although primitive cultures have a similar lack of emphasis on the individual, there are wide differences between them and modern totalitarian states. The two situations differ widely in origin and effect. In primitive societies man has not yet emerged sufficiently from his primary ties to his family and clan kindred to emphasize his own individuality. But totalitarianism attempts to negate the individuality of men who *have* broken these primary ties, who *have* known, and valued, freedom. The force of tradition offers very little choice to primitive man. The force of the modern police state also offers very little choice. Primitive cultures lack the knowledge and awareness of man's potentialities. Modern totalitarian societies fear and distrust them. Evolutionary thinking is not in style in the social sciences, but it is possible to view the history of man as a gradual freeing of himself from primary ties and becoming freer to utilize and develop his uniquely human characteristics.

In every society there are a multitude of patterns, some over-elaborated and others underplayed. The anthropologist is well aware that either process may be carried to such unnecessary extremes as to threaten the well-being and, occasionally, even the survival of the society. Among the aborigines of Australia the marriage regulations are worked out to such a fine point that it is almost impossible for a native to find a socially approved mate. His way out of this impossible situation is to elope. Some Eskimo tribes are not permitted to hunt seals in summer, and they will not touch seals in this season even if the land game fails and they are starving.

Hollywood has the elaborated totalitarian elements we have described: the concept of people as property and as objects to be manipulated, highly concentrated and personalized power for power's sake, an amorality, and an atmosphere of breaks, continuous anxiety and crises. The result of this overelaboration is business inefficiency, deep frustration in human relations, and a high number of unentertaining second- and third-rate movies.

There are, of course, other patterns in the U.S.A. which Hollywood could elaborate. They are the democratic ones of the dignity of man, the concept of freedom, a belief in man's capacity to think, create, and to exercise some control over his life — a belief that man is more important than property — all part of our cultural heritage. How far will Hollywood utilize them? It is not a matter of more brains and talent or of money, but of generating new modes of behavior and a system in which collaboration is more important than domination. Any changes that will occur will not come out of magical thinking or waiting for breaks. Nor is it possible to be sure of a "happy ending." No anthropologist ever expects a complete break from the past. But he does know that societies assume different forms through contact with others, through technological inventions, and through changes in values and goals. He can predict that Hollywood will not go back to its isolated position and that there will be new technological developments. The really difficult question to answer is, Can Hollywood change its ways of thinking and its values, so that the democratic concept of man becomes more important than a totalitarian one?

Index